Y2K—It's Not Too Late
Complete Preparedness Guide

Scott Marks

Karl Kaufman

Patrice Kaufman

187 Vester Street
Ferndale, MI 48220
mercurypub@aol.com

http://www.y2kredy.com

1-877-Y2K-REDY

ISBN 0-9669039-1-9

Library of Congress Catalog Card Number: 98-83022

Cover design by
Black Dog Design
903 North Main Street
Royal Oak, MI 48067
doghowze@aol.com

Printed by
Batson Printing
195 Michigan Street
Benton Harbor, MI 49022
batson@qtm.net

Published in the United States by
Mercury Publications
187 Vester Street
Ferndale, MI 48220
mercurypub@aol.com
http://www.y2kredy.com

Disclaimer

The material in this book is for information purposes only. It is intended to be used as a general guide and not as the absolute source of information. Information contained in this book regarding the Year 2000 computer problem is, at the time written, believed to be an accurate portrayal of facts. It is compiled from existing data and may contain technical inaccuracies and omissions. Neither the authors nor the publisher are professional consultants dispensing legal, medical, technical or any other services. This publication is not designed as a substitute for seeking the advice of professionals. Neither the authors nor the publisher assume responsibility or are liable to any person or entity for the use or misuse of the information contained in this book.

The authors receive a small referral fee from some of the suppliers listed here.

All product names mentioned in this book are the trade names of their respective owners.

To Tom Dickrell, who helped me out in my
Y2K preparedness. It was through these efforts
that I came up with the original idea for this book.
To my sister, Laurie Fielder, whose love and support
kept me going to completion. To Patricia Schaefer, for
her love, support, and caring. And to my son,
David Marks, for his belief in me.

Scott Marks

To my parents,
Marian Towne and Maynard Kaufman,
who taught me about writing and life.
To my soulmate, Patrice.
And to my loving children,
Ariana, Bernadine and Athena.

Karl Kaufman

To the memory of our parents,
Harry and Eileen Marks.

Patrice Kaufman
Scott Marks

Acknowledgements

We wish to thank all who helped with this project:

Tom Dickrell, for helping to conceptualize the book and design its contents.

Annabelle McIlnay, for your editorial assistance.

Kevin Serbus, Lisa Jeffrey, and Ko Wicke of Black Dog Design, for your great work on the cover.

Sherry Wells, for legal and publishing advice.

Suzanne DuMolin, Peter Hollerbach, Jerry Hollis, Maynard Kaufman, Greg Lynch, David Marks, Patrick Rogers, Patricia Schaefer, William Schmidt, Donna Sennott, Jon Towne, and Matthew Ward, for reading parts of the manuscript and/or offering feedback and suggestions.

Laurie Fielder, for your media help and suggestions.

Renee Lombardo, for sparking our Y2K awareness.

Patrice and Karl wish to thank Scott for coming up with the idea for this book, and for taking us on as partners in the project.

Karl expresses gratitude to God for life and opportunity, and to all beings for their assistance.

And to our daughter and niece, Athena Kaufman, for many patient hours spent waiting for us to finish this book.

Contents

Introduction

Let's stop pretending that Y2K isn't a major threat to our way of life. There is too much at stake for such uninformed wishful thinking.
Edward Yardeni
Chief Economist, Deutsche Morgan-Grenfell

Our concern about the Year 2000 computer problem motivated us to research the issue. Due to our findings, we spent the better part of 1998 getting ready for Y2K.

We asked ourselves, if the power goes out, how will we keep our families warm? If the water system fails, how will we drink, cook, and keep clean? We concluded it was a good idea to buy a generator for back-up power, and water purification equipment. But finding out where to buy these items, how much they would cost, and how to use them proved to be a different story.

The same thing was true about buying CB radios, long-term dried food packages, gold and silver bullion, and many other things.

Each time another aspect of the Y2K problem was revealed, we had more questions. The questions piled up faster than the answers. Gradually, after months of concerted effort, we eventually found the answers.

We decided it would be helpful to have a "one-stop shopping guide" to Y2K preparedness. The need for such a guide prompted us to write this book.

Our goal is to walk you through the Y2K preparedness process, showing you what you need to do, and how to do it. Unlike us, you won't spend months searching for information. Everything you need to know is in this book, or referenced here.

We learned how to prepare for Y2K, and so can you.

Scott Marks works as an electrician apprentice. He holds a B.A. in business administration with a major in Management Information Systems. For several years, he was a firefighter in the U.S. Air Force. Scott's expertise helped us sort through the information on power generation and safety. His background in computer information systems helped us better understand the Y2K problem.

Karl Kaufman is a Critical Care Registered Nurse. He grew up on the School of Homesteading organic farm, and spent many years living a self-sufficient lifestyle. He has worked with preparedness groups for 12 years. His experience qualifies him to comment on medical preparedness, food storage strategies, and alternatives to high-tech living.

Patrice Kaufman served in the U.S. Air Force. She holds a B.A. in Political Science. She is an author and publisher currently working on a series of books on spirituality and the evolution of consciousness. Her interest in issues impacting the new millennium led to her participation in this project. Patrice is Karl's wife, and Scott's sister.

Our book starts out with an overview of the Y2K problem. The overview presents a compelling look at how this problem will affect all aspects of our lives.

The text, arranged in twelve chapters, covers twelve steps to Y2K preparedness. We arranged the chapters in order of importance, according to the "hierarchy of needs" established by psychologist William Maslow. This list of human needs helps determine the focus and priority of preparedness steps.

Chapter 1 is on the planning process. This chapter is designed to help you create your Y2K preparedness strategy, and prioritize your action steps.

Chapters 2, 3 and 4 cover shelter, water and food. These are the human needs that form the base of Maslow's needs pyramid. Making sure your home will keep you warm if the power goes out, and that you have adequate water and food if supplies are disrupted, are your basic preparedness priorities.

Chapter 5 is entitled *Safety*. Since Y2K will likely disrupt emergency services at the local, state and national levels, you need to know how to keep your family safe.

The banking system, electric power grid and telecommunications network are three key infrastructure areas particularly vulnerable to Y2K consequences. In Chapters 6, 7 and 8 we examine what preparatory steps you can take to offset these Y2K impacts.

What can you do to keep healthy if the medical system fails after January 1, 2000? Read Chapter 9 to find out.

Chapter 10 looks at what you can do to keep mobile if Y2K affects the transportation sector.

In Chapter 11, we cover joining a community-wide effort to prepare for Y2K; possibly the most important step you can take.

Chapter 12 discusses how you can prevent your personal records—financial, medical, and legal—from being lost in cyberspace in the new millennium.

We titled our book *Y2K—It's Not Too Late* because we want to convey hope. Many Y2K books emphasize the serious nature of the problem, giving the impression that it's too late to prepare. We believe no matter when you find out about Y2K, you can still take positive steps to prepare. But remember, the hour is late, and you need to get started now!

There is a tremendous amount of information on Y2K preparedness on the Internet. Throughout the book, we refer you to websites which expand upon our material. If you don't have home access to the Internet, you can gain access through your local public library. Most have computer terminals you can use to surf the web for free.

One or more suppliers have been listed for each of the products discussed in the book. The first time a supplier is mentioned, we list contact information—toll free phone number and website if available. Also, in the appendix at the back of the book, this supplier information is arranged in alphabetical order.

We offer this book in hope it will help you achieve Y2K readiness. We wish you the best in your personal preparedness efforts!

The Y2K Computer Problem

If we don't fix the century-date problem, we will have a situation scarier than the average disaster movie you might see on a Sunday night.

Charles Rossotti
IRS Commissioner

On May 19, 1998, the Galaxy IV satellite spun out of control. Instantly, service to 90% of the nation's pagers failed. Millions of people struggled to implement alternative forms of contact, and maintain business and social communications. Fortunately, access to phones, fax machines, and e-mail kept the links alive during the two-day inconvenience.

This incident is often used to illustrate the kinds of problems that may await us at the change of century next New Year. When the clock ticks past midnight and 1999 becomes the Year 2000, every aspect of our modern technological infrastructure is potentially at risk of failure. Electric power, telecommunications, transportation, water treatment and distribution, banking and finance, government services, manufacturing and business—all may be threatened.

Pager failures may be the least of our problems when the Year 2000, or Y2K, time bomb goes off.

WHAT IS Y2K?

"Y2K" is an acronym for "Year 2000." *Y* stands for year and *K* stands for thousand. The Year 2000 problem stems from short-hand notation used by computer programmers to save space as they wrote computer software applications.

When programmers first began to write application code, they used a two-digit date code for the year to save space. For instance, the year 1967 was encoded as "67," 1968 as "68," and so on.

When the year rolls over from 1999 to 2000, computers will read "00" and interpret this as "1900." Why is this so, and why is this a problem?

Computers do not possess intelligence and reasoning ability. They rely upon the logic programmed into their applications. Peter de Jager, a Canadian computer consultant recognized as a pioneer in sounding the Y2K alarm, illustrated this at a C-Span conference: "I was born in 1955. If I ask the computer to calculate how old I am today, it subtracts 55 from 98 and announces that I'm 43....But what happens in the year 2000? The computer will subtract 55 from 00 and will state that I am minus 55 years old....If you want to sort by date (e.g., 1965, 1905, and 1966), the resulting sequence would be 1905, 1965, 1966. However, if you add in a date record such as 2015, the computer, which reads only the last two digits of the date, sees 05, 15, 65, 66....These are just two types of calculations that are going to produce garbage."

When computers are faced with the 00 date field, analysts state there are two potential outcomes. They may produce errors in calculating ages, sorting information by date, and comparing dates, thereby creating incorrect or garbled data. Or, they may crash, ceasing to operate entirely.

We know these outcomes are likely when the date rolls over from 1999 to 2000, because many computers have already faced the 00 date field and generated these erroneous responses. Nearly half of the Fortune 500 firms answering a 1998 Cap Gemini poll reported experiencing Year 2000 failures.

Examples of Y2K Glitches

Pre-2000 glitches which have already occurred serve two purposes—they prove that the problem exists, and they tip us off to the potential consequences if program code is not prepared to handle the 00 date rollover.

Some of these problems are almost funny. At a food services firm in London, the computer system read the expiration date on canned meat as 1902 instead of 2002. It decided that the food was 96 years old, and ordered it thrown out.

In another glitch, a 95-year old grandmother was ordered to report to kindergarten. Harmless enough.

Other problems are not so funny, or so harmless. The North American Air Defense Command in Cheyenne Mountain, Colorado, conducted a test to examine the effect of the Year 2000 on their nuclear attack warning computers. When the date rolled over at the stroke of midnight, everything froze. The screens that monitor early warning satellites, watching to detect an incoming missile attack, went blank.

Other critical services have shown signs of similar catastrophic problems. A Y2K-related problem caused a court computer to erroneously instruct a parole board to release an inmate, well before his appointed time. This prisoner was a convicted murderer, actually ineligible for parole until 2097.

While these glitches have been isolated failures, there is a potential for crisis if simultaneous, multiple failures occur after the century date change on 1-1-2000. As we approach the Year 2000, more and more computer systems will be dealing with dates in the

21st century. Systems not prepared to handle the date change can be expected to experience effects outlined above.

Components of the Y2K Problem

Consultant Peter de Jager has summed up the Year 2000 problem in four simple statements.

The code is broken: The first component of the Y2K crisis is that *the code is broken.* Computer code set up to recognize a two-digit year field cannot handle the Year 2000 without being repaired.

It is widely believed that Y2K is the biggest software repair project ever undertaken. What makes it unique and complex is that the majority of mainframe computers and PCs worldwide will be affected at the same time. It potentially affects all software.

Immovable deadline: The second fact, de Jager explained, is that the deadline for all repairs to be completed—January 1, 2000—is absolutely immovable. Whatever is not fixed by that date may not work.

In mid-1998, Senator Robert Bennett, chairman of the Senate Special Committee on the Year 2000 Technology Problem, said that "If today were December 31, 1999, and our systems were in the current state they are in today, tomorrow our economy worldwide would stop...You would not have dial tone tomorrow if tomorrow were January 1st, year 2000. You would not have air travel, Federal Express, the Postal Service, water, or power."

Delayed completion likely: Computer programming and repair projects have a history of delayed completion. As de Jager pointed out, more than 80 percent of all IT projects are delivered late or never. While many business and government Year 2000 project managers assert repairs will be completed on time, other experts state these assertions are not supported by the industry track record.

Y2K author Michael Hyatt stated, "Perhaps the scariest part of the whole Y2K repair effort is the miserable record that corporate software developers have in completing projects on time."

The embedded systems problem: De Jager's fourth and final point is that we have a problem even bigger than the software problem, which is the *embedded systems problem*. Not only do we have to fix the software code operating on computers, we also need to repair or replace the non-compliant computer chips that are embedded into electronic equipment and automated devices worldwide.

There are three additional issues, aside from software code and embedded systems repair, which must be considered in the quest for Y2K compliance.

Data exchange reliability: In today's interconnected world, computers constantly exchange data with one another. Businesses and organizations have computer connections with customers, suppliers, sales agents, financial service providers, insurance carriers, federal/state/local government agencies, and telecommunication networks. After 12-31-1999, non-Y2K-compliant data may corrupt computers which are Y2K-ready. Assuring that repaired systems successfully and safely exchange data in the new millennium is a job in itself.

Testing the repaired systems: It is widely believed that testing the repaired systems can consume up to 70% of the total time and budget of a Y2K project. Thorough testing poses various challenges, among which is completing the remediation work early enough to allow time for testing before 12-31-99. Once the expensive and intricate work of repair is completed, the lengthier and more costly job of testing has to be undertaken.

Contingency planning: Due to our reliance upon external computer-driven sources such as public utilities and the financial system, even the most Y2K-compliant businesses and organizations are likely to experience Year-2000-induced problems. Contingency plans are needed to deal with these inevitable problems.

Thus, there are five separate issues to consider in fixing the Y2K problem—software code repair, embedded systems repair, data exchange reliability, testing, and contingency planning. We'll look at each in turn in the following section.

WHY THE Y2K PROBLEM IS SO HARD TO FIX
Software Code Repair

The need to fix computer software is the part of the Y2K problem most people understand. The Year 2000 problem is defined as affecting computers at the level of their software code. Software code must be rewritten so it can recognize and read the correct date after January 1, 2000.

Rewriting code to make it Year-2000 compliant involves making changes to the *date fields*. In order to make these changes, each date field must be identified and located within the program.

Software programs consist of strings of programming instructions, called *lines of code*. Date fields are contained within them. It has been estimated that there are 180 billion lines of code worldwide that must be examined for date field correction.

No Silver Bullet

Many people have wondered why a software program can't be developed to scan these billions of lines of code, locate and correct the date fields at the speed of light. One of the reasons we're so behind in preparing for the Year 2000 is that companies tended to delay their Y2K projects, waiting for a silver bullet to be developed to do the work for them. But because software code is written in a large variety of programming languages, no one tool works for all programs.

The 1996 Software Productivity Research catalog of programming languages identified almost 500 different languages in current use. The computer language COBOL accounts for 70% of all current software running on mainframe computers today. While automated tools exist for COBOL programs, most of the remaining 499 computer languages don't have adequate support aids.

Even the COBOL-based programs, supported by numerous automated tools, aren't always easily repaired. Why? Because as many as 30% of all programs are written in multiple computer programming languages. This makes it much harder to find and fix Year-2000 problems. Also, software programs are often customized to fit the needs of a particular business; automated tools can't always be used to find date fields in customized software programs.

Challenge of Locating Date Fields

Even when automated tools can be used, there is no guarantee they'll find all the date fields. In many cases, the programmer must go behind the tool, and manually search for date fields that were missed. In August 1998, the Washington Post reported on the work of Randy Young, one of the Y2K programmers working on mortgage broker Freddie Mac's 1200 software applications. Young's efforts illustrate the complexity of date field repair.

For months, Young had been working on a program which compares information about mortgages stored in different databases to make sure the records match. He started the repair process by running the code through diagnostic software, scanning each line for date-related Cobol terms. The software looked for common programming words such as "Date," "DT," "Year," "YR" and "YY," and highlighted each occurrence.

But he discovered that some date-related information was stored in fields almost impossible to identify, named for the children, girlfriends, and favorite Star Trek characters of the programmers who'd written the code. He was forced to revert to manual tactics. Surrounded by stacks of printouts, he went through the program line by line, to see if the scanning software missed anything. He spent two weeks marking up printouts "like a teacher grading an essay."

As Randy Young and his peers know only too well, there is simply no quick fix for Y2K software repairs.

Lost Source Code

Y2K remediation is even more difficult when the original programming instructions, called *source code,* are unavailable.

Programmers write source code in the form of English-language-like statements. Source code is then compiled into *object code,* which makes it possible for computers to "read" it.

Programmers rely on their use of source code when they must make changes to object code. Without the original source code, they can't make sense of object code.

Much of the early computer code was written decades ago, and is still in use today. Unfortunately, many companies and government agencies have lost the original source code for these programs. In these cases, programmers are unable to "decode" the object code, making Y2K repair work even more difficult.

Shortage of Programmers

Because code remediation is so labor-intensive, another problem companies face is the shortage of computer programmers able to do the work. The National Institute of Standards and Technology reports that an experienced programmer working with automated tools can review and repair approximately 100,000 lines of code per year. If every one of the 550,000 COBOL programmers in the United States did nothing except work on Y2K projects, they could fix at maximum 55 billion lines of code this year.

Dr. G. K. Jayaram, co-founder and Chairman of the Y2K consulting firm Transformation Systems, stated that the number of people needed to remediate the billions of lines of code worldwide "is like building the pyramids." He believes the estimated shortage in America alone of 200,000 to 340,000 programmers represents a "global crisis in information technology human resources."

Clearly, Y2K software remediation is a complex and challenging task. Yet, it pales in comparison to another aspect of the Year 2000 crisis, embedded systems repair.

Embedded Systems Repair

Fixing computer software code is only the tip of the Y2K iceberg. The embedded systems problem looms below the surface.

What are Embedded Systems?

Simply put, embedded systems are tiny computers called *microchips, microprocessors* or *integrated circuits* These tiny systems are embedded deep in the heart of a variety of electronic equipment and automated devices. The average late-model car contains up to several dozen microprocessors which control and regulate systems from the dashboard clock to the anti-lock brakes and air-fuel mixture.

While estimates vary on how many embedded systems are in use in the world today, many experts believe there are 25 billion or more. How many of these 25+ billion chips are likely to fail at the change of century? Estimates range from 0.25% to over 1%. That would mean from 60 million to 250 million embedded systems failures could occur owing to the Year 2000-related non-compliance problems.

Some professionals believe a much larger proportion of the total chip population may be vulnerable to Year-2000 effects. Andrew

Bochman, senior analyst for Year-2000 services at Aberdeen, a Boston-based IT consulting company, expects to see a trouble rate of about 20% of all devices containing embedded systems.

However, the bigger problem is, how are those chips that are defective going to be identified, located, and repaired? Industry experts liken this to finding the proverbial needle in the haystack.

Where are Embedded Systems Located?

The word *ubiquitous* is often used to describe embedded systems. It means "being or seeming to be everywhere at the same time." This is an apt description of the billions of chips scattered across our planet.

Where are these chips found? They're in microwave ovens and VCRs, automatic sprinkler systems and security alarms. Elevators, automotive assembly lines, telephone systems, medical equipment and devices, electric power grids, nuclear power plants, public transit systems, and water treatment plants all run with the aid of microchips. They're located in undersea oil drilling rigs, air traffic control systems, and railroad track beds. Embedded systems control industrial machinery, communications satellites, and military command and control systems. The average American comes in contact with hundreds of microprocessors each day.

Potential embedded systems' malfunctions pose a great threat to our health and safety. Failures in many of the systems listed above could even lead to loss of life.

According to computer experts, a single faulty chip was to blame for the chemical leak in the industrial disaster that killed 7000 and injured 300,000 in Bhopal, India in 1984. The Y2K problem could present numerous such scenarios, if the non-compliant chips are not found and fixed in time. Many believe that the Year 2000 computer crisis poses the greatest environmental threat in history.

Difficulty of Solving the Embedded Systems Problem

To prevent a worst-case scenario from occurring, potentially vulnerable embedded chips must be located, repaired, or replaced. This is no small task. For example, one firm which has 10,000 embedded systems buried in the North Sea must spend approximately $75,000 to check *each chip* under the seabed.

Embedded systems on satellites orbiting the earth are nearly impossible to inspect for compliance. What about chips in pacemakers in patients' chests?

Locating, identifying, testing and repairing the millions of non-compliant embedded systems in use around the world is a job of monumental proportions. It involves combing through 25+ billion microprocessors in order to find those 250 million or so that may fail. *And all of this must be done by the end of this year.*

By far the biggest challenge to the process of embedded systems remediation is the time factor. Industry authorities state there is not enough time to find and fix all the non-compliant chips by the 12-31-1999 deadline date.

According to a recent report by Stamford, Connecticut-based Gartner Group, an Information Technology consulting firm monitoring global Y2K progress, only 11% of the 15,000 companies and government agencies they surveyed have begun to examine their potential embedded systems problem. If 89% had not yet started by the second half of 1998, what realistic chance do they have of completion by the deadline of December 31, 1999?

Having briefly examined the challenges of computer software and embedded systems repair, let's turn our attention to the third area of concern in the Year 2000 problem—connections between business partners, and the exchange of data between their computers.

Data Exchange Reliability

We've often marvelled at the switch from manual operations to computer operations, which took place early in our lives. In the business world today, financial transactions, retail sales, ordering and billing, communications, transportation, power generation—everything is done by computer.

Vast networks link computers locally, nationally, and globally. Your local bank may be in New York City, yet when you use an ATM machine in Los Angeles the transaction is entered automatically in your account.

What happens if these interconnections break down? How will the failure of a single business' computer systems impact upon those with whom its computers are networked? What will happen if multiple failures occur worldwide?

The question of computer connectivity opens up a whole new issue in the already-complicated Y2K minefield. Not only must organizations work to correct the two-digit date-field glitch in their computer software applications and find and fix all non-compliant embedded systems, they must also investigate all the ways in which their connections with outside suppliers, vendors, and business partners may impact their operating ability after December 31, 1999.

Will Suppliers Deliver Products After 12-31-1999?

"Modern business is completely reliant on networks," strategic planner John L. Peterson explained in an online article entitled *The Year 2000: Social Chaos or Social Transformation.* "Companies have vendors, suppliers, customers, outsourcers (all, of course, managed by computerized data bases.) For Y2K, these highly networked ways of doing business create a terrifying scenario. The networks mean that no one system can protect itself from Y2K failures by just attending to its own internal systems."

The example of General Motors, with over 100,000 suppliers and vendors worldwide, is often cited to illustrate the complexity of the Y2K connectivity issue. GM has experienced production stoppages whenever one key supplier has gone on strike. How many Y2K-induced delays and shutdowns are possible among 100,000+ suppliers?

Because software and embedded systems repair is so complicated, firms often leave their assessment of suppliers as the last step in their Y2K project. That means many firms will arrive at the December 31, 1999 deadline without having made sure key vendors and suppliers are Y2K ready.

This was underscored in a PC Week Online interview with Tim Morton, vice president of operations at Electronic Date Systems Corporation's CIO Services, in Plano, Texas: "Time is running out for many businesses just starting their assessment phase inside their own company. That means they may never get to the point where they know what their partners are doing."

The potential for Y2K-induced vendor and supplier firm failure is the first half of the connectivity problem. The second is the very real possibility that non-compliant computers will pass along incorrect data to others, corrupting even those systems that have achieved Year-2000 compliance. We'll look at this issue next.

Will Corrupt Data Infect Compliant Computers?

The transfer of information between computer systems is called *electronic data interchange,* or EDI. Information exchange is a common occurrence. Information is exchanged between departments within companies; between companies and their suppliers, vendors, and customers; between business partners and colleagues.

When two computer systems trade data, corrupted data in one system can corrupt the other. How does computer data become

corrupted? If just one line of code is missed by the Y2K programmers, that uncorrected code could cause havoc. If that data is
passed to other computers, it could corrupt them too.

Exactly how might this transfer of inaccurate data occur? It
all boils down to a computer's ability to handle the Year 2000 date
change. If a system reads dates in the year 2000 as 1900, it will
either freeze up or use its inaccurate reading to produce inaccurate output. We already know that a computer monitoring canned
meat expiration dates read the year 2002 as 1902. In this case inaccurate output was generated, as the computer tagged the meat
as outdated and ordered it destroyed.

When inaccurate data is passed from computer to computer,
it's like the "telephone" game we played as children, where a whis-
pered message is passed around a circle of kids. Each transmission changes a word here and there, until the original message
becomes totally distorted.

For example, a non-compliant computer may erroneously
decide that a payment should be made or a product should be
shipped. If it forwards that information to a Y2K-compliant computer system, the receiving computer may edit for accurate account number, valid amount, valid item number, and perform
debits and credits of the amount or issue a shipping manifest.
But, the data is wrong. The error is compounded. The receiving
system thus participated in an incorrect, non-compliant transaction. Its accounts are incorrect.

Such inaccurate calculations in the banking or securities industry could easily multiply into a serious crisis. Consider this.
The Federal Reserve System—the U.S. central bank—operates the
nation's payment system. It moves $1 trillion a day among finan-
cial institutions. FedWire, the Fed's electronic transfer system, is
used by 11,600 customers. In 1995 more than 27 million transfers

(over $220 trillion) were made using this computerized payment system. Errors in even a small percentage of these transactions could cause chaos in the world's banking systems.

This chaos could quickly hit where we each feel it most—in our pocketbook. Consider the monthly statements you get from your bank or other financial services provider regarding your checking account, passbook account, etc. What happens if you can no longer be sure these statements are accurate? Imagine if hundreds and thousands of bank customers all try at the same time to get customer service help to straighten out their accounts. If the computers are down, or miscalculating data, how will this be remedied?

It's not difficult to envision how this could impact upon the business sector. The systems in our modern world can't function without consistently reliable computer data.

It's not enough for any organization or company to bring its own computers into Y2K compliance. As long as any outside computer with which a firm exchanges data is not prepared for the century date change, its own internal computers are vulnerable.

Data filters and bridges: To make matters even more interesting, let's look at yet another piece of the Y2K connectivity puzzle. There are several different techniques computer programmers can choose from to bring software code into Year-2000 compliance. Unfortunately, none of these methods are compatible. This means if the technique used to repair a firm's internal computers is not the same as that used by a vendor, supplier, or business partner, the internal and external computers can not exchange electronic data safely or successfully.

In these cases, separate programs called *filters* and *bridges* must be written and installed. These allow the reprogrammed date codes to be exchanged between computer systems. However, even these stopgap measures are not fail-safe.

The U.S. Government General Accounting Office explained this in a July 1998 report entitled *Year 2000 Computing Crisis: Actions Needed on Electronic Data Exchanges.* "The solution—such as it is—involves creating a 'filter' or 'bridge' program that detects date patterns in the input stream. When a two-digit format is discerned by the system, it is converted before it is allowed into the system. This is similar to how antivirus programs work on microcomputers or how software 'firewalls' work on computers that are connected to the Internet.

"The problem is that filtering technology is still in its infancy. Given that so many of the programs that need protection are custom applications, these filters can be constructed only on an application-by-application basis. And, time spent writing and testing filters is time not spent converting and testing the actual code itself to make it Year 2000-compliant."

This report points out that as computer systems are converted to process Year 2000 dates, the associated data exchanges must also be made Year 2000 compliant. If the data exchanges are not Year 2000 compliant, data will not be exchanged, or invalid data could cause the receiving computer systems to malfunction or produce inaccurate computations.

The subject of electronic data exchange is particularly serious for the federal government. Federal agencies report they have a total of almost 500,000 data exchanges with other federal agencies, states, local governments, and the private sector. If Year 2000 data exchange problems are not corrected, public services many people depend on, such as welfare, medicare and medicaid, might be interrupted.

Imagine the work involved in inventorying 500,000 data exchanges. First you have to identify each of these half million connections between computers. Then you must contact each exchange partner, and determine if the data exchange will be compatible after 12-31-1999. You have to repair software code, negotiate the creation and installation of bridges or filters, or find a new business partner if a particular exchange can't be made compliant. If after all your hard work, one or more data exchanges fail, your computer system will be infected with inaccurate information.

These 500,000 data exchanges are for the federal government alone. Multiply this by state and local governments, the private sector, and the international scene. And don't forget embedded systems, testing the repaired systems, and formulating contingency plans, which we haven't even talked about yet.

It seems impossible that this feat can be pulled off by December 31, 1999.

Testing the Repaired Systems

After the work of repairing software code, fixing non-compliant embedded systems, and assuring the reliance of computer networks is completed, it still isn't time to say mission accomplished. From 50% to 75% of the total Y2K work has yet to be done.

Importance of Testing

Testing is the most important aspect of a Y2K project. As the House Committee on Government Reform and Oversight stated, "Testing is a major aspect of the Year 2000 problem...testing is also the hardest, most expensive, and most time-consuming aspect of fixing the problem."

Simply put, after the code has been fixed, it has to be tested to make sure that it still works right. Year 2000 repairs are designed to allow a software program to handle dates in the new millennium, but are not supposed to change the way the program functions. Yet programming professionals know only too well, code repair or modification often introduces new problems of its own.

Code Repair Introduces New Errors

Year 2000 repair is major surgery performed on software code. Each line of code is scanned, every date field modified. In such a process, unintentional errors are inevitable.

Whenever you change program code, something else will break. For manual remediation, the error rate is one error for every 1000 lines of code. If you use automatic tools, the error rate falls to one error for every 10,000 lines of code.

An average company with 10,000,000 lines of code will at best have only 1000 undetected defects after completing code repair. Even organizations whose programmers are on par with the very best in the world can't hope to complete Y2K remediation work with no residual bugs.

Chances for error are multiplied in most Y2K projects. In many cases, programmers work under extreme pressure, modifying computer programs written by someone else, working in unfamiliar programming languages without current documentation.

This is what makes testing so important. It's critical to find and fix the residual errors before sending the remediated software back into operation.

Many Plan to Do No Testing

Though one of the greatest risks for a company is to put its code back into operation without testing it first, many businesses and organizations plan to do no testing at all. Due to the difficulty of completing the repair phase alone by the December 31, 1999 deadline, they are not incorporating a testing phase into their Y2K projects.

Why? Because as mentioned above, testing is not only the most time-consuming part of a Y2K project, it's also the most expensive. Few companies have the time and money to thoroughly test their Y2K repairs.

In a recent survey of U.S. businesses and government agencies, Cap Gemini America found that fully half of those surveyed do not plan to test software code and systems to make certain they are ready for the Year 2000. Without thorough testing, you can't be assured that the goods and services you've come to rely on will continue to be there for you past the Year 2000.

Contingency Planning

The neglect of testing highlights the need for *contingency planning.* Since no one can guarantee 100% compliance, planning for problems that may arise post-2000 is the wisest course of action.

It's widely recognized that a certain percentage of mission critical computer systems will not be fixed before the 12-31-1999 deadline date. As a result, failures and disruptions will occur. We may lose electrical power in parts of the country. Water supplies may be disrupted. Delivery of food and other goods could be halted.

Contingency Planning Neglected

Developing work-arounds to permit continued functioning as these failures occur is what contingency planning is all about. Unfortunately, these plans are being neglected throughout the public and private sectors.

Business continuity and contingency planning across the government has been especially inadequate. In their May 1998 quarterly reports to the Office of Management and Budget, only four of 24 agencies reported that they had drafted contingency plans for their core business processes.

The government is not alone in its lack of contingency plans. None of the public utilities surveyed in mid-1998 had completed contingency planning. A survey of Fortune 250 companies shows that few have put together contingency plans to deal with the inevitable problems that will arise from Y2K.

Given the available information, it's clear that many computer systems, including some that are mission critical, will not be Y2K-compliant by 2000. It also appears that not all resultant problems will have advance plans in place for their solution.

This is the information we need to weigh as we determine the steps to take to prepare for potential Y2K problems. What will happen given the high probability of computer glitches, embedded systems failures, and inaccurate data exchanges? How difficult will it be to cope with and rebound from these problems?

In the next section, we'll examine the potential impact Y2K may have upon the various aspects of our lives.

Y2K RISKS TO OUR WAY OF LIFE

Y2K has the potential to disrupt every aspect of our daily lives. Not all critical systems will be repaired in time. Not every embedded chip will be found and fixed by 2000. Sporadic testing will leave some software bugs undetected. Lack of contingency plans will result in chaos in certain areas.

Where will these breakdowns occur? How severe will they be? How long will they last? While the details are open to question, we do know where the problems are likely to appear, and how they'll impact our way of life.

Risks to the Infrastructure

Our nation's critical infrastructures are telecommunications, electrical power systems, gas and oil production, banking and finance, transportation, water supply systems, emergency services, government services, business and manufacturing, and the health care sector. The greatest risk inherent in the Y2K problem is that critical segments of the national and international infrastructures may suffer debilitating disruptions.

Many experts are concerned about these potential failures. The Senate Special Committee on the Year 2000 Technology Problem has held numerous hearings exploring this risk. The GAO has issued over four dozen reports on the potential consequences of the Y2K problem.

Testifying before Congress in September 1998, the GAO's Joel Willemssen said, "The public faces a high risk that critical services provided by the government and the private sector could be severely disrupted....Financial transactions could be delayed, flights grounded, power lost, and national defense affected....Key economic sectors that could be seriously affected if their systems are not Year 2000 compliant include information and telecommunications; banking and finance; health, safety, and emergency services; transportation; power and water; and manufacturing and small business."

Life after 2000 could resemble a real-life disaster film, if these predicted disruptions occur.

Public Utilities

The foundation of modern civilization rests upon the "iron triangle" of electric power, telecommunications, and running water. If either leg of the triangle goes down, it can take the others with it.

Electric power grid: The Y2K risk to the electrical generating and distribution system is the most critical of the three. It's been said, "if the power grid goes down, it's all over." Without power, it doesn't matter if computers are Y2K compliant or not.

In the United States, electrical power is generated and distributed from coast to coast by an interconnected network of 7800 electric utilities and power producers. About 75% of the nation's power capacity is generated by 200 large investor-owned utilities; the remaining 25% of our power comes from 7600 municipal utilities. These power plants are fueled 51% by coal, 20% by nuclear power, and 15% by natural gas. Once generated, the electrical power is moved across the country via half a million miles of high-voltage power lines, passed through 112,000 substations. All this is tied together in one gigantic mainframe-controlled system containing countless embedded chips.

The U.S. energy industry is one of the most technologically advanced and heavily computerized industries in the world. This complex network moves fuel and power from coast to coast. For the most part, it is controlled and maintained by computer. When the calendar changes at the millennium, the software is liable to interpret the date as 1900 and fail to operate.

Similar problems exist on the hardware side involving embedded chips. A Y2K glitch could affect the microprocessors in thousands of embedded systems just at one power plant. Kathleen Hirning, CIO for the Federal Energy Regulatory Commission, admitted "the potential impact of Year 2000 errors could cause some embedded systems to malfunction, possibly resulting in a ripple effect across the grid."

The potential vulnerability of the power grid was thrust into the national spotlight this past June when Senator Bennett publicly stated that Y2K-induced regional brownouts and blackouts are all but certain after the century date change. He predicted that if January 1, 2000 came that weekend, there would be a 100% chance of the power grid's failure. With 18 months to repair it, his predicted odds dropped to 40% failure.

Results of the June 12, 1998 Special Y2K Committee hearing on the power grid show that prospects are slim of fixing the grid's hundreds of millions of chips, microprocessors, and computer programs in time. Senator Christopher Dodd, co-chair of the Special Y2K Committee, said "we're no longer at the point of asking whether or not there will be any power disruptions, but we are now forced to ask how severe the disruptions are going to be."

Chapters 2 and 7 examine alternative means to provide your home with light and heat, should you lose electrical power.

Telecommunications: The second hearing held by the Senate Special Committee on the Year 2000 Technology Problem was an in-depth look at the Y2K status of the telecommunications industry. In his opening statement, Senator Bennett stated,

"The global telecommunications infrastructure is the central nervous system of modern society. Daily, 270 million Americans depend on this complex web of voice, data, and video services that enable their telephones, radios, fax machines, computer networks, televisions and other information appliances. Major national and international enterprises, such as emergency response, national security, finance, transportation, health care, government, energy distribution, and others, are critically dependent on reliable, 24 hours a day, seven days a week telecommunications."

Without these services, our ability to receive, gather and respond to information would be as limited as it was before Alexander Graham Bell invented the telephone.

Whether our global telecommunications infrastructure can ride out the millennium date change without significant disruptions is doubtful. First, it's a highly complex network of systems. Second, there is no identifiable U.S. public or private body taking the lead on the global aspects of the Y2K telecommunications problems. Third, successful communications depend upon being able to both send and receive information.

Today in the United States, there are five long distance carriers not including the growing number of long distance resellers, five major national television broadcasters, six Regional Bell Operating Companies, more than 1000 small phone companies,

16 communications satellite providers, more than 4500 Internet Service Providers and hundreds of cellular phone companies. This doesn't include thousands of radio stations and over 11,000 cable services companies.

This infrastructure relies on hundreds of millions of lines of computer code. Telephone companies are as computer dependent as is the electric power grid. Complicating the problem is the extensive use of embedded chips throughout the telecommunications industry. It is difficult to believe all elements of a system this complex will be ready by December 31, 1999.

The consequences of not resolving Year 2000 problems in the telecommunications infrastructure will be broad based. National and global financial institutions and brokerages won't be able to function. Air traffic control systems will grind to a halt. Credit card transactions won't be processed without working phones.

What about emergency services? You can't call 911 if the phone doesn't work. You won't be able to call in sick for work or notify your child's school of an absence. These are but a few of the myriad things you won't be able to do.

In Chapter 8, Communications, we'll examine how you can safeguard yourself and your family against these potential outages.

Water treatment and distribution: If the municipal water treatment and distribution system fails, even temporarily, the effect upon us would be immediate and severe. While a water outage doesn't carry the business implications of a power or telecommunications failure, its physical impact is greater. People can survive only a few days without water.

Like so many aspects of modern life, we take drinkable water flowing from our faucets for granted. Yet like other amenities, the water system is highly computerized. It is dependent on embedded systems to control its operations.

What is the status of Y2K remediation efforts in our nation's water supply systems? In November 1998, the results of the first industry-wide survey to determine this were released. Some of the findings were alarming.

Of 725 water treatment and distribution companies surveyed, 36% reported they had no formal Y2K plans in place. Of those working on compliance, only 10% had been working at it for more than one year. The assessment phase of the project had been completed by no more than 58% of the companies. Just 23% were developing contingency plans.

Will there be safe drinking water at the tap on January 1, 2000, and each day thereafter? You can't count on it. If delivery of treatment chemicals is upset by computer or microprocessor failures, the water that flows from our faucets could make us sick.

Worse yet, if water delivery fails, we won't receive any water at all. That would make it impossible to drink, cook, bathe, wash clothes, or even flush toilets.

None of us want to consider this possibility. Yet, no public official at this time offers guarantees that we'll all continue to enjoy safe running water after the turn of the century. We each must consider the personal steps we can take to ensure an uninterrupted supply of water for ourselves and our families. In Chapter 3, Water, we'll look at these steps.

Transportation

In the first Senate Y2K Committee hearing to discuss Y2K's impact on the nation's airports, railways, waterways, and roadways, the consensus was that major disruption of U.S. transportation was inevitable.

Prior to this hearing, the Committee surveyed 32 airlines, airports, railroads, maritime shippers, trucking companies, and metropolitan transit authorities. One hundred telephone calls to offer assistance and encourage results were made; 50% responded.

Of that 50%, only a third had completed their Y2K assessment process. None had fully assessed the scope of their Y2K problem, only half were working on contingency plans, and none had completed this process.

Overall readiness in the U.S. transportation industry gives cause for concern. Transportation is the lifeline of our global economy. Thousands of American corporations and businesses depend on air, rail, maritime shipping, trucking, and mass transit to move millions of people and goods safely and economically. Even temporary disruptions could cause chaos.

Senator Bennett expressed concern that the transportation sector as a whole may not be able to make the Y2K transition without major disruptions. He warned "interdependencies of these companies with their partners and suppliers—both foreign and domestic—make the transportation sector extremely complex and, thus, make the Year 2000 issues difficult to address."

One such example is the possible interruption of rail-transported coal shipments to the nation's electrical generating plants. Coal-fired power plants receive two rail-delivered coal shipments per day. Because these plants do not warehouse fuel, they are totally dependent upon these daily shipments for continuous operation. City Utilities of Springfield Missouri plans to have a large enough stockpile of coal by the end of 1999 to generate electricity for three months. This is the only public utility company so far to have announced such contingency plans.

Another vulnerable area is the distribution of our nation's food supply. Grocery stores typically stock a 72-hour supply of merchandise. They depend upon the continued reliability of the trucking industry to keep foodstuffs on their shelves. Their inventories, delivery routing and schedules are run by computers.

On July 29, 1998, the Westergaard Year 2000 online news service wrote, "The low level of Y2K preparation in America's farms could leave grocery store shelves bare come early January, 2000. Due to a very high lack of concern in the agricultural community, grain could end up rotting in silos and animals dying in their pens due to unremediated transportation and storage equipment."

Agricultural Committee Chairman Richard Lugar worries that in late 1999, consumers will panic and empty grocery shelves.

Parts and supplies deliveries to manufacturers also depend upon trucking, rail, ship, and air transportation. The transport of finished goods to market, business travel, and all forms of travel in general could also be impacted.

On September 2, 1998, the Department of Transportation, charged with the overall responsibility of our nation's transportation industry, was given a "D" rating in Y2K preparedness. This agency is not expected to have its mission-critical computer systems Y2K-ready by the change of century.

This brief overview shows there is significant reason to believe our nation will experience Y2K-induced problems within the transportation industry after December 31, 1999. We should each use this information to assess the potential consequences of these upsets on ourselves and our families. See Chapter 10, Transportation, for steps you can take to offset these consequences.

Financial Services

At the end of 1996, the U.S. banking industry consisted of 9500 main offices and 55,000 branch offices, plus 2000 credit unions, thrifts, and other savings institutions. Most of us utilize the services of these financial institutions to cash paychecks, operate checking accounts, obtain credit, and accumulate savings.

Everyday more and more Americans become involved in the securities industry. Before the Great Crash of 1929, trading on

Wall Street reached record volumes of five million shares per day. Now, stock market volumes often exceed 500 million shares daily.

Over 84 million Americans participate in pension plans. The Department of Labor reported that of $3.6 trillion held by private pension plans, nearly half—$1.8 trillion—is invested in equities. Since 1991, individuals have invested $1.1 trillion into stock mutual funds and that amount is increasing at a rate of $21 billion a month.

Worldwide, over $3 trillion in electronic payments is moved daily in millions of separate transactions. Computer dependence within the financial services industry is total.

Computer code is the vehicle for these transactions. No errors can be tolerated in the industry's computer calculations. Alan Greenspan, Chairman of the Federal Reserve, observed that "99% accuracy won't do, it must be 100%."

The financial services industry is particularly vulnerable to Year-2000 computer breakdowns. Each of the more than 9000 FDIC insured commercial banks in the U.S. has a software portfolio averaging 100+ million lines of code. Estimates are that for every million lines of code, there are between 20,000 to 50,000 date fields to find and fix. Inevitably, some bugs are missed, others are introduced in the process of code repair.

Computer expert Ed Yourdon pointed out, "A typical bank's remediated software will likely have 10,000 errors at the end of a Y2K project. While the majority will be minor in scope, some of these errors will set off serious consequences."

Uncorrected date fields and bugs not caught in the testing process will generate corrupted data, which will be passed between financial institutions. Bankers will no longer be able to trust their general ledger, funding position, and account balances of depositors and trading customers.

What are the possible effects of these Y2K timebombs? What

happens if the banks cannot clear checks? What happens if there can be no electronic transfers of funds? We personally don't want to see any portion of our stored, saved, and/or invested funds caught—or lost—in a Y2K glitch. We're sure you don't, either.

Most analysts regard the financial services industry as leading the pack in Y2K preparedness. In general, the majority of financial institutions are doing an adequate job in addressing the Year 2000 issue. Yet, Senator Bennett cautioned, there are no guarantees that complete Y2K compliance will be achieved.

BankBoston, the 15th largest bank in the United States, began its remediation work in the spring of 1995. Its Y2K project is viewed as the model for the industry. Yet in early 1999, BankBoston's Y2K effort is still incomplete, and its project staff works diligently on contingency plans. The concern is with the rest of the financial services industry—those who have not adopted an aggressive program.

Complete industry compliance means all financial institutions must achieve 100% readiness. Is this a realistic assumption? Can we believe that all members of the global financial sector will complete their Y2K work before the Year 2000?

As with other industries, the financial services sector is vulnerable to issues of vendor and supplier compliance. Compounding these risks is the industry's critical dependence upon public infrastructure such as telecommunications and electric power networks. Peter Miller, CIO of J.P. Morgan, testified before Congress that the ripple effect from a large disruption in industries such as telecommunications, transportation, or power could severely impact the financial sector. Federal regulators in the financial services industry are being urged to develop contingency plans anticipating Year-2000-related disruptions to the public infrastructure.

Y2K glitches in the financial system could threaten the money you have saved and invested. Consider the safety of your funds as they are presently allocated, and determine what steps if any you should take to better secure them. See Chapter 6, Finances, for more information.

Business and Manufacturing

One of the greatest personal threats Y2K presents is the impact it could have on your job. Why is this so? If your employer doesn't take care of his Year 2000 problem, he could go out of business. And if he goes out of business, you're out of a job.

Y2K-induced business failures: It's estimated that between 5% to 10% of businesses nationwide will fail because of Y2K woes. Of the 20 million small to medium businesses in the U.S., one to two million will close. A lot of employees will be out of work; unemployment compensation will likely be unavailable. The effect upon the national economy will not be inconsequential.

Many businesses are ignoring Y2K, neglecting to consider its impact upon them. The federal government is gearing up efforts to raise the level of Y2K awareness among business owners and corporate management, but many feel these efforts are coming too late to stave off the projected business closings.

Throughout 1997 and 1998, less than 25% of small businesses were taking the problem seriously. Half say they have no intention of doing anything about it. Analysts are gravely concerned about the implications for our national economy. The health of our small businesses is considered one of the measures of our economy's vitality. If small businesses suffer, we all suffer.

Fortune 500 companies aren't in the clear either. While a higher percentage of large companies have begun their Y2K work, many are not moving fast enough to complete repair work and accomplish testing in time. As of July 1998, Congressional testimony revealed that an astonishing 73% of companies had not yet begun their code remediation.

Many companies, up to 40% of all surveyed, report having already experienced Y2K-related failures. Those that don't achieve compliance in time, will hurt those that do. Supplier-vendor problems will ripple across the country.

Litigation concerns: A complex offshoot of the Y2K problem is an estimated one trillion dollars in lawsuits preparing to be filed after 1-1-2000. Even now, company lawyers are studying who they can sue if Y2K glitches hit their companies.

Software and equipment manufacturers are particularly vulnerable. Companies will seek to place blame and recoup losses if their equipment fails. Some analysts believe that post-Year 2000 lawsuits will dwarf the tobacco, asbestos, and silicone-implant lawsuits of recent years.

Whether your employer fails to achieve Y2K compliance, or has a business partner that misses the deadline, you're bound to feel the crunch.

Government Services

The uninterrupted functioning of government agencies is crucial to the maintenance of our societal infrastructure and our way of life. For that reason, the slow progress of the U.S. federal government's Year 2000 compliance efforts worries many.

One of the most Year 2000-challenged agencies of the federal government is the Internal Revenue Service. While you might think that nobody cares if the IRS goes belly-up, if their computers fail and the government can't collect taxes, all public services which we depend on will suffer.

Federal government's poor Y2K progress: In an October 1998 Congressional report, the House Committee on Government Reform and Oversight found, "The federal government is not on track to complete necessary Year 2000 preparations before January 1, 2000." This assessment mirrors that of the Senate Y2K Committee. After hearing numerous expert witnesses testify, Senator Bennett concluded "In reviewing the status of federal agencies, what is most striking is that it appears highly unlikely that any agency will be completely Y2K-compliant by January 1, 2000."

GAO assessment: The GAO acts as the investigative arm of Congress, auditing and evaluating government programs and activities. Since 1997, they have published over 50 reports detailing Y2K's risk and the federal government's slow response.

In August 1998 the GAO reported "the government's 24 major departments and agencies are making slow progress in fixing their systems....Unless progress improves dramatically, a substantial number of mission-critical systems will not be compliant in time."

Agencies within the federal government are sorted into three groups, based on the progress of their Y2K programs. *Tier three* agencies are making satisfactory progress, nearing completion. They include the Social Security Administration and the SBA. *Tier two* agencies, including NASA and HUD, are making some progress, but not enough. *Tier one* agencies include those in which there is insufficient progress. This last group includes some of the most critical agencies in the U.S. government.

Representative Stephen Horn's Government Reform and Management Committee ranks government Y2K progress and issues quarterly grades to 24 U.S. agencies. Seven of these agencies consistently receive failing assessments.

Among these tier one agencies are the Department of Treasury, which disburses the millions of government checks monthly; the Department of Transportation, responsible for our nation's air traffic control system; the Nuclear Regulatory Agency, overseer of America's nuclear power plants; the Department of Energy, regulator for the national power grid; and the Department of Defense, in charge of our military forces, conventional and nuclear armaments, and national defense. These important agencies currently fail in their Y2K-compliancy efforts—clearly cause for alarm.

State and local Y2K efforts: State and local governments are doing no better. They also face a major risk of Year 2000-induced failures to the many vital services—such as benefits payments, transportation, and public safety—they provide.

In a July 1998 survey of state Year 2000 readiness, just one-third of the states reported at least 50% of their critical systems had been completely assessed, remediated, and tested. Another survey found that approximately 3200 of 3673 cities, ranging in population from 2500 to more than one million, were lagging in their Year 2000 efforts. Many small municipalities are still trying to understand the problem.

At the state and local level, little or no progress has been made in dealing with embedded systems, data exchange issues, and contingency planning. Overall, the magnitude of the Y2K problem is beyond the capacity of state and local officials to address.

Should government operations at the federal, state, or local level be impacted by the millennium bug, we can expect disruptions in many areas of our lives. Think what could happen if welfare, food stamps or medicare checks weren't mailed. What if public transportation weren't available, or if police, fire, and 911 service disappeared? All of this and more is at risk if our government fails to achieve Y2K compliance by December 31, 1999.

Risks to National Security

The implications for national security as a result of the Year 2000 computing crisis are of increasing concern. Those at top levels of our military services have made fixing the Y2K problem their highest priority.

Will America's Superiority in Combat Arms Survive Y2K?

Pentagon specialists have voiced serious doubts that Department of Defense compliance will be completed in time. Given its current rate of progress, DoD's 1.5 million computers and 25,000 systems will not be totally compliant until 2012.

Speculation abounds as to the impact DoD's inability to reach Y2K compliance may have on our military capabilities. The Pentagon lists 30 mission-critical systems not expected to be Y2K-compliant by the Administration's deadline. These include the Army's Enhanced Tactical Combat Service Support Computer System, the Defense Attache Worldwide Network, and the Army Standard Installation/Division Personnel System.

Life-threatening computer glitches have already occurred in our nation's combat systems. In a 1996 Computerworld article entitled *Year 2000 May Ambush U.S. Military*, retired Air Force General Thomas McInerney stated that the Clinton administration should declare the Y2K crisis a "potential national emergency."

In an August 1998 memorandum to top defense officials, Defense Secretary William Cohen admitted that the Pentagon was making insufficient progress in solving its Y2K problem. Will our nation's crucial military defenses make it intact past the year 2000 boundary? Who knows!

Threat to National Defense

In the Computerworld article an Air Force Y2K project director said "There's a real risk some wacko in another country...might decide to launch an attack against the U.S. a few seconds after midnight just to see if our defenses can handle it."

This possibility can't be lightly brushed aside, since our nation will be at its most vulnerable when the technology crisis hits.

Terrorists or leaders of rogue nations, avowed enemies of the United States, could see this as an opportune moment to strike.

Global Nuclear Threat

Analysts debate whether Y2K might trigger a nuclear event. Could a missile be launched intentionally, as a preemptive strike to take advantage of Y2K vulnerability? Could a Y2K glitch activate an automated response to false data, leading to an unintentional launch?

There is also the possibility that computer problems could scramble nuclear missile monitoring capabilities, leading a country to believe it is under attack and purposefully counterlaunch in error. Concern for the fragility of Russia's early warning system prompted U.S. officials to approach their Russian counterparts to discuss plans to offset this possibility.

A report published in late 1998 entitled *The Bug in the Bomb* highlights the vulnerability of the planetary stockpile of nuclear weapons. Many of the countries lagging in Y2K awareness are without the inclination or resources to assure their military computer systems will handle the date change.

Another threat is that Y2K errors in a nuclear power plant could trigger a Chernobyl-like accident. Many of the 400-plus nuclear plants, worldwide, are in nations with inadequate Y2K programs. In the former Soviet states alone, there are over 65 nuclear plants, none of them Y2K-ready. These nations only began to assess their Y2K status in late 1998. Now reeling under the devaluation of the ruble, they are financially unable to achieve compliance.

To many analysts, these nuclear concerns are among the gravest Y2K dangers we face.

International Risks

There are only a handful of countries that approach our level of Y2K readiness. Given our problems, if we are in the lead, that doesn't say much for the rest of the world.

Canada, Great Britain, Australia, Sweden, Singapore, and Israel have Y2K projects in place. Like the U.S., their governments established task forces to increase Y2K awareness in the public and private sectors. The remaining countries are either asleep to the issue, or lag far behind in tackling it.

Why should this concern us? Don't we have enough to worry about within our own borders?

The problem is, today's world is a global village. What happens post-2000 in other parts of the world will affect us in the United States. What happens to computers in any industrialized nation will affect those in many other countries. We are inextricably linked across countries and continents.

Many of GM's 100,000+ suppliers are outside of the U.S. Think about all the products we use daily that are made in other countries. When foreign companies fold because of Y2K problems, their products and services will disappear. U.S. companies will collapse when their overseas business partners close.

Economist Ed Yardeni and others predict a global recession or worse triggered by Y2K. They see the Asian and Russian financial crises as the tip of the iceberg.

The Gartner Group warns that most of Western Europe is neglecting Y2K remediation. Russia and China only began to look at the Y2K problem in mid to late 1998. Japan, with the second largest economy in the world, also waited until last year to gear up. The CIA claims Latin America is "way behind the power curve." Half of the world is reeling under financial depression, unable to mount the billions of dollars necessary for Year 2000 remediation work.

More than 75% of the world's nations are doing nothing to prepare. A June 1998 World Bank survey found that only 18 of

127 countries—14%—had a national Year 2000 program. Senator Bennett predicts that entire countries will "drop off the radar screen" as they lose electrical power, telecommunications, and banking services.

Ed Yardeni summed it up. "Even if we fix everything in our country, even if we all together get alarmed about it and get the message out and make this the top priority that it needs to be...the rest of the world would still be in trouble."

We're in for a wild ride. We'd better fasten our seatbelts.

Y2K—IS IT TOO LATE?

We've examined the components of the Year 2000 problem, looked at the challenges inherent in software, embedded systems, and business connectivity remediation, and surveyed the potential impact upon key areas of our national and global infrastructure. Let's turn now to the question everyone who learns about Y2K wants answered—*can it be fixed in time?*

Can We Fix the Problem in Time?

Computer experts concur, the problem fixing Y2K is not that it's too hard to do, the problem is the time constraint. It must be finished by December 31, 1999, with no margin for error.

Most say we should have geared up globally for Y2K remediation 10 years ago. Instead, with less than one year remaining, we haven't fully geared up in one single country.

Too Late to Achieve 100% Compliance

For this reason, it is too late to achieve 100% national and international Y2K compliance. As we've seen, too many companies and organizations have either not yet begun, or are not far enough along in their Y2K projects to finish before next January.

Analysts state it usually averages about 30 months for a mid-size company—2000 to 20,000 employees—to get their mission-critical systems compliant. This implies that companies who initiated their Y2K projects after July 1997 will be unable to finish in time. Large numbers of companies and organizations fall into this category.

Dr. Ed Yardeni said in his testimony before Congress on July 22, 1998, "We also know that we are running out of time....I believe that with so little time left, it is very unlikely that all mission-critical systems will be properly fixed in time....I believe that only naive optimists can assume that there won't be any significant malfunctions, and consequently major disruptions to our global economy."

At this point, there is no way to avoid this situation. It is a given. How many computers will not be fixed in time is another question.

How Many Computers Won't Be Fixed in Time?

At the time this book went to press, in early 1999, not one company or organization had publicly proclaimed it had achieved Y2K compliance. With less than one year to go before the January 2000 deadline, this is alarming.

Also alarming is the growing number of reports stating companies that thought they were compliant are now finding their corrected code is riddled with errors. Date errors at rates as high as 900 for every million lines of code are turning up in many programs already tested and pronounced compliant.

As each day falls through the year's hourglass, we have 24 less hours to work toward compliance. When the last day of 1999 concludes, how many computers will still have uncorrected date fields? How many unrepaired embedded systems will remain?

In mid-1998, Senator Bennett said it was highly unlikely any federal agency would achieve complete Y2K compliance in time. Government analysts believe no more than 2/3 of government computers will be ready. Y2K author Ed Yourdon predicts that a best-case scenario would be 75% of our computer systems repaired, globally. Many countries will finish so far behind as to lose their modern infrastructures entirely.

"Fix on Failure" Gaining Ground

As this reality sinks in, focus is shifting from pre-2000 code remediation to post-2000 damage repair. This is illustrated in the Y2K strategy of the city of Denver, Colorado. The city's plan is, "Let it break, then fix it." Officials say there's no way Denver can reprogram every computer chip in every piece of city equipment on time. So they're concentrating on repairing things deemed critical to public safety—and rolling the dice on the rest.

While this may seem logical and unavoidable, it doesn't make it safe. No one can predict the impact of thousands—or more—of computer systems failing in the new millennium.

While we can only guess how many mission-critical systems may fail, we do know large numbers of sub-critical systems will fail. These failures will cascade, creating greater problems in combination than any one would in isolation. Analysts believe the effect of cascading failures will threaten the stability of even those systems which successfully make the date rollover.

Y2K commentator Michael Lindemann said, "In a world that is defaulting to Fix on Failure, individual preparedness becomes more urgent than ever."

It's Not Too Late for You to Prepare!

There is a bright spot. While it may be too late for business and government to achieve Y2K compliance, it's not too late for you and your family to get ready for the consequences.

You have within your power the ability to take steps to assure your family can weather the Y2K storm ahead.

If you start today, with the assistance of this book, you can lessen the impact of Y2K consequences in your life.

Read on! See what you can do!

If you're interested in researching the Y2K problem further, see Appendix B, pages 367 to 369, for a listing of recommended websites.

12 Steps to Y2K Preparedness

1. Planning
2. Shelter
3. Water
4. Food
5. Safety
6. Finances
7. Power
8. Communications
9. Medical
10. Transportation
11. Community
12. Records

CHAPTER I

Planning

The size and scope of the Y2K crisis is still unknown. What is known is that it has the potential to be a major national disaster. We can hope for the best, but we must not rule out preparation for the worst.

Senator Robert Bennett
Chair, Senate Y2K Committee

Our desire is that this book will give you hope. It's not too late for you to prepare for Y2K! While many computer-related systems and processes may end up not being ready, *you can be prepared.*

Your Y2K preparations begin with the realization that you should take preparedness steps. Having purchased this book, you have already realized this.

To prepare for Y2K, you need to create a plan and prioritize your steps. All successful endeavors require planning. Your success in preparing for Y2K will be more effective if you take the time to consider the planning strategies outlined in this chapter. How accurately you identify risks, evaluate their likelihood, create strategies to offset them, and develop effective fallback plans will determine in large part the level of your mental and physical preparedness for the century date change.

This chapter is about that planning process. It is designed to

help you organize your thoughts and focus your Y2K preparedness. Chances are you have no idea where to begin. But after reading this chapter, you will be ready to undertake the practical steps
outlined in the remainder of the book, and implement your plan.

THE PLANNING PROCESS

The idea of preparing for Y2K disruptions is entering the
mainstream. On October 2, 1998, the Senate Y2K Committee held
a hearing on the ability of the nation's emergency services to handle
a wide range of potential Y2K-induced scenarios. Bob Cass, city
manager of Lubbock, Texas, testified on the results of a drill simu-
lating New Year's Eve 2000. In the Lubbock Y2K drill, the scenario
included a police officer being shot while trying to break up a riot
at the civic center, the local prison doors being opened by a computer glitch, and a jet making a Y2K-induced emergency landing
at Lubbock International Airport.

This is an example of the planning process on a city-wide level.
The Lubbock authorities are studying how Y2K will affect their
city, and are planning to offset these disruptions. Lubbock will fare
much better than the 65% of cities and towns with no Y2K plans.

Personal Y2K Planning

Lubbock authorities are deciding what steps they need to take
to prepare for Y2K impacts in their city. Your personal Y2K planning will utilize much the same process, applied to your individual
situation.

The Year 2000 computer problem poses a threat to many areas of life we depend on and take for granted. Y2K preparedness
entails putting alternatives in place and establishing backup plans
so that we will still have access to what we need, even if the delivery of goods and services is interrupted.

Y2K preparedness is an insurance policy. You hope that problems won't happen, but you don't want to lack coverage in case they do. The planning process is deciding what backups to put in place for yourself and your family—what type, and how much, Y2K insurance coverage to buy.

How to Use This Book

Each chapter in this book illustrates specific risks, demonstrates how they could impact you, and provides a range of options to choose from in preparing your response.

At the end of each chapter, you'll find a checklist of action steps based on the material covered. The checklists aren't meant to indicate everything you should do, rather, they are meant to outline the options available.

Make copies of the checklists and use them as worksheets. As you read each chapter, decide if it contains areas of concern to you. Mark the checklist with what you plan to do. Then, when you've finished the book, you'll have 12 checklists marked with the steps you've identified. Highlight the items and steps you feel should be part of your preparedness plan. It will be a simple matter to then prioritize the highlighted items and establish a budget for your plan.

Evaluating the Information

As you read this book, view the information through the following mental filters:

• How important is this preparedness aspect to me?
• Will my budget permit my taking this particular step?
• Does my life allow for these specific changes?

Look at each risk, threat, and area of concern. Then, determine if you need to respond with preparedness steps. Identify if it is a major or minor issue for you. For which areas will you establish contingency plans?

Review the different levels of responses listed in the book, and decide which you can use based on the specifics of your circumstances. Family responsibilities and employment issues will largely shape your particular options.

Planning Considerations

The old adage is "Those who fail to plan, plan to fail." Take the time to write out your plan and the steps to accomplish it. By doing so, you will be less prone to miss anything important in your preparations, and increase the likelihood you'll complete the necessary tasks. Writing down your plans makes them more concrete, and is the first step toward realizing your goals.

Establish a blueprint and timeline to accomplish your preparedness plan. It's helpful to work with a planning partner or team. Sit down with your spouse, planning partners or group of friends, and brainstorm solutions unique to your circumstances. Write down the ideas which come to you. From these write out a personal preparedness plan. Review the checklist at the end of each chapter as a guide.

Prioritize Your Preparedness Steps

It's important to prioritize your preparedness steps. This is especially so if you are on a budget.

First take care of the physical needs of shelter, heat, water, food, and life-sustaining medication. Once you have sufficiently secured these, you can proceed as your funds allow, to address other concerns and purchase other supplies. These include currency reserves, gold and silver coins, barter items, electrical power generators, radios and alternative transportation.

Budget Your Preparations

Once you decide the extent to which you would like to prepare, the next question is, "How do I pay for all this?" Preparing for Y2K can be expensive. Storing additional food and water and setting aside some ready cash can cost a lot of money. Purchasing a generator or solar panels, a wood stove, communication equipment, and a variety of other Y2K supplies can cost thousands of dollars.

Determine how much money you can raise for your preparedness by evaluating your assets. Establish priorities and a budget. Consider what you presently own of value that could be converted to cash, so you can reallocate these assets for Y2K preparedness purposes.

For example, you might own a late-model car with a sizable monthly payment. Consider selling your car, and in its place purchase a used or otherwise less expensive model. The money saved could be invested in a food storage program for your family, to purchase water purification equipment, or other supplies.

Many people are planning to relocate to a vacation home or the more rural home of relatives in the event of serious Y2K disruptions. For the time being, they are remaining in their city residence, near their place of employment. If this is your situation, you could sell your city property and temporarily move into a rental home or apartment. By selling real estate now, you could invest these assets in preparedness equipment and protect the funds from future loss if real estate values drop.

If you're interested in this idea, make a list of your personal possessions that have value today, but may not after the Year 2000. Put these items up for sale, by advertising, having yard sales, estate sales or auctions. Then, use these funds to purchase the supplies and equipment you need to secure your family's safety and well-being in the event of societal disruptions.

Another alternative is to increase your income. Many people can earn an extra $1000 over a few months. Take a part-time job and dedicate the money earned to your Y2K preparations.

The question of debt: Some Y2K experts recommend doing everything possible to stay out of debt in preparation for Y2K. Others feel your primary consideration should be providing for your family first, even if it means going extensively into debt. Then, work to pay off the debt as quickly as possible.

We feel that it is unwise to burden yourself with debt, as this can be a vulnerability in the time period after Y2K. If you have a mortgage on a house and can't pay the monthly payment because you were laid off, for example, your home could be repossessed. Likewise, collection actions could go against you if you default on a large credit card debt generated while investing in preparedness supplies. Life will continue after 2000 and you can be sure that your lenders will keep good records of what you owe them and won't forget you.

However, we agree that your first priority is providing a stable source of shelter, water, food and medicine for your dependants. Other preparedness supplies are less important. If you need to go into debt to accomplish that level of security, we feel it is appropriate. Likewise, prices will be rising, and supplies of preparedness items will be shrinking as we approach Y2K. Buying items on credit now will ensure that you can still find them and that prices are low, even though you will have interest to pay on the purchases.

Once you've gotten your Y2K safety net in place, then work hard to pay off debts and become debt-free before 2000.

Make Time for Preparedness Work

Everything takes time, and usually more than you anticipate. If you are fortunate to have abundant finances, you may only have to spend a week or two on your preparedness, ordering your supplies and then storing them when they arrive.

If you are going the budget route, you can save a lot of money by buying your food in bulk and preparing it for storage yourself. Likewise, you can get some great bargains on preparedness items if you shop around and/or visit secondhand stores and yard sales. Be ready to spend a significant amount of time in doing this legwork.

Where to Store Everything

Efficient use of your space may become necessary as supplies accumulate. Use shelving to maximize your available space. Drums of water can be lined up along a wall and plywood placed on top to create a large shelving area. Boxes of canned storage food can be stacked floor to ceiling.

You may want to sell unneeded items in your home to make room to store the water, food and equipment which you will be acquiring. Reinvest these funds in your preparedness plans.

Supplies vulnerable to freezing, such as water and wet-canned goods, should be stored in the heated area of your home or be buried below the freeze-line in your area.

Use wise security measures to keep your preparations and supplies unadvertised and safe. See Chapter 5, pages 199 to 204, for tips on storing valuables in secure locations.

DURATION AND RANGE OF Y2K DISRUPTIONS

Your personal assessment of the risks Y2K poses to you and your family will determine the steps you'll take to minimize exposure to those risks. Chief among the factors to consider are, how long will each disruption last? How widespread will be its effect?

If you lose power, will it be out for a day, a week, a month, or longer? Will it go out in your neighborhood, your city, your state, or a group of states? Consider the loss of water, food, telecommunications, banking services, access to health care, etc. How you prepare will be influenced by how long you expect the problem to last, and over how wide a geographical area you expect it to occur.

No One Knows For Sure What Will Happen

Some say Y2K will present only minor problems, thus we need to make only minimal preparations. Others believe it will be "The End Of The World As We Know It" (TEOTWAWKI). They believe we will lose our entire infrastructure and advocate preparing for a return to a 19th century life-style.

No one knows for sure what will happen. In preparing for Y2K, you have to come to grips with uncertainty. Unlike planning for a hurricane, we can't extrapolate the likely consequences based on what past storms have produced. Instead, we can only consider what experts predict is likely to occur after the date rollover, and extrapolate the possible consequences.

While no one can say with certainty what will happen, there is also no assurance these predicted consequences won't happen. Unfortunately, many people won't prepare, or will prepare minimally. If the Y2K consequences are more severe than they expect, they will not be ready.

Some will store a little water and some extra canned goods. Others, ourselves included, don't feel preparing for a minimal period of disruptions is enough. We don't believe life will quickly return to normal. This forms the basis of our decisions.

Should you store a few extra gallons of water and some canned goods, or buy a farm with a well, livestock, a wood stove, and hand tools?

For most of us, buying a farm in the country is out of the question. Even if we had the inclination, we don't have the money. Yet even in the city it's possible to prepare for a severe Y2K scenario.

We believe the wisest course of action is to hope for the best, but prepare for the worst. We would rather make preparations we may not need, than not make preparations that could mean the difference between safety and serious consequences.

Risk Management

The most difficult part of Y2K planning is deciding what preparedness steps to take. Since no one knows for sure what's going to happen after 2000, it can be hard to know what to do.

Risk management is a scientific process of examining problems, evaluating how best to handle them, and then taking the indicated steps to address them. Risk management can help us determine the actions we need to take to prepare for Y2K.

The four phases of risk management are, *risk identification, risk analysis, risk treatment* and *risk evaluation.* We'll look at them briefly in the context of preparing for Y2K.

Risk Identification

Risk identification is defined as locating and measuring possible sources of loss. Before you can plan a response to a risk, you must first identify it.

Y2K is a dynamic, systemic risk because it potentially threatens every aspect of modern life in ways which will shift and change depending on global influences. This level of risk is not easily identified, until you grasp the interconnectivity of our technologically-dependant culture. By studying the Y2K problem, you identify and gauge the risks you believe could impact you.

How you personally measure the risks will be further influenced by *risk analysis.*

Risk Analysis

Before you decide what level of preparedness is appropriate for you, look at the factors which influence your vulnerability to Y2K.

What is the probable frequency of Y2K-induced losses that could impact you? For example, a succession of electrical blackouts and brownouts is likely. Since electricity powers the water treatment and pumping facilities, water may be supplied to your home only intermittently, and the safety of the water may not be dependable.

What is the probable severity of losses to you? No one can predict with certainty, but observers feel Y2K will be a problem for weeks, months or years. The severity of the harm to our society will depend on the duration of these disruptions.

What is the greatest possible severity of the losses? Y2K impacts could rank as a worst-case scenario. It is possible that we could experience a general breakdown of the social order.

Finally, *what effects could the potential losses have on you physically and financially?* In this regard, consider what the losses could be ranging from a worst-case to a less damaging scenario. If you are still in the stock market, could you lose everything from a Y2K meltdown? How much would you be hurt by an extended global depression?

These issues are all uncomfortable to consider, but using the risk analysis process helps us examine and think clearly about them.

Risk Treatment

The techniques by which you control your potential losses and minimize your exposure to Y2K risks include *loss prevention, loss reduction* and *risk avoidance.*

Loss prevention: In loss prevention, take steps to prevent potential losses from occurring. For example, if you are dependent on a municipal water treatment system, you are at risk that the water delivered to you may be improperly treated. However, you don't have to expose your family to water-born diseases. If the treatment system fails and water is contaminated, you can filter and purify it yourself.

Loss reduction: Loss reduction means you decrease the potential severity of loss exposure. If your bank limits withdrawals or closes due to bank runs you won't be able to get your cash. But if you have stored some extra cash you'll have the ability to buy a last bag of groceries as the supermarket empties.

Risk avoidance: Risk avoidance means staying away from activities which increase your risk. Avoiding risk motivates some people to get entirely out of the stock market. The chance of gains over the next months when weighed against potential losses makes them nervous. This is also the perspective of those who opt to move away from metropolitan areas. They aren't comfortable staying in the city, where Y2K effects could be most severe.

These are just some examples of the steps you can take to minimize and offset Y2K consequences in your life.

Risk Evaluation

After all your plans and Y2K preparations are in place, you still need to continually reevaluate risks as they evolve, along with your response to them. Your risks may change and new responses may be required.

Examining the risks Y2K poses will help you determine your planning steps. Next, we'll look at three levels of preparation, based on our risk analysis: preparing for problems lasting a few days to a few weeks; preparing for a three-month disruption; and preparing for long-term Y2K consequences.

Short-Term Preparations

The American Red Cross has advised people to store one week's worth of emergency food, water and other supplies for Y2K.

http://www.redcross.org/disaster/safety/y2k.html

For other disasters, the Federal Emergency Management Agency recommends storing two weeks' worth of supplies.

http://www.fema.gov/library/emfdwtr.htm

The Gartner Group recommended having two weeks' worth of cash and five days' worth of consumables going into Y2K.

http://gartner11.gartnerweb.com/public/static/home/ 00073955.html

These scenarios do not leave any room for error. While it is commendable these organizations recommend preparations, many experts believe one or two weeks is inadequate. If disruptions are severe, food and water will quickly be depleted. We know from past experience with natural disasters such as hurricanes, grocery stores are emptied of goods within hours.

We believe it is unwise to assume only minimal consequences will occur from Y2K. Both computer glitches and transportation problems could interfere with the distribution of supplies. Water treatment and delivery could be interrupted for an extended period. If these outages last longer than one week, what will people do when their supplies run out?

Emergency planning expert Chuck Lanza recommends preparedness for 14 days. He believes most people can meet this goal.

http://www.y2ktimebomb.com/GL/CL/gl9850.htm

Lanza says a more prudent 90 day self sufficiency strategy "provides the government with the time and opportunity to reestablish infrastructure and essential services." However, he believes the majority of people can't afford the purchases necessary to prepare for a 90 day period. Therefore, he believes it's more practical to aim for the attainable level of 14 days of preparations.

Our concern is that short-term preparation may lead to a public belief that Y2K will have minimal effects. No one can guarantee minimal effects. Thus we reassert that hoping for the best and preparing for the worst is a more prudent course of action.

We agree many people are unable to finance an extended period of preparation. We also agree, any amount of preparation is better than none at all. Begin with a solid two to four weeks of stored water, canned and dried food, medication, and cash for each person in your family, plus supplies and fuel for heating your living area. Then add to that supply as you are able.

Mid-Term Preparations

A mountain of evidence points to the possibility of moderate to severe disruptions to essential services upon which we all depend. Without a modern-day miracle, it seems unlikely these problems will be minor. A period of upheaval lasting several months appears highly probable.

For those who can afford it, we recommend three months of canned and dried food, water purification equipment, medical supplies, cash, alternative heating supplies and fuel, electrical power generators, lighting supplies, emergency two-way radios and other supplies such as gold and silver coins and barter items. Several months' worth of supplies would be preferable.

If your level of funds requires proceeding in stages, first get three months' worth of everything listed, then gradually increase supplies as you are able. If you delay in purchasing these items, certain supplies may become unavailable due to the intense demand.

Long-Term Preparations

A credible body of experts believe massive, long-term Y2K-induced disruptions in our basic infrastructure are possible. In this case, life-style and economic recovery could take months or years. If this level of severe disruption occurs, preparations sufficient for a few weeks or months will be woefully inadequate.

If problems are serious enough, the infrastructure could be interrupted through the spring planting season, preventing normal crop production and cutting the ability to restock national and global food reserves. Therefore, a one-year supply of stored food could be crucial. Your stored food can also be supplemented by food supplies which become available during 2000, thereby extending your reserves well beyond a year.

Likewise, having access to sufficient supplies for the long term purification of water is important. Heating fuel for the first three months of 2000 would insure warmth throughout the winter. Having six months' worth of stored cooking fuel will provide time to establish alternative cooking supplies and strategies.

Food stamps and other social services may not be available. Several months' worth of cash, gold and silver coins, and a supply of barter items will be valuable if large-scale disruptions occur in the banking and financial services sector. If the basic economic infrastructure collapses, many people's employment would disappear. Family breadwinners could be unemployed for months. What goods or service could you provide as a temporary second career, if a severe Y2K scenario comes to pass?

A one-year preparedness plan will give you a significant buffer. Plus, it will help you achieve a self-sustaining life-style afterwards. If your reading of the situation convinces you we're in for severe Y2K consequences, consider implementing a long-term plan.

The Y2K Newswire offers "The Real World Contingency Plan" with a 30-day Minimum Plan and a one year Worst Case Plan.

http://www.y2knewswire.com/plan.htm

In the Final Analysis, It's Your Call

Only you can make this call. Your personal Y2K insurance policy must be crafted by you, for you and your family.

You must decide how severe you believe Y2K consequences could be, and take the steps you deem necessary to protect your family. Continue to keep your ear to the ground, and update your plans as new information warrants.

BACKUP PLANS

Since no one can anticipate exactly what will happen when Y2K occurs, be ready to implement alternative plans for your family.

Don't lock yourself into only one response to Y2K. We recommend having at least two backup plans you can implement on the fly.

If conditions signal that a move would be prudent, think about going to stay with family members in rural areas or small towns in advance of 2000. If you expect to stay in your current home, have a plan to leave your area if conditions deteriorate.

Work out where you will go and make agreed-upon arrangements with friends and family. Evacuate only if you have a clear destination in mind. Don't just leave and become a refugee. Have routes picked out and obtain detailed county maps. You may want to have an alternate retreat site relatively nearby, as well as a more remote one.

You could invest in a vehicle sufficient to carry enough fuel to get you to your destination in an emergency. A four-wheel drive vehicle will be useful if roads are clogged with other retreaters.

You can also establish a group plan with people you trust such as members of your church. Pool your resources with theirs, and you're likely to have a better outcome than if you try to go it alone.

You may not be able to take all the steps needed to handle every possible Y2K risk. It might not be practical or possible. But you can identify potential risks and plan to minimize their impact.

For example, you may not be able to afford to purchase an alternative heating system. Instead, you can plan to move into the basement and employ emergency heating and insulation techniques if the power does go out. See Chapter 2, page 86, for details.

It would be far better to have such a reactive plan, than to have no plan at all. As you read the following chapters, take mental notes or write down your ideas and observations. Make notes of what you feel will work for you and use these in formulating your unique strategies to deal with Y2K disruptions.

COPING WITH Y2K

Our discussion of the Y2K planning process would not be complete without acknowledging how stressful this process can be. The potential ramifications of Y2K are greater than most of us have ever had to face before. It can make us feel powerless, frightened, and overwhelmed.

When we learn enough about Y2K to understand its possibly serious consequences, we face a number of difficult questions.

What are the steps needed to prepare for a crisis on the scale of Y2K? With many different consequences possible, how do I get ready to deal with them?

What costs are involved in preparedness? Can I afford it?

What do I do first? How much preparation is enough?

What will my friends and family say? What about my job?

Psychologists tell us that all people respond to significant emotional events with a predictable pattern of responses known as the *grieving process.* Y2K certainly qualifies as a significant emotional event!

The Grieving Process

The grieving process has five distinct stages—denial, anger, bargaining, depression and finally acceptance. Each person experiences these stages in his or her own way and time.

It's important to remember, as you deal with Y2K, experiencing the feelings associated with the grieving process is normal and healthy. We're all coping with the emotional aspects of this subject.

You'll note an infinite variety of personal responses to the stresses of Y2K. One woman we told about Y2K responded, "Well, I guess I won't dust anymore."

Another acquaintance heard someone say "Y2K was not really a problem after all." This one comment was seized upon as the gospel truth, despite the fact that it contradicted all the previous information she'd heard from several different sources. She just *wanted to believe* Y2K wasn't a problem.

When co-author Patrice Kaufman first started studying Y2K, she went into a blue funk and became depressed. She'd just finished writing her first book—her long-held dream of writing and publishing was finally becoming a reality. And now, Y2K could take out the power grid, upset the economy, and affect her way of life. The work she loved could be put on the back burner, just as it was coming into fruition.

Her sister Laurie had a similar reaction. It took her several months to face the reality of Y2K. When she finally did, fear took hold and immobilized her. She was overwhelmed with the possibility of losing her familiar way of life, and having to face a frightening, uncertain future. How could she protect herself and her daughter from what might lie ahead?

But these reactions passed. Both sisters have taken steps to prepare, and in the process worked through much of their depression and anxiety. You can, too!

Coping Mechanisms

The issue of Y2K shouldn't dominate your life, but be kept clearly in sight. The key is not to panic.

Talk about the issues and your feelings. Verbalize your anxieties to friends in a supportive environment. Don't try to rush the grieving process. Coping has to run its course.

If you feel you're not handling the emotional dimensions of Y2K well, it might help to speak with a therapist. Professional counseling is commonplace in dealing with issues such as a divorce or a death in the family. Y2K, with its potential for life-altering consequences, is no different.

Taking concrete preparedness steps is another means of dealing with the Y2K unknowns. You will feel empowered and less anxious if you take physical steps to safeguard your family.

Many people testify to the benefits of prayer. Faith in God's power to intercede on your behalf can be a powerful coping mechanism. Many spiritual leaders advise us to pray on a daily basis. You can pray for yourself and your family. You can also pray for immediate solutions to the Y2K problem as well as mitigation and aversion of the predicted disruptions. Prayer is one way to feel you are doing something about an issue you may otherwise be powerless to influence.

An Internet site which is addressing the issue of coping with Y2K is:

http://www.readyfory2k.com/52staying_sane.html

Another looks at "How the Year 2000 Problem Impacts Children."

http://www.dfiy2k.org/y2kkids.html

The Utne Reader's highly recommended *Y2K Citizen's Action Guide* has a section on Inner Preparedness with an article on "The Psychological Challenges of Y2K" by Gordon Davidson and Corrine McLaughlin. It also has a piece by Doc Childre and Bruce Cryer from the HeartMath Institute entitled, "From Chaos to Coherence: the Emotional Challenge of Y2K."

http://www.utne.com/y2k/psychological.html
http://www.heartmath.org

To sum up, take the time to consider Y2K-related risks and plan your responses. Review the 12 preparedness steps and their checklists.

Talk it over with your family members and planning partners. Place a star next to those items you feel you should address.

Next, prioritize the starred items. Then, start on the list. There is something on that list you can do today, right now.

Y2K is a serious issue. Recognize that people, including yourself, can have difficulty dealing with it. Talk it over, and help each other come to terms with the task at hand.

PLANNING CHECKLIST

____ Make copies of the checklists at the end of each chapter

____ Read the entire *Y2K- Its Not Too Late: Personal Preparedness Guide*

____ As you read, highlight the checklist items that are important to you

____ Join up with a planning partner or team

____ Review the 12 preparedness steps

____ Establish your priorities

____ Decide what duration of disruptions you will prepare for

____ Apply risk management to clarify your preparedness steps

____ Evaluate your assets

____ Obtain extra income to invest in preparedness supplies

____ Establish a budget for each of the preparedness steps

____ Write out a personal preparedness plan

____ Establish, prioritize and write down concrete action plans for each step

____ Create a sequential time line for each step with dates

____ Develop effective fall back plans

____ Utilize coping strategies, as needed

CHAPTER 2

Shelter

The size and scope of the Y2K crisis is still unknown. What is known is that it has the potential to be a major national disaster. We can hope for the best, but we must not rule out preparation for the worst.

Senator Robert Bennett
Chair, Senate Y2K Committee

"Now is the winter of our discontent!" Richard III's lament from Shakespeare's play may be the common refrain of those who didn't prepare for the winter of '00. The expression "Home is where the heart is," is a variation of the old saying "Home is where the *hearth* is!" If your home furnace doesn't function because of Y2K related electrical power and natural gas supply problems, your house won't feel like much of a home.

Shelter is defined in the dictionary as, "The state of being covered or protected." As the foremost human need, shelter from the elements comes even before water and food in importance. You can perish from exposure within minutes or hours, but you'll survive days without water and weeks without food.

You need a personal contingency plan for the possible interruption of municipal services. This may be a question of survival for your family. How will you heat your home in the winter of 2000 if you lose power?

LOCATION

The first thing to consider when preparing your home for Y2K is, where do you want to be on January 1, 2000? That's the cornerstone of the foundation on which to build your plans. First, decide if you are going to remain in your current location or relocate.

Many people, aware of the Y2K problem, are equipping their city homes to withstand the potential loss of power, water, and telecommunications. They are planning to work cooperatively with family and friends to help each other through any crisis. Some are coordinating with neighbors and others in the local community.

Others, concerned that urban areas could experience social disruptions due to potential economic and infrastructure difficulty, plan to relocate before 2000 to areas they feel offer more stable and supportive environments.

Location Factors

Several factors will influence your relocation decision, including your personal Y2K risk assessment, financial situation, and responsibilities to friends and loved ones.

Risk Assessment

Whether to stay in your present residence or to relocate depends upon your Y2K risk assessment. No one can tell you how severe the Y2K consequences will be. As stated in the previous chapter, there is wide-ranging debate about the potential consequences. Among the prominent Year 2000 spokespersons, opinion varies greatly.

Consultant Peter de Jager believes there's no need to relocate, claiming disruptions won't be bad enough to warrant such a step. Y2K author Ed Yourdon disagrees. He feels the large metropolitan areas may be unsafe, and has moved his family from New York City to the small town of Taos, New Mexico.

At the further end of the spectrum, computer programmer Scott Olmstead, featured on Nightline, 60 Minutes, and the CBS Evening News, sees the possibility of great upheaval. He's purchased a home in an isolated area of the California desert, and stocked it with equipment and supplies.

Finances

Your financial situation also plays a major role in determining whether or not to relocate. Can you afford to move? Are you willing to give up your present job, to relocate? Do your skills or profession permit you to go to a rural area and still find employment?

If you desire to relocate and your finances allow it, consider buying an inexpensive rural retreat property. Some recommend locating up to 200 miles away from major population centers.

Pick property which has a good water supply, decent soil and the capacity for gardening. A few acres should be sufficient.

Personal Responsibilities

Your family dynamics—ailing parents, a spouse who doesn't share your level of concern, or child custody arrangements—may be such that even if you wish to move, you must stay where you are. Given these situations, your choice will likely be to remain in your present location and take steps to provide for the safety and well-being of your dependent family members there.

Location Fallback Planning

If after reviewing your options, you choose to stay where you are, consider having at least one fallback plan to activate in emergencies. If you remain in the city, plan in advance to relocate if necessary.

If a friend or relative has a remote cottage or home, discuss the possibility of joining them if Y2K makes staying in your current location difficult. Some people are planning to visit rurally located relatives or friends over the holidays. Then, if severe problems occur on the New Year, they could stay on for the duration.

Whether you stay in an urban residence or relocate to a rural property, there are similar steps you need to take to prepare your home for Y2K. Some of these preparations involve purchasing supplies and equipment, and some involve altering the structure and function of your home.

A comprehensive approach to getting your home ready will involve elements of heating, cooking, lighting, sanitation, and maintenance. Let's look at each of these issues now.

HEATING AND COOKING

Y2K-induced electric power, natural gas, and heating oil shortages could make it impossible for you to use your conventional furnace to heat your home. In 8 to 12 hours without heat in the winter months, the temperature inside your house will drop to near the outside air temperature. You should decide on a backup method to heat your home. This is a critical aspect of Y2K preparedness planning.

Problems such as intermittent rolling electrical brownouts or blackouts could require alternative heating at intervals for unknown periods of time. In some locations, power outages may last a week. However, Y2K-induced problems could be long-lasting, requiring the use of alternative heating strategies until things warm up in the spring of 2000.

In this section we'll cover what is required to keep your family warm during a period of potential infrastructure problems during the winter of 2000. Our fuel requirement estimates will be for three months of heating, through early spring 2000.

These requirements assume that you will be heating a single section of your home during the period of Y2K disruptions. By heating only one large room during the winter, a family can with minimal discomfort and only minimal to moderate expense, successfully use alternative heating strategies to stay warm.

A large room of 400 sq. ft. can be kept comfortably warm with a heater producing 10,000 British Thermal Units (BTUs) per hour. If you chose to heat a smaller room, your heating fuel requirements will be proportionately less. This heat can be supplied, for example, by a single burner from a camp stove.

Any cooking stove will put out heat sufficient to warm a room. If left burning, a cooking stove burner could put out enough heat to keep a single room quite comfortable. For the sake of efficiency, we recommend you plan to use one stove for both heating and cooking.

Fuels and Stoves

There are several considerations in selecting your heating and cooking method. You must decide on a fuel source, and procure and store the fuel. You need to purchase and install the stove in which the fuel will be burned. Learn and implement the necessary safety precautions for the method you select.

Many different materials—such as wood, coal, kerosene and liquefied propane (LP)—can be used as fuel. They all have advantages and disadvantages.

It would be wise to have at least two alternative heat sources available, in case one fails.

Wood

The most popular option for heating and cooking in case of Y2K disruptions is wood. It's readily available, wood stoves are easy to get, and people are familiar with burning wood in fireplaces.

If you opt for wood heat, stock up on wood now. Buy four full cords, enough to easily get you through the winter. Wood costs about $150 per cord; a winter's worth would cost $600.

Wood is usually sold by the "face cord," a stack 16 in. deep, 4 ft. high and 8 ft. long. This is only 1/3 of a true cord, which is 4 ft. deep, 4 ft. high and 8 ft. long. Specify that you want a full cord when you buy wood, to get your money's worth.

Different woods are of different densities. These fall into two general categories, slow growing and denser hardwoods and quicker growing soft woods. If possible, buy hardwoods as they are nearly twice as dense as soft woods, therefore they take up half the space and burn twice as long. Make sure your wood will be good and dry before you need to burn it. Store it in a well ventilated, covered and dry area.

Wood cutting tools: Wood cutting and splitting tools are important to have. Buy a good ax, splitting wedge and maul or sledge hammer. Purchase tools with steel or fiberglass handles, for extra durability. All these supplies can be purchased from hardware stores.

Lehman's sells one and two man hand crosscut saws for $150. Hand buck saws are $60. They also sell a kit for sharpening the blades, which comes with a *Guide to Crosscut Saws*, for $140. You can reach Lehman's at 330-857-5757.

http://www.lehmans.com

Cumberland General Store, 800-334-4640, sells buck saws for $43. Be sure to buy extra blades, which are $9 each.

http://www.cumberlandgeneral.com/country.htm

McCulloch, Stihl and Homelite are dependable chainsaw brands. Buy them at any small equipment supplier. Look them up under "Saws" in your Yellow Pages directory.

Wood stoves: If you have a fireplace and plan to burn wood as your alternative heating source, realize that using an open fireplace as your main source of heat is extremely inefficient. Most of the heat escapes up the chimney.

Purchase a wood-burning stove instead, and properly vent it through your chimney. If you don't have a chimney, you will need to vent it through the ceiling or an outer wall.

Don't attempt to vent it yourself. Hire a professional to install your wood stove, to assure all safety considerations are addressed and all code requirements met. Place the stove on a noncombustible code-specified or listed floor protector.

Wood stoves for home heating can double as cook stoves unless they are the high efficiency style which only get warm on top. Buy models with cooking capacity.

Purchase a stove with a big fire box that will accept lengths of wood longer than 18 inches. Longer pieces require fewer cuts during wood preparation. This is an important factor if you have to make each cut by hand.

Catalytic stoves are popular. Catalytic converters increase the efficiency of your stove. Inquire locally from wood stove retailers as to what types are recommended for your area.

Don't buy a wood pellet stove. Pellets are very expensive compared to cord wood and the stoves require a source of electricity to operate the auger which pulls the pellets into the fire.

Many stove manufacturers have websites. Several are listed at: **http://www.cairns.net.au/~sharefin/Markets/Alternative.htm** Lehman's "Non-Electric Catalog" is a wonderful source for wood and other fueled stoves. Their catalog offers 26 pages of a variety of wood stoves, from a $200 steel stove to a fancy $3750 kitchen stove. The catalog costs $4 and is well worth the price.

For $80 you can buy a kit from Lehman's to build an airtight wood barrel stove. This homemade stove can be constructed from a 55 gal. drum.

Northern Tool and Equipment, 800-533-5545, sells inexpensive wood stoves. They sell a two-barrel stove kit for $50. A cast iron Boxwood Stove sells for $140, and a cast iron Pot Belly Stove sells for $300. Visit their website at:

http://www.northern-online.com

Cumberland General Store sells a wood or coal kitchen stove for $1000.

Battery powered wood camp stoves: The Zip "Sierra" wood burning camp stove burns twigs, bark, pine cones, scrap wood or charcoal. It puts out 18,000 BTU per hour. The system requires one AA battery to power its fan. It can be purchased for $43 from Jade Mountain, 800-442-1972, or for $58 from Campmor, 800-230-2153. Use these stoves outside.

http://www.jademountain.com
http://www.campmor.com

The Zip "Eagle" puts out twice the heat, 35,000 BTU per hour, for $59. The "D" cell power supply provides over 35 hours of cooking time. It can also be used without the battery.

Care of wood stoves: Have your chimney professionally cleaned in 1999 and make any indicated chimney repairs. This is vital for fire prevention and safety. Check your chimney and stovepipe frequently during the heating season for creosote buildup and clean when necessary. Keep combustible curtains, chairs and firewood at least three feet away from the stove. Use only proper fuel in the stove and be sure that ashes are removed in a metal container with a tight-fitting lid.

Information on wood, BTU values for various tree species, wood stove safety, and proper care of wood stoves can be found on the Chimney Safety Institute of America website. CSIA certifies chimney sweeps and can refer you to reputable companies.

http://www.csia.org

Information on fire building, how to install a wood stove, and fuel cost comparisons is available from HearthNet:

http://hearth.com/what/heatvalues.html
Propane

The types of heaters commonly used in recreational vehicles (RVs) and to heat garages burn propane. There are many varieties of propane heaters. All are fueled with liquefied propane gas (LPG).

Propane is a clean-burning fuel. Its only by-product is carbon dioxide. Propane is stored in cylinders or tanks which commonly come in 1 lb., 20 lb., 40 lb., and 100 lb. sizes. It doesn't deteriorate over time and lasts indefinitely since it is sealed in a pressurized tank. You can purchase the tanks from a propane supplier. Locate your propane container outside of the house and pipe the gas in for safety.

Normally, when a tank is empty you return to the supplier for a refill. During the period of Y2K disruptions, it may not be possible to do this. Decide how much propane you want to have on hand and purchase it while the supply is still abundant. Follow all zoning regulations with respect to propane and other fuel storage.

An empty 20 lb. cylinder costs $40 new and can be filled for $10. A 20 lb. cylinder will last 26 hours with continuous use, and keep a large room warm. By running the heater on low or using it intermittently and turning it off for most of the night, you may be able to make one 20 lb. cylinder last two days. You would need 45 of the 20 lb. cylinders, at a cost of approximately $2250, to heat one large room for a three month period.

Forty lb. cylinders are the most practical size. The cylinders cost $50 and are $12 to fill. Buy a 5 ft. long LPG stove kit for $20 to connect the tank to a $40 stove. A 40 lb. cylinder will run a small heater for 100 hours. You would need 23 of the 40 lb. cylinders, at a total cost of $1485, to heat one large room for three months.

An empty 100 lb. cylinder costs $100 new and can be filled for $40. These cylinders weigh 70 lb. empty and 170 lb. when filled, making them difficult to move easily. $1280 would buy 90 days' worth of LPG.

If your zoning allows, you can rent tanks ("pigs") which range in size from 120 lb. to 1000 lb. for the back of your house. This is the most economical way to purchase propane.

Your LPG supplier will rent you a tank for $140 per year and a gas flow regulator for a one time fee of $50. You'll have to pay $45 per hour for installation labor, and $1.50 per foot for the copper tubing to take the gas inside. A 1000 lb. cylinder will last more than three months, enough to get you through the winter. 1000 lbs. of LP gas costs $413 for a total cost with heater of about $720.

There are many suppliers of LP gas. Look them up in your Yellow Pages under "Gas-Propane." AmeriGas, 610-337-7000, sells LP gas in 44 states.

http://www.amerigas.com

Propane heaters and stoves: Purchase a propane cook stove and use it for heating. Cooking burners put out from 15,000 to 35,000 BTU/hr., depending on the stove model, and cost $60 to $100.

LP gas heaters cost $40 to $300 and can be purchased from your LPG supplier, any discount retailer or RV equipment dealer. Most LP heaters are designed to be vented into your chimney.

Direct-vent heaters vent directly through an outside wall. They use outside air for combustion, reducing drafts and preserving fresh indoor air. The Eco-Therm Direct Vent is a 5,600 BTU model sold by Jade Mountain for $460. No electricity is required for their operation. Direct-vent models can be as large as 50,000 BTU.

Vent-Free LP gas heaters as approved by the American Gas Association and certified by the federal government can be burned directly without venting the exhaust gases outside, much like your kitchen stove. They are 99.9% efficient and use interior air for combustion. All vent-free models must have an oxygen sensor which shuts off the heater if the oxygen content of the room drops below safe levels. Unvented heaters less than 10,000 BTU are approved for use in sleeping rooms. The Valor Infrared Vent-Free Gas Heater sold by Jade Mountain is a 5000 BTU heater for $220. Model sizes go up to 30,000 BTU.

The Glo-Warm Blue-Flame Vent-Free Gas Heater from Harbor Freight Tools, 800-423-2567, is a 20,000 BTU heater which costs $180. It requires no electricity to operate.

http://www.harborfreight.com

Kerosene

Kerosene heaters are the most common non-electric space heaters in use. Both heaters and fuel are inexpensive.

Kerosene heaters require a constant fresh air supply because they put out more fumes than most heaters. Have excellent ventilation and a functioning battery-operated carbon monoxide detector when using a kerosene heater. Turn the heater off while you are sleeping and never leave it unattended. Place an unvented heater out of traffic areas so it will not be knocked over.

Always burn crystal clear grade one kerosene (K1). It costs $2 per gal. and can be purchased at some gas stations. Other grades of kerosene have excessively high amounts of sulfur which can cause health problems.

One gal. of kerosene produces 10,000 BTUs per hour for 12 to 16 hours. That's about 2 gal. per day or a consumption of from 45 to 60 gal. per month. For $330 you could store enough to heat your living room for three months.

Kerosene will last for 10 years in storage. All kerosene containers must be painted blue and labeled "kerosene" to keep them from being mixed up with red gasoline cans. Even a little gasoline in a kerosene heater can cause a fire.

Plastic or steel closed-head buckets and drums should be used for kerosene storage. See Chapter 7, pages 252 to 254, for information on fuel storage container suppliers.

Total costs to heat your living space with kerosene for three months including fuel, fuel storage, venting (if necessary) and heater would be from $540 to $870.

Kerosene heaters and stoves: Many hardware stores and most discount retailers sell both ventable and unvented kerosene heaters.

The 15" high Alpaca unvented kerosene stove is sold by many preparedness suppliers. With a cooking surface on top, 8500 BTU per hour rating, and 16 hour burn time, it costs $100. Similar stoves can be purchased for $150. This stove and a variety of other expedient cook stoves can be obtained from Major Surplus & Survival, 800-441-8855.

http://www.majorsurplusnsurvival.com

Lehman's and Walton Feed, 800-269-8563, also sell kerosene stoves.

http://www.waltonfeed.com

The kerosene heater's wick builds up carbon deposits when used constantly for about a week. Read your manual regarding how best to remove these deposits. One technique is to let the heater run out of fuel every third tank. This burns the deposits off. But this creates a lot of soot, so be sure to do it outside. Have several extra wicks available.

Fuel Oil

You can use #2 grade home heating oil for space heating. Diesel fuel is the same thing as #2 fuel oil. Fuel oil costs $1 per gallon and you can obtain a permit for a 250 gal. steel exterior fuel oil tank. Alternatively, you can use steel or HDPE plastic buckets or drums.

Fuel oil or diesel can be treated to last for several years. See the information on fuel life extenders in Chapter 7, page 250.

Fuel oil heaters and stoves: Franco Belge #2 fuel oil heaters are sold by Jade Mountain beginning at $975. They burn from 0.066 to 0.25 gal. of fuel per hour. At the lowest settings, these heaters use 143 gal. of fuel over 90 days. They require a 5 in. vented flue and a remote, gravity fed fuel tank. The larger models, costing $1560 to $1900, have a built-in 3.7 gal. fuel tank.

Coal

Because of storage space requirements, coal may not be a practical alternative fuel for city residents. If you live in a rural area, and have the room to store a dump truck load of coal, you might want to consider it.

Three tons of coal if used sparingly will heat a large room through the winter. Coal costs vary depending on availability. In metro Detroit, soft and hard coal is priced at $200 per ton, and there are few suppliers. Use hard coal, as it produces little smoke.

You will need at least one ton of coal per month if used for heating and cooking. If feasible, store the coal out of contact with sunlight and air. With exposure to air, coal begins to disintegrate and crumble over time. A plastic lined buried pit is the best storage. Lidded barrels or cans are another option.

Coal heaters and stoves: Coal stoves need to be vented through the roof, like wood stoves. You may be able to find a used coal-fired cook stove in your area. Or, buy a stove with special heavier firebox grates which will burn either wood or coal. Either of these can do double duty as both a heating and a cooking source.

A potbellied or Ben Franklin type stove does the job. It needs to have a cast iron or firebrick lining to be safe for burning coal. Northern Tool and Equipment sells a 200,000 BTU pot belly coal stove for $300.

Information on hard coal is available from:

http://hearth.com/blaschak/blaschak.html

Charcoal

Charcoal is a hot, relatively clean fuel when compared to coal and wood. It is a space saver but expensive when compared to wood per BTU. Buy bags at discount retailers or wholesale markets. Links to buying it by the 40 lb. bag or in one ton super bags are available at:

http://forestry.miningco.com/library/weekly/aa051798.htm

You can even make your own charcoal. To find out how it was done in bulk hundreds of years ago, visit the web site:

http://www.ftech.net/~regia/charcoal.htm

Charcoal stoves: Use a hibachi or common charcoal grill for cooking. You will need at least 25 lb. of charcoal per week. Buy it from a discount retailer. Use charcoal stoves outside to provide adequate ventilation.

A Pyramid portable cook stove efficiently reflects heat back onto the cooking surface and works well when heated with charcoal. They cost $35 to $180 from B&A Products, 918-696-5998.

http://www.baproducts.com

White Gas

The white gas stove uses traditional lantern fuel. This product is a more refined, cleaner burning fuel than gasoline. White gas burns easily in any type of liquid gas stove.

Sealed cans of Coleman brand white gas may last as long as three years. In comparison, unleaded gasoline will only last 12 months with additives.

You can burn unleaded gas in any white gas camping stove. Unleaded fuel runs about 1/4 the cost of white gas and 1/20 the cost of propane. Its availability can't be beat as it can be found at any gas station, or in a car's gas tank.

By Federal law, from mid-October to spring, gasoline distributors add butane and other additives such as benzene to keep the fuel volatile in cold weather. These additives may not be completely combusted and can be unhealthy for you to breath. If you choose to use unleaded gasoline for cooking or heating, be sure that you have excellent ventilation.

Using two burners four hours per day, white gas stoves consume 5 pt. per day or 100 gal. per year of unleaded gasoline. Using one burner continuously for heat, they'll use at least 2 gal. per day or 180 gal. for the first three cold months of 2000, producing about 8500 BTU/hr.

Untreated unleaded gas will store for about four months, then begin to lose octane. Loss of octane won't prevent you from burning it in a cookstove.

Store cans of white gas as an extended backup supply, as it will last up to three years. Check for local laws restricting the amount of fuel you can legally store on your property.

Store your gas in a cool, shaded area in sealed, airtight containers painted red and marked "gasoline."

White gas stove: The Coleman white gas camping stove is the most common brand of this type, and is available from any camping supplier. Two or three burner models are available. Major Surplus sells them for $90 and $150, respectively.

Multifuel Stoves

Some brands of stoves are designed to burn any type of available liquid fuel. Such a stove may be a good backup if fuel supplies and fuel quality deteriorate.

Expedition gear supplier MSR makes shaker jet models. When shaken upside down, these stoves self-clean any clogs resulting from poor fuel. Their Whisperlite Internationale burns white gas, kerosene, auto fuel or jet fuel. The MSR XGK II also burns diesel, aviation gas and Stoddard solvent.

Multifuel stoves are available from Campmor. For $130 they sell the MSR Whisperlite with an extra parts kit, kerosene wicks, 2 fuel bottles and a heat exchanger for greater efficiency. The $108 Dragonfly with 22 oz. fuel bottle burns white gas, aviation gas, kerosene, naphtha and auto fuel. It is a fully adjustable stove which can be turned down for simmering foods and includes a windscreen and heat reflector. The Apex II costs $77, with kerosene and maintenance kits.

Optimus offers excellent information on fuels and stoves at its website.

http://www.optimus.se

Suunto USA, 800-543-9124, distributes Primus and Optimus stoves.

http://www.suuntousa.com

Gelled Alcohol

Alco-Brite gelled ethanol fuel is similar to Sterno. It comes in 1 lb. steel cans, burns for 4 to 7 hrs., and produces up to 2500 BTUs of heat per hour. It will keep an average room of 100 sq. ft. at about 65° F. This fuel when burned gives off only carbon dioxide, which makes it a good choice as a heat source in a confined space. Snap-on steel top and bottom pieces convert the cans to stoves. Alco-Brite, 800-473-0717, sells its products through independent distributors.

http://www.alco-brite.com

Cans cost $3.25 each or 12 for $38 from B&A Products.

Another non-explosive, safe-to-store gelled alcohol fuel is EcoFuel. It has two sizes of can openings, permitting slower burning. A can lasts 8 hrs. at 200° F, and 4 hrs. at 450° F. A stove and two cans of fuel are sold for $29. A case of 24 cans costs $70 and will burn for up to 192 hrs. of cooking time.

http://www.coolandunusual.com/y2k/cgi-bindeliver.cgi?
ecofuel-y121twok-1

Expedient Stoves

Basic stoves can also be made from a metal bucket or a #10 can. These stoves can burn twisted paper or small sticks. Directions can be found in James Talmage Stevens' book *Making the Best of Basics*. The excellent source book *Roughing it Easy* by Dian Thomas has ideas for dozens of expedient stoves.

Such open stoves would have to be used outside due to the large amount of smoke they produce.

Radiant Heaters

Heat some golfball-sized rocks inside a covered dutch oven. Bring the dutch oven into your sleeping area and place it on a noncombustible surface. It will radiate heat for hours and help you to sleep comfortably without concerns about fumes from a fueled heater in your sleeping area.

Passive Solar Air Heater

Install a passive solar system on the south side of your home. This collects warm air and allows it to flow into the house via a thermostatically-controlled valve when the air is warm enough. Using plexiglass to cover a series of wooden baffles or channels painted black allows a good deal of energy to be delivered to your home. A solar system can be installed with a minimal initial investment. Other good suggestions and techniques can be found in the book *The Passive Solar House* by James Kachadorian.

Jade Mountain sells solar air collector systems which give a quick investment pay back and last for years. A Sun Aire 4 ft. by 8 ft. solar air collector provides 25% to 50% of the heat needed for a 400 to 800 sq. ft. space and costs $435. The installation kit costs $132.

You can mount a Sun Mate 2 ft. by 4 ft. solar air collector on a south wall for $315, and heat 150 sq. ft. of living space. It requires a 14 watt fan which can be powered directly by a small solar panel.

Fuel Comparisons

Compare home-heating fuel costs by entering your regional fuel prices in HearthNet's calculator.

http://chi.hearth.com/addcalc.html

Fire Starters

While it is possible to start a fire by rubbing two sticks together, modern technology does it easier and better.

Butane Lighters

Buy a case of cheap butane lighters from a dollar store or discounter. Sam's Club, 888-733-SAMS, sells them for $10 per case of 50. Lighters will be very valuable as barter items and are great fire starters.

http://www.samsclub.com

Piezoelectric Camp Stove Lighter

This stove lighter creates 100,000 sparks via piezoelectricity for just $8. You can get one from Campmor.

Magnesium Fire Starter

Scrape off some magnesium shavings and ignite them with sparks from a built-in flint. Magnesium burns at 5400° F. These can be purchased for $7 from Campmor.

Matches

Buy an abundance of kitchen stick matches from the grocery store. This is another good barter item. Store boxes inside two ziplocked plastic bags, one inside the other. You can order cases of strike-anywhere stick matches for $40 per case of 9000 from Diamond Match Co., 800-777-7942.

http://www.diamondbrands.com

Buy waterproof matches as well. Waterproof matches are available from Major Surplus, Campmor and most camping suppliers. They cost $4 for 450 matches. You can waterproof your own matches by dipping the heads in paraffin wax.

Safety Considerations

All stoves require specified clearances from combustible surfaces. Wall clearances can be reduced with a properly designed and installed brick or metal wall shield. Your stove manual will state what the requirements are, and you should take advantage of a professional installer's knowledge of local codes.

Coal and wood stoves require a fireproof floor. This is typically tile, slate or brick over a layer of sheet metal or Durock cement board. The floor protection must extend a foot or more beyond the stove, depending on the model. Specifics are also available in the *National Fire Protection Association Manual*, available from Lehman's for $40.

Metal floor and wall shields used for wood stoves are an excellent safety application for your portable cook stove. Expediently, use a platform built with concrete blocks or bricks placed edge to edge under any heat source. Be sure that this platform extends at least one foot beyond the heater in all directions, and keep all heat sources at least three feet away from walls.

Minimize your risks if you decide to have supplemental space heaters available for the winter of 2000. The U.S. Consumer Product Safety Commission provides recommendations and checklists to use with various types of fueled space heaters.

http://www.cyber-north.com/tipnet/homefire.html

Be sure to permit sufficient ventilation and air exchange when burning fuels for heating. Crack a door to the upper portion of your home if you are in the basement, to permit fumes to travel up and out.

Have a battery-powered carbon monoxide detector in your living and/or sleeping quarters when using these alternative heat sources, especially if your room's air movement is limited by plastic and insulation. They cost $24 and can be purchased from any hardware store or discount retailer. Battery-powered smoke detectors can be purchased for $10 for use in your living area, and on each floor of your home. Stock up on extra alkaline batteries.

Be sure to take steps to prevent fires if you need to use flammable liquids for heating and lighting. Always keep a large ABC fire extinguisher at hand, located between the stove and your exit. See Chapter 5, pages 187 to 192, for instructions on Fire Safety.

Heat Retention

It can be quite a challenge to heat your home using an alternative method. Storing fuel is difficult and expensive, and you may not have sufficient quantities to run your heater continuously. Thus, taking steps to retain the heat you generate is essential.

Consolidate Living Quarters in One Room

By heating just one room of your house, you can dramatically decrease the amount of fuel you'll need.

Setting up house in the basement may sound alien, but it provides an advantage in a winter Y2K emergency situation. These lower level quarters have natural earth sheltering, and if properly insulated, provide the best heat retention of any room in the house.

Basements require less fuel to maintain at a comfortable temperature and are easier to insulate. If you decide to use your basement in this manner, mound extra dirt against the exposed upper portion of the walls, to increase the natural insulation effect.

If you don't have a basement, consider moving in with someone who does. Two families can easily share such a space and total heating costs are cut in half.

Insulation and Weatherproofing

Insulate and weatherproof your home to maximize your ability to retain precious heat. Cover all windows with plastic to reduce air exchange. Drape coverings over the walls, as they used to do in castles with woven murals. Anything can be used to cover the walls, even newspaper. These coverings create insulation by trapping dead air. Just be careful; those wall coverings could become a fire hazard.

See Susan Conniry's discussion on maximizing warmth in an emergency situation, at the Westergaard website:

http://www.y2ktimebomb.com/Computech/Management/ sconn9843a.htm

Body Insulation

When preparing to deal with cold temperatures, take advantage of your own internal furnace, your metabolism. Properly insulated sleeping bags and layered clothing keep your own heat next to your body and decrease the amount of heating and fuel required to keep your home comfortable. If you have warm bedding and/or a sleeping partner, you can turn off your heater at night and save fuel.

Bedding: Winter-rated sleeping bags are important items. Purchase sleeping bags rated to at least -20° F for every family member. If your bags are warm enough, you can sleep comfortably even in freezing environments. Out n' Back, 888-533-7415, sells military surplus mummy bags for $70. These are rated to -20° F. New ones cost $150. Avoid down or feather bags, as they lose their effectiveness when wet. Buy bags insulated with Hollofil or its equivalent which stays warm when wet.

http://www.citysearch.com/slc/outnback

Layering your bedding increases the thermal efficiency. Inner liners add significant warmth to a lighter sleeping bag. An inner liner made from a flannel sheet will increase any bag's rating by 10° to 15° F.

A bivouac outer bag is an excellent investment. When used as a cover, it increases the warmth of your bag by 10° to 20° F. In warm weather, it can be used by itself as a lightweight sleeping bag.

Major Surplus sells a military body bag for $20. This makes a good sleeping bag cover, and can also be used as an expedient stretcher. Out n' Back sells a G.I. sleeping bag cover for $8.

American Freedom Network, 800-205-6245 sells Wiggy's extreme cold weather gear, including a -60° F Antarctic sleeping bag with Lamilite insulation for $284. The Super Light 0° F sleeping bag and Patrol Overbag shell, providing an additional 30° to 40° F protection, sells for $286.

http://www.amerifree.com

Clothing: Be sure to have proper clothing. In northern areas, buy cold weather gear for each member of your family. Snowmobile or one-piece winter work suits are the warmest and make good cold weather gear. Carhart makes a good durable product. You'll need work gloves. We also recommend lined leather mittens, which are warmer than gloves.

Sweatshirts and sweatpants are useful for both winter and summer use. In addition to being unisex, their sizing characteristics allow almost anyone to wear them. This makes them especially appropriate for children, as they continue to fit for longer periods of time and require fewer size adjustments.

Since you may be working hard outside, heavy duty, durable clothing will be very important. Military surplus clothing like U.S. Marine wool field pants take a lot of abuse and are inexpensive at $13. These can be purchased from resellers such as Out n' Back, Major Surplus & Survival and The Sportsman's Guide, 800-888-3006.

http://www.sportsmansguide.com

Wiggy's is known for making the warmest parkas in the world. Their Antarctic Parka is $292 and the accompanying Bib Overalls are $224. You can buy them from the American Freedom Network.

Footwear: Waterproof boots with felt liners work well in subfreezing temperatures. Military surplus white arctic snow boots, called Mickey Mouse boots because of their appearance, are warm to -30° F. They are sometimes available from surplus suppliers. The Sportsman's Guide sells -100° F boots for $45.

Also, buy some heavy work boots and heavy socks.

Raingear: Have a heavy-duty set of waterproof fabric rainpants and raincoat. A good set of raingear costs $50 for a hooded top and bottom. All camping suppliers sell them.

Emergency insulated clothing: Staying warm without an external heater is simply a function of trapping enough dead air around yourself and cutting down heat convection to retain your own body heat. You can keep from freezing by layering and crumpling up newspapers or leaves to create insulation under clothing. Towels or sheets of newspapers wrapped around your limbs and trunk create necessary dead air spaces and provide insulation. Use windbreakers such as paper bags to prevent warm air from being blown away from your body.

Expedient Shelter

Outside: Climbers survive on Mount Everest in expedition tents. With the proper equipment, you could also fare well if you have to do extended winter camping in 2000. High quality, four-season expedition tents of various sizes cost $200 to $400 from Campmor.

If a tent must become your temporary home, a larger tent will be more comfortable. But, smaller tents are easier to warm with a small heat source such as a single burner stove. Tents with "double wall" construction provide an insulating air space between the walls and are significantly warmer. Place an inexpensive tarp over the tent and rainfly to protect it from sunlight. Ultraviolet rays will damage the nylon of a tent which is in continuous use.

Inside: You can also use a tent inside your house or another structure to create a super-insulated space. Securely string the tent from the top of two opposing door or window frames. Then pile all the insulating material you can find around and on top of the tent. It will stay quite a bit warmer than the surrounding air due to the retention of your body heat. You can also make an emergency warming shelter by building a little structure using mattresses propped against each other.

LIGHTING

Light provides an important psychological boost. It gives you a sense of control over your environment, and during times of emergency it is crucial to be able to see what you are doing. Therefore, it is important to have some basic forms of lighting available if electricity becomes unreliable.

Fueled lamps provide a measure of heat as well as light. In a single room, this may be all that is required to keep the temperature well above freezing. Bundle up in layered clothing, and you will be comfortable with temperatures in the 40° to 50° F range.

There are a variety of lighting sources to be used in case of power outages.

Lamps

Kerosene/Oil Lamp

For $64, buy an Aladdin lamp which burns liquid paraffin, vegetable oil or kerosene. Get extra wicks, mantles and chimneys.

Get the model with the unbreakable metal base from Major Surplus or other suppliers.

Lehman's sells kits for $8 to make any glass container into an oil lamp. Olive oil is 99% fuel and creates no smoke or odor.

Major Surplus sells an old-fashioned flat-wick hurricane lamp which burns kerosene for $8. Real Goods, 800-762-7325, sells a sturdier brass model for $50, which burns lamp oil or kerosene.

http://www.realgoods.com/products/outdoors/35-363.html

Paraffin lamp oil can be purchased at Meijers or most discount retailers or hardware stores. It costs $3 per quart and will store more than 10 years.

Lanterns

Lanterns pressurize their fuel and are up to five times brighter than lamps.

Dual-Fuel Lanterns

Peak and Coleman both sell lanterns which burn white gas or unleaded gasoline. For $70, the Coleman models burn from 7-14 hours on 1-2 pt. of fuel and produce 2700 to 4000 BTU/hr. The Peak model is smaller and sells for $40. These dual-mantle lanterns are unaffected by temperature ranges from 0° to 100° F. Store extra $2 lamp mantles, Major Surplus and Campmor sell them.

Lehman's sells the "Best Kerosene Lantern" for $130. It puts out 180 foot candle power, as much as a 400-watt electric bulb. It burns white gas, unleaded gasoline, kerosene, lamp oil, naphtha or mineral spirits. Lehman's has 12 pages of oil, kerosene and white gas lamps in its catalog.

The PetroMax multi-fuel lantern from Nitro-Pak, 800-866-4876, is all brass and burns any fuel. Use kerosene or paraffin lamp oil inside your house as their fumes are the safest. The PetroMax is the brightest lantern available, putting out 500 candle power. A quart of fuel lasts 8 hrs. at full brightness. These lanterns cost $135 each; a deluxe kit including extra parts costs $225.

http://www.nitro-pak.com

Propane Lanterns

With an adapter, propane lamps can be fueled with 20 lb. or 40 lb. LP tanks. These don't produce as much light as the dual-gas models, but are more convenient.

Most sporting good stores sell the Coleman 2-mantle propane lantern. Campmor sells it for $30. Buy extra mantles.

Candles

Candles are an expedient source of light in an emergency. However, due to their open flame, candles are the most dangerous of all lighting sources. Care must be taken if you use them.

Nuwick makes 120 hour canned candles which are also a source of heat. The nontoxic slow burning wax is contained in a stable metal can, is reusable, and is waterproof. Campmor sells them for $8.

Liquid Candles

Major Surplus also sells what they refer to as a liquid candle. It is a form of expedient oil lamp. Three cans sell for $7 and provide a total of 120 hours of light and heat.

Emergency Essentials 100 Hour Candle burns liquid paraffin for $4.50. Contact them at 800-999-1963.

http://www.beprepared.com

Candle Lanterns

These lanterns hold solid wax candles in a glass case, and have a carrying handle. This is safer than using non-enclosed candles. Campmor sells a three candle Candlelier model for $30, as well as a Uco single candle model for $14. Buying a case of extra candles is recommended.

Electric Lighting

Direct current (DC) and alternating current (AC) lighting sources require an alternative power source, but are much safer than fuel-source lighting.

LED Lamps

The best lamps are Light Emitting Diodes, as they require the least amount of power. By using LEDs, battery life can be extended several dozen times as compared to conventional light bulbs. White, yellow or red LEDs can be obtained for flashlights.

LEDs don't have a filament, so they are very long-lasting. LEDs will last for 68 years if used for 4 hrs. per day, and use only 1.2 watts of power or less. Their fantastic efficiency means you will need much smaller and less expensive solar modules and battery sizes for photovoltaic systems! Off Line and Jade Mountain sell LEDs, for use in 120 VAC as well as 12 VDC light systems.

Multiple LEDs can be used in 12 volt applications for room lighting. One source for these LEDs is Delta Light, 612-980-6503. Their ML-2 for $10 is designed for the MiniMag Light flashlight, which is our AA battery flashlight of choice.

http://www.stpaulmercantile.com/deltalit.htm

Nitro-Pak and Jade Mountain sell LED solar flashlights costing $26 to $35.

Fluorescent Lights

Next to LEDs, fluorescent bulbs are the most efficient. They are available for 120 VAC or 12 VDC lighting systems. All solar supply companies sell both.

Portable Coleman fluorescent lanterns are available from Campmor for $40. They are rechargeable from a 12 VDC source and provide steady lighting for 9 hours. Extra fluorescent tubes are $4.

Incandescent Lights

If you are running a 120 VAC generator or have an inverter on your 12 VDC battery, you can use regular incandescent or fluorescent lighting. See Chapter 7 for information on generators and inverters.

Solar Lights

Get a simple solar panel, a voltage regulator and a deep-cycle battery to hook up to some 12 VDC lamps and you've got light for the whole night! Several hundred dollars buys a complete solar power setup which will last for years and which is sufficient for small loads such as lighting and radios. Check with Mr. Solar, 435-877-1061. His website is excellent.

http://www.mrsolar.com/solardesaltinators.html

Lehman's sells a solar indoor light kit for $470.

Simple portable solar lanterns are sold by Jade Mountain, starting at $24. The Kyocera solar lantern gives six hours of light from one day's recharging, for $125.

See Chapter 7, pages 257 to 259, for more information on solar powered alternative energy systems and suppliers.

Kinetic Flashlights

The Freeplay kinetic lantern lets you wind an internal spring which powers a generator inside the flashlight. This creates electricity to light the bulb. Thirty seconds of winding provides three minutes of light. An internal battery can also be charged to provide up to two hours of light. It can also be run in flasher mode, turning on and off every other second. This saves power, and doubles the run time. Off Line sells them for $70, as does B&A Products.

One of our favorite kinetic energy products is the Dynamo hand crank flashlight. The Dynamo flashlight has no means to store a charge, its sole means of power is derived from your hand cranking the lever. Surprisingly, it doesn't take that much energy to operate. It produces quite a bright beam and works under any conditions, with no batteries to go dead! It's available from The Sportsman's Guide for $6.

A similar, more durable product, is the Russian-made Forever flashlight, which has an adjustable beam. One squeeze every two seconds provides continuous light. It costs $12. Major Surplus, Nitro-Pak and Lehman's sell them.

SANITATION

Cleanliness is important for physical and psychological health. Both hygiene and waste disposal are important considerations if public utilities are unavailable for any duration. Waste disposal must be handled properly, to prevent contagious diseases.

Hygiene

Cleanliness is important to maintain health. Plan on having supplies available for taking sponge baths. Also, be sure to have a large container for heating water for bathing.

Clothes Washing

The manual Wonder Washer from Emergency Essentials can clean clothes in less than two minutes without electricity. The eight cup capacity washer can wash three shirts per cycle and costs $46.

Wood-Fired Water Heaters

Hot showers would be a comfort in the stressful situation created by Y2K. Jade Mountain sells several wood-fired hot water heaters priced from $185. Other models which can retrofit wood stoves run from $185 to $225 and require some plumbing skills. A multiple-fuel water heater which burns kerosene, diesel, alcohol, wood, pine cones or corn cobs, has a 15 gal. tank, and sells for $260. Hot Products, Inc. makes a wood-fired hot water heater for $629. Contact them at 707-444-1311.

http://www.hotpro.com

Solar Water Heaters

Jade Mountain and other suppliers sell solar water heating systems. These systems can provide part or all of a home's hot water needs.

You can make your own 6 gal. solar collector by looping 1/2" Kitec tubing back and forth on your roof inside a glazed cabinet. The heated water then goes to a backup water heater or directly to the point of use. This Solar Thermal Pipe system is available from Jade Mountain for $400.

Thermomax Solar Collectors beginning at $2450 can provide the hot water needs of a small home. They will pay for themselves many times over with a 5% to 10% return on your investment.

Showering: A simple black plastic bag attached to a hose and shower head will work as an expedient solar water heater for showers. The Super Sunshower II with insulation and reflector to reduces heat loss from the back of the bag provides 14 minutes of showering from 5 gal. of water. Available from Campmor for $16.

Nitro-Pak sells shower water heaters which can be heated with a campfire or camp stove. The $40 Super Trail Shower holds 3 gal. for an 8 minute shower and heats in 20 minutes with a copper coil in a campfire. The Hotman is a pressurized steel tank which holds 3 gal. and heats in 7 minutes with a stove. It costs $116.

Toiletries

Have an abundant supply of bathing accessories. Following is a short list of must-have supplies. Evaluate how much you use of each in a month, or several months. You can go to a discount warehouse and load up with bulk packages of everything.

- Toilet paper: Buy extra, it will be your best barter item!
- Soap: Bar or concentrated liquid.
- Shampoo: Alternatively, you can use soap.

• Feminine hygiene supplies: The website "Y2K for Women" discusses long-term solutions for alternative feminine hygiene products. See their web pages at:

http://www.y2kwomen.com/keeper/index.htm
http://www.y2kwomen.com/archives/DK6.html

• Deodorant: The mineral rock or crystal type lasts for over a year and kills the smell by killing bacteria. Available from health food stores or drug stores.
• Toothbrushes
• Toothpaste, or a 50/50 mix of salt and baking soda.
• Dental floss or tape
• Denture care supplies
• Disposable diapers: A big expense, but can you imagine being without? Monitor how many you use in a week and buy enough to last.
• Washable diapers: If you have a good supply of water.
• Moist towelettes: Good for baby care and general cleanup when water is scarce.
• Ointments
• Contact lens solution and supplies
• Hair cutting supplies
• Shaving supplies

For complete lists of recommended household supplies to stock up on, see the websites:

http://www.utne.com/y2k/individual.html
http://www.y2klinks.net/Y2Ksupplies.htm

Waste Disposal

Electric sewage pumps and processing plants may not function after Y2K. Human waste disposal could become a major health issue if power for sewage system pumps and water for toilets is not available. You must have a strategy to safely deal with waste. Improper disposal could allow rains to create contaminated run-off and spread diseases such as hepatitis and cholera to surface water sources. Disease from contaminated water can be an outcome of the loss of municipal sewage treatment systems.

How To Shit in the Woods by Kathleen Meyer is oriented to creating wilderness toilets which protect the environment from contamination. This is important, since you'll want to continue living in your neighborhood and not be forced to move after you've fouled your nest!

A good discussion of sanitation issues and a clear schematic of a latrine and an outhouse is available in David Werner's book, *Where There Is No Doctor.*

Types of Toilets

There are a variety of satisfactory expedient toilets available.

Bucket Toilet: Get a lid formed like a toilet seat for your 5 gal. lined bucket and you're in business! $13 from Out n' Back.

Bag Toilet: Major Surplus sells a portable folding toilet that holds a bag for waste. It is effective and costs just $12. Buy a case of 13 gal. kitchen garbage bags with which to line it.

Chemical Toilet: PortaPotti's model 135 has a 2.6 gal. water tank for flushing. Put chemicals in the water and you have a toilet which solves the smell problem, can be carried away and dumped as needed. Store extra chemicals and you're all set. Major Surplus sells it for $110.

Composting Toilets: This type of toilet does not require water for flushing, nor a functioning sewage system. By adding peat moss to the toilet, wastes are converted to compost. Liquids are evaporated via a vent stack or drained out. Eventually, a few gallons of compost are removed and can be used for nonfood plants. Optional 12 volt DC fans speed the evaporation process and create a partial vacuum to help prevent odors. A small solar panel can directly power the fan on an intermittent basis.

Keep the toilet in the warmed area of your home, as composting slows down below 50° F. Read David Del Porto's definitive *The Composting Toilet Book* to get an in-depth understanding of the topic; available from Jade Mountain.

Composting toilets are approved by the National Sanitation Foundation. For $1000, a Sun-Mar system handles the continuous use of two to three adults. Larger systems are available.

While up-front costs may seem high for a composting toilet, you save the expense of installing a conventional septic system and drain field. Contact these manufacturers for information:

BioLet Composting Toilets, 800-5BIOLET

http://www.biolet.com

Clivus Multrum, 800-962-8447

http://www.clivusmultrum.com

Sancor Industries, 800 387 5126

http://www.envirolet.com

Sun-Mar Corp., 800-461-2461

http://www.sun-mar.com

Lehman's, Jade Mountain, and Off Line Independent Energy Systems, 209-877-7080, sell composting toilets.

http://www.psnw.com/~ofln

Latrine: Locate latrines at least 60 to 100 feet away from wells. Dig a slit trench one foot wide, several feet long and as deep as you can go. Improvise a seat or some poles to lean on. Buy a supply of hydrated lime to sprinkle over the waste to help keep flies off, use ashes, or cover the waste with soil after each use.

Alternately, you can burn the contents for disinfection, but this requires the use of fuel, which may be precious. Flies spread disease and should be kept out by building an outhouse.

Outhouse: An outhouse is a covered pit toilet. Flies stay out and odors stay in. It is built over a 6 to 9 ft. deep pit which is 3 ft. in diameter or 3 ft. square.

A wooden or reinforced concrete slab with a 10 in. to 12 in. hole in it is placed over the pit to seal it off. A toilet seat with a tight fly-proof lid is secured over the seat to prevent flies from entering and leaving and transmitting disease.

Surface water is diverted away from the pit, to prevent water contamination. Put some topsoil in the bottom of the pit to speed the composting process. The pit gradually fills up and a new one has to be dug. When the pit is filled to within 2 to 3 ft. from the top, remove the slab and fill the hole with dirt.

The best style outhouse has a ventilation stack to let out odors, with a fly screen on the stack's exit to trap flies. Outhouses should be located at least 60 to 100 ft. away from wells. A description of how to build an outhouse is available at:

http://tortugas.idir.net/~medintz/surv_faq/gid.html

Septic System: If you have a septic system, take care of it now. Have your septic tank pumped out in 1999 to be sure it has the maximum useful lifespan ahead of it. Repair the drain field if it hasn't been working properly. Use biodegradable toilet paper and feed it with composting bacteria periodically. You can buy commercial beneficial bacteria products at most hardware stores.

MAINTENANCE

Every household should have a basic tool kit. It's better to have a tool and not need it, than to need a tool and not have it! Your tool kit should include everything needed to be self sufficient in an emergency situation. Many of us already have enough tools to take care of the majority of common chores.

The best way to ensure your tool kit is complete is to review your equipment. Assess your individual situation. Make a written checklist of all the possible tasks you may have to do, paying particular attention to maintenance tasks that must be performed. Make a list of all necessary tools, focusing on manual tools so you won't be dependent on electricity. Purchase and organize them.

A basic tool kit should consist of the following items:
- Crescent wrench, to shut off utilities
- Ax and hatchet
- Hand drill with drill bits
- Socket and ratchet sets, metric and standard
- Hand saws—rip saw, crosscut saw, hack saw, etc.
- Open end wrenches, metric and standard.
- Pliers—Channellocks, Vise Grip, needle nose, etc.
- Wire cutters and wire strippers
- Files—round, flat, rasp, etc.
- Tape—masking, electrical, duct, etc.
- Fasteners—nails, screws, nuts and bolts, etc.
- Manual can opener
- Good quality pocket knives
- Screw drivers—Phillips and slotted in various sizes
- Hammers—ball peen, claw, rubber mallet, etc.
- Power tools—circular saw, reciprocating saw, electric drill, etc.
- Spare blades and parts for the power tools

Power tools can be run with a generator or an inverter if you have an alternate power source.

To sum up, carefully choose where you will locate during Y2K. Establish strategies for heating and cooking. Buy winter bedding and clothing. Establish alternative lighting. Buy extra toiletries and establish alternative sanitation. Finally, invest in good quality hand tools. Make your home a haven in which to weather Y2K!

SHELTER CHECKLIST

____ Choose where you will locate for Y2K

____ Establish an alternative plan for emergency relocation

____ Consolidate living quarters into one room

____ Establish strategies for heating and cooking

____ Choose which fuel you'll use

____ Store at least three months' worth of fuel

____ Buy a stove which can be used for heating as well as cooking

____ Have the stove professionally installed

____ Store a back-up heater and fuel

____ Store a supply of matches or fire starters

____ Buy two fire extinguishers

____ Buy battery powered smoke detectors, carbon monoxide detectors, and extra batteries

____ Buy -20° F winter sleeping bags for each family member

____ Buy winter clothing for each family member

____ Establish alternative lighting

____ Buy a lamp, a lantern and candles

____ Buy extra mantles and wicks

____ Store at least 3 months' worth of fuel for the light sources

____ Buy and store extra toiletries

____ Store plenty of toilet paper and soap

____ Establish good alternative sanitation

____ Buy a portable chemical toilet and supply of chemicals

____ Buy a portable bag toilet and an abundant supply of bags

____ Dig a latrine

____ Buy a 50 lb. bag of lime to be used with the latrine

____ Invest in a supply of good quality hand tools

CHAPTER 3

Water

Every person needs to address this at a personal and local level. They need to be asking about their local power company or water purification plant.

John Koskinen
Chairman, President's Y2K Council

Clean water is the most essential substance we require to sustain life and health. You can live for weeks without food, yet only days without water. If your water is contaminated, even brushing your teeth can transfer debilitating water-born diseases which can leave you sick for weeks or months, and can even kill you. Especially vulnerable are infants, the elderly and the immune-compromised.

Highly automated municipal water treatment plants are at risk from Y2K. Loss of electric power could short circuit water distribution systems. Automated equipment dispensing chlorine used to purify water could fail, resulting in a contaminated water supply. Fatal levels of fluoride could also be released.

Sewage treatment plants are also at risk. Treated sewage effluent is discharged into surface reservoirs such as rivers and lakes, from which municipal fresh water is drawn. If the sewage treatment plants malfunction, untreated sewage could contaminate downstream fresh water sources.

Given these considerations, a clean water supply should be high on your list of priorities when making Y2K preparations. With some basic planning, you can deal with these problems.

There are two considerations to make to secure an abundant supply of safe water for your family. First, you must have a dependable water source. Second, the water must be pure.

In this chapter we'll look at the issues of water storage, short-term alternative sources of water, water purification, and long-term renewable water sources.

Some frequently asked questions about water are available at: **http://www.millennium-ark.net/News_Files/INFO_Files Water_FAQs.html**

A Safe Drinking Water Hotline is offered by the Environmental Protection Agency at 800-426-4791.

WATER SUPPLY STRATEGIES

The Red Cross and the Federal Emergency Management Agency recommend that everyone store at least a week's worth of water in preparation for Y2K. How much water you decide to store will depend on your evaluation of the degree of risk to the water system from Y2K and the length of time you feel you may have an interrupted supply of healthy water.

We recommend you store a minimum of 2 gal. of water per person per day. In hot weather, a full gallon or more per day may be required for drinking alone. We typically use 2 gal. each time we brush our teeth! If you want enough for drinking, cooking, washing dishes and clothes, and for personal hygiene, increase your amount of stored water to 4 gal. per person per day.

Short-Term

If you feel that Y2K will only bring short-term problems to

your water supply, follow the recommendations of the Red Cross and FEMA and store one or more weeks' worth of water.

If you believe a one week supply should be enough, store a minimum of 14 gal. per person in your home. For a two week supply, store 28 gal. per person.

Store 60 gal. per person for a one month supply. A family of four would require 240 gal. for one month. That's four 55 gal. drums plus four 5 gal. buckets full. If you use just 5 gal. buckets, 240 gal. will require 48 buckets.

On Dec. 31, 1999, fill up all containers in your home, including the bathtub, just in case you lose water after 2000.

Mid-Term

If you are concerned that potential problems with the water system could take longer than a month to be resolved, store 60 or 90 days' worth of water per person.

To store 60 days' worth of water for one person, at 2 gal. per day, you will need a minimum of 120 gal. This will fit into two 55 gal. drums, plus two 5 gal. buckets. Two months' water for a family of four is 480 gal., which will fit into nine 55 gal. drums or a small water storage tank.

To store 90 days' worth of water for one person, 2 gal. per day, you need 180 gal., or four 55 gal. drums. Three months' water for a family of four is 720 gal., requiring thirteen 55 gal. drums or a small water storage tank.

If you are preparing for a disruption lasting several months, also purchase water filtration or purification equipment, and chemicals for water disinfection. These will be necessary in case your stored water supply runs out before safe, reliable municipal water service is restored.

Long-Term

If you are concerned that Y2K problems could disrupt water supplies for several months to a year, plan in advance to secure a long-term, renewable supply of clean water.

For a stable long-term supply of water, consider relocating to a site where you are free to have your own well. Acquire property with an existing well, or drill one as early as possible before 2000. Well drillers are getting busier all the time!

A good well can provide clean water for several families and can be pumped by hand if you don't have stable electricity from the power grid after Y2K. Clean water also won't require the addition of chemicals for disinfection, which is much healthier.

WATER STORAGE

Keeping water on hand is one of the best and simplest things you can do to prepare for Y2K.

Water Containers

Decide what kind of containers to store your water in. Use food-grade containers that won't deteriorate. The Food and Drug Administration considers the following container materials to be food-safe and appropriate for storing water.

Two-liter polycarbonate plastic pop bottles are convenient, inexpensive and readily accessible. A moderate number of 2-liter bottles will be useful due to their portability and ease of handling, but are inefficient for storing large quantities of water. It would require 480 2-liter bottles to store enough water for a family of four for a month. Collecting, disinfecting, filling and storing that number of containers would be cumbersome.

Bulk storage container options include buckets and drums in 5, 15, 30 and 55 gal. sizes, made of food-safe plastic. Steel and fiber buckets and drums of equivalent size can also be used as long as they are fitted with food-safe plastic liners. Alternatively, large water tanks are a handy way to store all your water in just one or two containers.

We recommend using 55 gal. drums with a few 5 gal. buckets for the bulk of your water storage. All are inexpensive and easily obtained anywhere in the U.S.

Your cheapest bulk water storage option, if available locally, is a used 55 gal. fiber drum with a drop-in 55 in., 55 gal. plastic liner. For 18¢ per gal. you'll have good quality, inexpensive water storage.

Another cost effective storage container option is to buy dirty open-head plastic food containers from food processors or distributors. Clean them with a power washer and rinse with a 10% bleach solution before use. Look in your Yellow Pages under "Food Processing and Manufacturing" or "Food Products–Wholesale."

If you are on a budget, use whatever food-safe containers you can obtain for free, such as the 2-liter bottles. Sometimes restaurants will give away dirty 3 or 5 gal. food containers to save the cost of disposal. Don't use 1 gal. plastic milk jugs. They are difficult to get completely clean, are biodegradable and may not last longer than six months. Avoid glass containers as they break easily and are a hazard for children.

Some container sizes and prices follow. These costs were the lowest we could find in our area. Some require volume purchases to get the listed prices, in which case you could buy in bulk with your friends. A list of suppliers follows these container prices.

Polycarbonate Containers

Two-liter clear polycarbonate pop bottles are available free or for the deposit.

1, 2, 3 or 5 gal. polycarbonate plastic jugs cost $1 to $8 respectively from retail purified water sellers or supermarkets.

High Density Polyethylene Containers With Covers

Buckets and drums can be purchased with either tight-head or open-head construction. The plastic tight-head variety is made from one piece of molded HDPE plastic. Tight-head drum tops have two small openings which close with threaded plugs called *bungs,* you'll need a bung wrench to open them. Get a bung wrench from a drum supplier or Emergency Essentials for $9.

Only new tight-head plastic containers are available. Used ones are not, due to the difficulty in cleaning them for recycling.

5 gal. tight-head HDPE bucket with lid. New: $7.

15, 30 and 55 gal. tight-head HDPE drums, new: $10, $26 and $30 respectively.

Open-head buckets and drums look like a barrel, with the entire top being open. Their lids are flat and round, clamping onto the drum with a metal band. Since these are easily cleaned, they are available used and are a good buy.

5 or 6 gal. open-head HDPE bucket with lid; new: $3 to $4, used: $2.

Ordinary bucket lids won't reseal properly once removed. Buy a few resealable Gamma Seal lids from Major Surplus and Survival. The outer ring seals the 12 in. top of a 5 or 6 gal. bucket and a screw-in airtight lid seats within it. They are $6.25 each.

30, 55 gal. open-head HDPE drums w/ lids. New: $36, $42; reconditioned: $15, $25.

Steel Containers With Covers

5 gal. open-head steel buckets. $3 each, on pallets in lots of 120.

30 or 55 gal. open-head steel drum. New: $23 or $35. Used: $12 or $20.

Fiber Containers With Covers

Various sized fiber (heavy cardboard) containers ranging from 10 to 55 gal. Used: $2 to $8.

Plastic Liners

Plastic liners are food-safe heavy bags which drop into a sturdy open-head container. All steel or fiber containers must be lined with these FDA-approved HDPE or LDPE plastic liners before being used to store water. Tie the liner shut before sealing the container. Alternatively, drape clean polyethylene plastic sheeting into the container to line it, as long as it extends well above the sides and can be tied up before sealing.

5 gal. HDPE or LDPE liners for buckets, available for $1.02 each in lots of 100 from CDF.

55 gal. LDPE liners; 40 in. tall, cost: $1.39 each; 55 in. tall: $1.59 each. Sold in boxes of 100 from CDF.

Single 55 gal. liners can be purchased from Cover-Your-Basics, 509-935-0375, for $2.50 each.

http://www.theofficenet.com/~covyrbas

GlitchProof sells sets of four for $15, 877-302-0706.

http://www.glitchproof.com

Mylar Bags

4 gal. Mylar bags with a built-in plastic spout are available for $5 each. They store in accompanying cardboard boxes and can be stacked three high. Emergency Essentials sells them in lots of five.

Tanks

Water tanks designed for or adaptable to basements are efficient ways to store large amounts of water. It would be much better to have excess water than too little. Consider adding enough drinking water for an extra person or two, if you have relatives or friends nearby whom you may need to help out.

Rectangular 55 to 300 gal. HDPE tanks which fit through most doorways for basement water storage are available from Jade Mountain for $166 to $425 respectively.

"Kolaps-A-Tank" 73 to 1340 gal. collapsible containers, fit in

a pickup, flatbed truck or the corner of your basement. $250 to
$799 from Jade Mountain.

"Terra Tanks" from watertanks.com, 877-H2O-TNKS are 100
to 2000 gal. waterproof industrial fabric containers costing from
$400 to $1200, respectively. Larger sizes are also available.

http://www.watertanks.com

Omega Systems, 301-735-8373, sells 300 and 500 gal. black
water tanks for $370 and $400 respectively.

http://www.omega-inc.com/water.htm

CDF's "Flexotainer" Flexible Intermediate Bulk Container, 160
gal. round or 300 gal. square collapsible resin containers, each
cost $60. FIBCs require external support such as a wire cage. CDF,
800-443-1920, will recommend a cage supplier, or just add two
plywood walls onto the corner of your basement to make a support structure.

http://www.cdf-liners.com

Maxi Container, 800-727-6294, e-mail maxirsr@aol.com, sells
reconditioned square 275 gal. FIBC's in steel cages on a steel pal-
let, for $150.

Polyethylene vertical tanks cost from $125 for a 100 gal. tank to
$985 for a 2000 gal. tank from Jade Mountain or watertanks.com.

Redwood water tanks, 300 to 5000 gal. are available for $580
to $3200 respectively from Jade Mountain.

White plastic resin underground cisterns cost $520 for 500
gal., or $885 for 1200 gal. from Jade Mountain.

Container suppliers: Many distributors sell both new and
reconditioned standardized buckets and drums. Due to the added
shipping costs from non-local suppliers, you will find your best
deals close to home. Look in the Yellow Pages under "Barrels and
Drums." National container suppliers include those already listed,
plus Freund Can Co., 773-224-4230.

http://www.freundcan.com

Expedient Water Containers

Expedient water storage is as simple as a plastic-lined pit in the ground. When properly protected during construction, it will remain free from contamination and be an inexpensive way to store large volumes of water. Otherwise, clean glass, food-safe plastic or any containers lined with clean polyethylene plastic bags or sheeting can be safely used. Rigid or collapsible 5 gal. water containers for camping are also good and can be found on sale at your local discount retailer for under $5.

Transporting Water

You'll need ways of transferring your water to smaller containers and moving it from place to place. To get your water from its source to your place of use, you'll need extra 5 gal. buckets with lids or other containers small enough to carry.

Hand Pumps

Buy a self-priming siphon pump for easy, sanitary transfer of water from your 55 gal. drums or larger containers to smaller buckets. Available from hardware stores; Major Surplus & Survival, $17; Emergency Essentials, $12.

watertanks.com sells a Drum Dispensing Pump which fits 15, 30 or 55 gal. drums and dispenses 16 oz. per stroke. Cost: $23.

Siphoning

Use a hose to transfer water from one storage container to another lower one. Keep the hose length 25 ft. or shorter, to permit adequate suction. 1/4 in. inner diameter surgical tubing, flexible 1/2 in. hose from a recreational equipment dealer, or garden hose will all do the job.

Drum Hand Cart

If you plan on using 55 gal. drums to store your water, you

may want to invest in a drum hand cart. A 55 gal. drum full of water weighs 440 lbs. Without a hand cart, it's difficult to move.

To purchase a drum hand cart, check your Yellow Pages for suppliers under "Material Handling Equipment" or "Barrels and Drums." We found one locally for $160.

A regular hand cart will work, especially if the back is concave to receive the barrel. Harbor Freight Tools sells the Bigfoot Hand Truck for $50.

Wagons

Harbor Freight Tools sells Heavy Duty Garden Carts with 6.5 or 11.3 cubic ft. of capacity, 20 in. or 26 in. tires, carrying 300 lbs. or 400 lbs., for $70 or $100 respectively.

Harbor Freight also sells a 2 ft. by 4 ft. steel mesh deck wagon with 10 in. pneumatic tires that will carry 1000 lbs for $100. Bolt a sheet of plywood on top to carry larger loads.

Expedient Water Carriers

You can create soft-sided containers out of plastic bags inside smaller fabric bags or pillow cases. An adult can easily carry 80 lbs. of water in this way, if the bag's corners are tied together and draped over a shoulder.

Treating Water For Storage

To stop the growth of micro-organisms in stored water, add a teaspoon of unscented bleach for every 5 gal. of water. Keep the container tightly sealed as chlorine evaporates quickly, permitting recontamination. Before using water, let small amounts sit uncovered for a day, so that the chlorine can evaporate. Drink it when you can no longer smell the chlorine, but remember that it won't keep fresh for long once the disinfectant has evaporated.

When filling 2-liter pop bottles, add four drops of bleach per bottle. Keep an eyedropper with full-strength unscented bleach at your sink. Rinse out the bottle, add four drops of bleach, fill with water, seal, and store.

Change your stored water every six months if possible. Alternatively, recharge the water with the same amount of chlorine or other disinfectant as when you first stored it.

The use of opaque blue plastic or steel buckets or drums for water storage will cut down or eliminate the amount of light exposure, and minimize the growth of algae. Otherwise, keep your water in a covered container in a dark location.

Other suggestions regarding water storage can be accessed at: **http://www.millennium-ark.net/News_FilesLTAH_Water_ Store(3).html**

Winter Water Storage

In the northern climates, Y2K hits in the middle of winter. Water not kept above 32º F will freeze and expand 10%. For water stored outside, use containers which won't be damaged by freezing.

Plastic or metal containers subject to freezing should be filled to no more than 90% of capacity, to permit expansion of the contents. We've found that 2-liter pop bottles don't burst when frozen. Don't use glass; it will break when the contents freeze.

Containers that are vulnerable to freezing should be stored in your heated living area. Frozen water storage containers can be brought into this area to thaw out.

Remember that freezing does not kill all bacteria or parasites in contaminated water; many just go into suspended animation. Some are still dangerous after being frozen for six months. Do not use melted ice for drinking water unless you disinfect it first.

Water Stored In Your Plumbing System

Don't forget that your hot water heater and the hot and cold water pipes of your home are always full. Up to 50 gal. of clean water is stored in your home's plumbing system. If you lose power and heat, drain your water pipes, or they may freeze and burst.

For those of us living in colder climates, the water shutoff valve is located indoors. Turn the water valve at the meter off by turning it clockwise. Open the valves in the sinks upstairs and drain the water out from the drain valve at the lowest point in your water system. Trace the pipes from the water meter or hot water heater, if you aren't sure where to begin. Drain out the hot water heater at the bottom where the drain valve is. The other pipes will also have drain valves which look like outdoor faucets.

ALTERNATIVE WATER SOURCES

If water supply problems persist after you've used most of your stored water, you will need to utilize other water sources. Since those sources will probably be contaminated, use water filtration, purification or disinfection.

There are many sources which can provide an alternative supply of water for your family and which are not dependent on a municipal water system. These sources include collected rainwater or melted snow, and purified surface water from streams, springs and lakes.

Don't neglect to use the water in your stored food supply. All wet-pack canned foods contain a large percentage of water in the food as well as in the canning water. Use it as soup stock or just drink it as is.

Canned or fresh fruit, fruit and vegetable juices, and fruits or vegetables themselves, will help to meet your metabolic needs for water. Desert survivors have long known about getting the water stored in cactus flesh, and we all know about watermelon, which is 95% H_2O!

Other ideas on finding sources of water are discussed at:
http://www.millennium-ark.net/News_Files/Finding_Survival_Water1.html

Rainwater and Snow

Rainwater and snow is condensed, precipitated water vapor, and is considered clean until it hits the ground. Only areas with significant air pollution will experience impure rainwater. Rain and snow condense most readily around a particle of dust in the air bringing that dust to the earth. Filtering or distilling your collected rainwater will solve that problem.

In *Rainwater Harvesting: The Collection of Rainfall and Runoff in Rural Areas*, Arnold Pacey describes a variety of rainwater collection techniques. As Pacey states, underground cisterns have long been used for rainwater collection. Cisterns are buried underground and require structural integrity to prevent them from collapsing under the weight of the soil on top of them.

Using the roof of a home or a catchment basin made of plastic sheeting, asphalt, or concrete is one way to collect as much as 75% of the rainfall which descends on a given area. Sand filters and roof washers are techniques used to insure the water is less contaminated before being diverted into the cistern.

Diverting your eavestrough into 55 gal. drums is a simple way to accomplish rainwater harvesting. To be sure of the water's safety, filter or purify it.

Jade Mountain sells 500 or 1200 gal. white plastic resin underground cisterns, for $522 or $885.

They also sell the book *Rainwater Collection for the Mechanically Challenged*, a 50-page primer on rainwater harvesting and other aspects of water management, for $15.

Surface Fresh Water

Freshwater creeks, rivers, lakes and ponds are all examples of collected surface runoff. Preferably draw your water from a fast-flowing source or from the middle of a pond. Whenever water runs along the ground, it can become contaminated with parasites, bacteria, viruses, and toxic chemicals or metals. It will then require purification, or filtration and disinfection prior to drinking.

Springs

A spring is any place where water comes up out of the earth due to gravity or artesian pressure. Count your blessings if you have an artesian well which flows up from an underground aquifer.

Unfortunately, springs usually don't produce water consistently year-round and are easily contaminated. If you have access to a spring, try to isolate the flow so you can keep the clean subsurface water from mixing with the surface runoff. Be careful, since some spring water is surface water that has flowed into and through underground channels without being filtered by the soil. Get your water professionally tested to be sure it is safe.

Finally, "capture" your spring by making a waterproof cover to keep out surface water. Often this is done by encasing the spring in concrete blocks or large round pre-cast concrete tiles. Clay is tamped down around the top of the cover to keep surface water out. This process is described in detail in *The Home Water Supply* by Stu Campbell.

Saltwater or Brackish Water

Seafarers use reverse osmosis or distillation systems which extract fresh water from seawater. Likewise, those living in areas where water is brackish or saturated with mineral salts can utilize similar strategies.

Tree Sap

In the spring, sap from maple, box elder, sycamore and hickory trees can be drunk like water. It's pure and safe and can produce hundreds of gallons. Using the techniques of maple sugaring, drill a 1/2-in. hole through the bark and insert a piece of metal, called a *spile,* to direct the flow of sap into a bucket.

WATER TREATMENT

Contaminated water from Y2K-disrupted municipal water treatment systems, or alternative sources of water such as surface runoff, require treatment prior to use. Obtain supplies for treating at least 1000 gallons of water per person in your group.

The most common disease-causing micro-organisms in water are enteric pathogens from infected human or animal waste. Enteric pathogens come from the digestive tract and include bacteria, protozoa and viruses. Bacteria are the most dangerous, causing dysentery, cholera and typhoid fever.

Much municipal water is already chronically contaminated with low levels of Giardia lamblia and Cryptosporidium parvum protozoa. These low levels are currently not much of a threat in the U.S. except to immune-compromised individuals. For example, 30 people died during a 1976 outbreak of Cryptosporidium from municipal water that affected 400,000 people in Milwaukee, Wisconsin. Amebic dysentery from protozoa may become more of a danger to the general population if our water treatment is compromised.

Water-borne viruses aren't much of a threat for healthy adults. Hepatitis A is the primary concern. It causes a stomach flu lasting a few days. After exposure, you will have immunity from this virus.

If you want further information on water-borne pathogens, see the Centers for Disease Control, 404-639-3311.

http://www.cdc.gov

Treatment Options

Partial purification of water is appropriate for post-Y2K situations. This involves using techniques which help disinfect water, but which can still leave small amounts of the less pathogenic micro-organisms. Partial purification techniques include *handheld microfilters, disinfection with chlorine, disinfection with iodine, pasteurization,* and *expedient filters.*

Complete purification removes or kills all the disease-causing micro-organisms in water—bacteria, protozoa and viruses. These methods are *boiling, distillation, use of a handheld purifier, disinfection with hydrogen peroxide,* and *disinfection with colloidal silver.*

We recommend filtration with specially designed microfilters as the simplest method of water treatment for healthy adults. All bacteria and protozoa are eliminated. Filtration leaves viruses in the water, but this doesn't pose an unacceptable risk.

Chemical disinfection is the most cost-effective solution, and is an appropriate second choice. All water treatment chemicals when properly used will kill bacteria, but some won't kill all protozoa and/or viruses. Since chemical treatments require more attention to detail, there is a greater margin for error, possibly leading to inadequate disinfection.

When large amounts of treated water must be used for extended periods of time, the safest chemical disinfectant is food-grade 35% hydrogen peroxide. The most renewable treatment option is colloidal silver, since with proper equipment you can make your own supply of this disinfectant indefinitely. Both kill every disease-causing microorganism, including viruses.

A complete listing of water treatment chemicals and suppliers is available from the National Sanitation Foundation, 800-NSF-MARK.

http://www.nsf.org

All of these water treatment options will be discussed in the following sections.

Partial Purification

Handheld Microfilters

A water microfilter is one of your most important preparedness purchases. Microfilters remove bacteria, fungi, protozoa cysts, parasites and other debris from the water, but not viruses. If you want to eliminate viruses from your water supply, a sterilizing agent such as iodine, hydrogen peroxide or colloidal silver which kills viruses can be added after filtration.

Protozoa cysts are from 2 to 15 microns or millionths of a meter in size. Pathogenic or disease-causing bacteria are 0.2 to 0.6 microns and water-borne pathogenic viruses are the smallest at 0.02 to 0.03 microns.

Katadyn is the only microfilter approved by the International Red Cross for field work. Their filters have a 0.2 micron pore size. This prevents all disease-causing microorganisms from passing through the filter except viruses. The ceramic filter is impregnated with silver which prevents bacteria from growing through it. The outside of the filter can be brushed hundreds of times and cleaned for reuse before it has to be replaced. Katadyn is the most cost effective of all filter brands. Katadyn filters purify large volumes of water, at a cost of about 2¢ per gal.

http://www.katadyn.ch

If you would like to buy a Katadyn filter, put it at the top of your list and order it today. They are on back-order with all suppliers. As of December 1998, the delays in delivery were projected to be from six weeks to several months.

The Katadyn KFT Expedition Filter is a hand-pumped version which processes a total of 26,000 gal. at one gal. per minute.

Cost: $875, replacement filters, $90. A smaller handheld Pocket Purifier sells for $250. It filters 13,000 gal. at the rate of one quart per minute, and weighs 1.5 lbs. Spare filters cost $165.

The Katadyn "TRK Drip Filter" has three parallel filters and will handle 26,000 gallons for $240. The water flows through the filter under the force of gravity only. Extra filters are $70 each.

The Katadyn Siphon Filter filters up to 13,000 gal. of water for $100, making it the most cost-effective Katadyn product. Jade Mountain and most preparedness suppliers sell Katadyn products. The shortest delivery time and cheapest price we found for Katadyn filters was at the Special Op's Shop, 877-852-2486.

http://www.compfxnet.com/opshop

Another brand is the British Berkefeld Gravity Filtration System. It uses the same type of high quality silver-impregnated ceramic filters as Katadyn does. The filters are made from diatomaceous earth. The absolute pore size is 0.9 microns, but it removes 98% of the smallest 0.2 micron bacteria. This level of removal is technically considered to be bacteriologically safe. A two-filter model costs $200, a four-filter one costs $260. Each filter element will handle from 2600 to 15,000 gal., depending on water quality. The Berkefeld is sold by Y2K Grub, 877-Y2K-GRUB.

http://www.y2kgrub.com/waterfilter.htm

The PUR Hiker 0.3 micron microfilter sold by Campmor filters 200 gal. for $60. Extra filters cost $25.

The SweetWater Guardian microfilter costs $50 and filters up to 200 gal. Extra cartridges are $20.

A SweetWater "Silt Stopper II" which prefilters the water going into your filter will help extend the filter life, or time between brushings. It costs $10 from Campmor, replacements are $9.

Disinfection With Chlorine

Have you ever noticed a smell of bleach while taking a shower?

That smell is chlorine. Chlorine is an inexpensive and common water disinfecting agent. The U.S. military uses chlorine in its "water buffalo" storage containers. However, it is the least effective chemical discussed here. Chlorine will not kill viruses nor Cryptosporidia protozoa.

Proper disinfection with chlorine can't be guaranteed unless you are able to measure the amount of free chlorine available after treatment. Moderate doses of chlorine may otherwise not be enough, especially with surface water. Ammonia nitrogen, minerals and organic matter all bind with chlorine, diminishing its ability to kill micro-organisms and disinfect water.

One solution is to superchlorinate the water and add more chlorine than necessary. This excess chlorine can later be removed via evaporation, the addition of hydrogen peroxide, or through the use of a charcoal filter. Once the chlorine is removed, however, the water is at risk of being recontaminated and must be used immediately.

Swimming pool supply companies offer inexpensive test kits to test the concentration of free chlorine in the water after treatment. It's a good idea to use them if possible. For $8 you can buy a small bottle of reagent which turns color when added to the treated water, depending on the amount of available or free chlorine. The World Health Organization standard for residual chlorine in treated water is 0.2 to 0.5 mg per liter after 30 minutes of contact time.

For water disinfection, buy several bottles of unscented Chlorox brand or generic bleach from your supermarket for $1.40 per gal. Read the label to be sure the only ingredient is 5.25% sodium hypochlorite, with no additives. The potency of the chlorine in sodium hypochlorite deteriorates about 10% every six months, so be prepared to increase the amount used if your bleach is old.

After treatment, there should be a chlorine smell to the water. If you wait a day or two to drink the water, the chlorine will have killed any microbes and should have dissipated, as it readily evaporates. Leave the container lid ajar to enable this to occur. For long-term water storage, keep the container sealed to prevent chlorine evaporation.

Use eight drops or 0.4 ml of commercial household bleach per gal. to disinfect clear water. For cloudy water, double the concentration to 16 drops per gal. Wait 30 minutes after treatment before using the water, 60 minutes for cold water, to allow complete disinfection to occur. One gal. of bleach treats 7680 gal. of water, or half that amount of water if the water is cold or cloudy. If you can't measure the free chlorine and want to superchlorinate your water, double the amount recommended for cloudy water.

Swimming pool suppliers sell 15% liquid chlorine for $2.50 per gal. You can also purchase dry calcium hypochlorite or High Test Hypochlorite from a water treatment supplies distributor, such as Culligan, or a swimming pool equipment supplier. Suppliers can be found in the Yellow pages under "Water Treatment Systems." Dry HTH is more stable and stores much better than bleach for long periods. It comes in crystal form, is 70% available chlorine and costs $5 per lb.

Chlorine is a powerful chemical and has unhealthy effects on people if consumed over an extended period of time. It's a known carcinogen and promotes heart disease and stroke. While we have it in our municipal water systems, and may need it for water storage purposes, try to avoid consuming chlorine for extended periods if you have appropriate alternatives.

Disinfection With Iodine

Iodine is a poisonous element which in small amounts of 8 parts per million kills micro-organisms in clear water after 10 minutes. It will kill all micro-organisms including viruses except Cryptosporidia protozoa. Iodine will disinfect effectively until a water's pH reaches 10, versus chlorine which only works with a pH of 8 or less. However, iodine costs 20 times as much as chlorine.

You can use less iodine if you filter out the bacteria, Giardia and Cryptosporidia with a microfilter. You'll only need to use 0.5 ppm iodine to kill the residual viruses. That's 1/16th as much.

Vitamin C or sodium thiosulphate can be added after the water has been sufficiently treated to eliminate the iodine taste but not the residual iodine. Vitamin C is added in the amount of 90 mg. per qt.

Military-style iodine tablets can be purchased from Army surplus stores. If they are old and have lost potency, they turn brown. If they are still grey, they are OK. The same compound, tetraglycine hydroperiodide, is sold as Potable Aqua in 50 tablet bottles which treats 50 quarts for $5. Potable Aqua with P.A. Plus is a two-step product which includes Vitamin C tablets to eliminate the iodine taste after water disinfection, it costs $7.

Polar Pure is a crystalline iodine product which makes a saturated iodine solution. The package has a built-in thermometer to help calculate proper iodine dosing when iodine is used in cold temperatures. Campmor sells it for $10. You can also buy your own USP iodine crystals from a chemical supply house.

Use iodine only for short-term water disinfection, since with prolonged use it is unhealthy. Avoid using 2% Tincture of Iodine and Lugol's Solution, since they contain additional iodine compounds which have no disinfectant benefit, but increase the load of iodine in your body. If you're pregnant or might be, don't use iodine for water disinfection; fetal deformation or miscarriage could occur. If you're allergic to seafood or iodine, or have a thyroid gland disorder, don't use iodine as a water disinfection agent.

Chlorine Dioxide

"Aerobic O7" permits storage of tap water for up to 5 years. 2.3 ounces treats 126 gal. of water for $20. Available from Nitro-Pak Preparedness Center.

Pasteurization

If water temperature is raised above a certain level for sufficient time, pathogenic organisms are killed. The hepatitis virus is the most heat resistant intestinal pathogen. It requires temperatures of 158 degrees F for 10 minutes to kill it, or 176 degrees F for 5 seconds. Certain bacterial cysts can withstand these temperatures, but they are not disease causing.

A solar cooker is an ideal way to heat and maintain the water at these temperatures for the appropriate time without the expense of fuel. A "Water Pasteurization Indicator" is available which indicates that pasteurization temperatures have been reached. Details about obtaining the WAPI and a great deal of other information on water pasteurization is available at:

http://www.accessone.com/~sbcn/metcalf.htm

Jade Mountain sells solar and wood-burning pasteurizers as well as a hybrid solar/wood model. The Family Sol Saver model, at $100, will produce 3 to 5 gal. of pasteurized water in 2 to 3 hours of direct sunlight by heating it to 170° F. The Wood Saver costs $1150, is only heated by wood and will make 30 gal. daily. For $2000, the full-size Sol Saver makes 200 gal. of safe water daily. With a $400 add-on it burns wood to pasteurize 25 gal. daily when there is no sunshine, making it an alternative for groups.

Expedient Filters

Slow sand filters: Slow sand filters also will remove microorganisms from water. This technique is used in conventional water treatment facilities. By slowly passing water through at least two feet of fine sand with gravel and a drain pipe at the bottom, micro-organisms are removed as they naturally die off, are eaten by other micro-organisms, or are mechanically filtered.

Infiltration galleries can be used near streams or other standing water. They are another form of slow sand filter. Ten ft. away from a source of surface water, dig a trench 3 ft. deep. Water will filter through the soil, collect in the trench, and can then be collected or drained through a pipe to a holding tank.

Water must pass through at least 10 ft. of earth before it is considered completely filtered. Information on slow sand filters and good FAQs about water are available at:

http://tortugas.idir.net/~medintz/surv_faq/waterfaq.txt

Diatomaceous earth: Diatomaceous earth specially processed for swimming pools will work as an expedient water filter or prefilter. Swimming pool equipment suppliers sell it. It will filter contaminants larger than 1 micron. Many municipalities use it on a large scale in their water treatment facilities.

In an emergency, you can use swimming pool filter equipment. Connect a holding tank onto the filter unit. Let the water flow by gravity through the filter and collect it at the other end. It will filter out all protozoa and some bacteria.

Complete Purification

To eliminate all microorganisms from water, use the following complete purification techniques. If you have vulnerable young, elderly or sick individuals in your group, you would be better off using complete purification techniques which will eliminate all potential pathogens.

Boiling

No form of chemical purification is as safe as boiling. Water boiled vigorously for 10 minutes plus an extra one minute for every 1000 feet of altitude is considered totally purified. Boiling for less time may not kill all organisms. Certain bacterial cysts can withstand several minutes of boiling. To be on the safe side, we recommend the longer boiling times.

If boiling is to be your primary method of water purification, make sure you have a working stove, pots and enough stored fuel to do the job. A pressure cooker is the most efficient pot to boil water in. It takes about 2 lbs. of wood to boil 1 qt. of water. Review the fuel usage for cooking discussed in Chapter 4 and double your amount of stored fuel if you'll be boiling all drinking water.

A solar cooker is an ideal tool for boiling water, without the expense and problems of fuel storage. For information on solar cookers, see Chapter 4, pages 173 to 174.

Distillation

Steam distillation: The Federal Emergency Management Agency pamphlet entitled *Emergency Food and Water Supplies* is free and gives a clear, basic description of what you should do for your water-related preparedness. Expedient steam distillation of water is discussed. This and other preparedness information can be found on-line at:

http://www.fema.gov/library/emfdwtr.htm

Solar stills: Water distillers most appropriate for use after Y2K will be those that don't require electricity. Solar stills come in several types. Some float on top of ponds, lakes or seas and collect small amounts of distilled water daily. Fixed units are larger and produce the most pure water.

A solar still evaporates water below the boiling point. The water vapor then recondenses in another part of the still and the pure water is collected.

You can build your own, inexpensive solar distiller. The $10 *Solar Still Manual* by Breslin & Clark offers plans for building your own inexpensive three gal. per day still. *Understanding Solar*

Stills by McCracken & Gordes, offers guidance on instruction, maintenance and uses, and costs $12. Both books can be purchased from Jade Mountain.

Commercial solar stills can also be used to desalinate water. The cheapest one we found, at $100, is available from Solar Solutions, 888-44SOLAR.

http://www.solarsolns.com

The Agua Del Sol $685 fixed solar still is 3 ft. by 6 ft., and makes 3 gal. per day. It is available from Mr. Solar, who discusses solar stills in depth on his website.

Sunlight Works, 520-282-1202, has other solar stills.

http://www.sunlightworks.com

Information and plans for building your own solar still are available from:

http://www.epsea.org/stills.html

http://www.solarsolns.com/free.htm

Handheld Purifiers

Portable handheld water purifiers are microfiltration systems with added iodine resin cartridges. Buy some spare filters for your purifier and you'll enjoy safe drinking water from any source, even polluted surface water. PUR and MSR are good brands. Get one now, as purifier supply shortages are increasing.

First Need's Deluxe Direct Connect Purification Device removes standard microbes as well as cysts and viruses without using chemicals, and purifies a total of 100 gal. Available for $75 from Campmor. Recreational Equipment, Inc., 800-426-4840 also sells it.

http://www.rei.com

The PUR Explorer removes all microorganisms and kills viruses with an iodinated resin filter. It will purify 500 gal. of water for $130. Available from Out n' Back.

The SweetWater Guardian Plus microfilter has an iodine-based add-on cartridge which upgrades a filter to a purifier by killing any viruses that get past the filter. Available from Campmor, it will purify 200 gallons of water for $75.

Most preparedness and sports equipment suppliers, plus the food suppliers listed in Chapter 4, offer water purification and disinfection equipment. Other suppliers of Katadyn, MSR, PUR or SweetWater purifiers are listed at:

http://www.millennium-ark.net/News_Files/LTAH_Water_ Pure(2).html

Reverse Osmosis Purifier

Reverse osmosis water is almost as pure as distilled water. Life rafts carry emergency hand-pumped reverse osmosis desalinators which produce small amounts of fresh water from salt water. The PUR Survivor models make either 1 qt. or 1.2 gal. of water per hour. They cost $585 and $1550 respectively from Mr. Solar or from SafeTrek, 800-424-7870.

http://www.safetrek.com

PUR also sells 12 volt DC pumped desalinator purifiers which could be used in conjunction with a solar collector.

A regular kitchen-model reverse osmosis unit could be used for water purification if you had an elevated water tank or a solar powered pump which was able to deliver 40 pounds per square inch of water pressure to the RO unit.

Hydrogen Peroxide

Peroxides deliver high concentrations of oxygen to water which kills micro-organisms including viruses. Hydrogen peroxide (H_2O_2) is beginning to be used extensively in municipal water treatment facilities. It doesn't have the negative health effects which can come from the extended use of iodine or chlorine. In fact, many alternative health practitioners believe it has a health-promoting effect. An information packet, *Hydrogen Peroxide H_2O_2* is available for $3 from Kansas Wind Power, 785-364-4407, which references 5000 medical journal articles on the benefits of hydrogen peroxide.

Use only food-grade 35%, 50% or 70% hydrogen peroxide for water purification. Avoid the pharmaceutical-grade 3% hydrogen peroxide which you buy in the drug store because it contains additives. Use 1 oz. of 35% H_2O_2 to purify 60 gal. of water. One oz. will treat 120 gal. of water for long-term storage if the container is tightly sealed after treatment. H_2O_2 is a very volatile compound and will dissipate rapidly if the container is not kept sealed. Use an eye-dropper and purify 1 qt. of water with 10 drops.

Look up suppliers under "Chemicals- Dealers" in your Yellow Pages. The National Sanitation Foundation site referenced earlier on page 118 lists several H_2O_2 suppliers.

Centipede Industries, 800-433-0348, sells a quart of 35% food grade H_2O_2 for $38 and a gallon for $72. Fisher Scientific, 800-766-7000, also sells food grade H_2O_2.

http://www.fishersci.com

The preparedness book *How To Start Your Emergency Preparations Even If You Only Have A Dollar To Spare* by Cindy Chase, 406-848-7728, e-mail chase@gomontana.com, discusses H_2O_2 in some depth.

Colloidal Silver

Silver can be used in its colloidal form as a safe and nontoxic water disinfectant. Katadyn, the premier water filter manufacturer, uses silver-impregnated ceramic filters in its products. Metallic silver historically has been used for its bactericidal properties and today is used medically in Silvadene, a topical burn treatment. The Greeks used silver-lined containers to preserve food and early

American pioneers used a silver dollar dropped into a milk jug to help keep the milk fresh.

Katadyn manufactures Micropur tablets and fluid, a nontoxic silver compound water preservative which will keep water disinfected for 6 months. Major Surplus & Survival sells both. $10 buys 100 tablets, which treat 100 quarts. Ten drops of fluid will treat a gallon, a total of 250 gal. can be treated per $12 bottle. Micropur crystals which will treat 12,500 gal. can be purchased for $70. Let the treated water sit for two hours before use.

Silver compounds have been documented in the U.S. as being effective in killing pathogens including bacteria and protozoan cysts. Research indicates that silver also kills viruses. According to researchers at the Runcorn Health Laboratory in England, sterilization of water requires 0.04 to 0.2 parts per million of silver.

Use only low dose electro-colloidal pure silver solution of 3 to 100 ppm, which has the ultrafine 0.005 to 0.015 micron particle size. Colloidal silver generators create solutions of 3 to 5 ppm within 20 minutes. This amount of 3 ppm colloidal silver solution safely sterilizes a volume of water 75 times larger. 16 oz. of 3 ppm colloidal silver treats 9 gal. of water.

Avoid the use of silver salts, mild silver protein or powdered silver. We recommend using only pure colloidal silver for human consumption. The effectiveness of colloidal silver is dependent on the size of the silver particles. The smaller the particle, the more effective is the product.

The best quality colloidal silver is made with high voltage generators, which make a smaller silver particle. We recommend the high voltage generators made by CS Pro Systems, 888-710-2773, a standard in the industry. They make the generators which commercial producers use to make CS for the market. Their 180 VDC system costs $780 and can be run on a DC to AC power inverter.

CS Pro Systems guarantees that their products are Y2K compliant, and will put that in writing.

http://www.csprosystems.com

You can also make colloidal silver with low voltage inexpensive electrolytic colloidal silver generators. The quality is good enough for water purification. Silver Solutions, 888-505-6005, has models for $130 which use AC power, as well as DC power models using three 9 volt batteries for $80. These products and a $12 booklet, *Colloidal Silver, Making and Using Your Own* are available from Mark Metcalf.

http://www.silversolutions.com

Elixa, 800-766-4544, sells the 36 VDC model CS-300C colloidal silver generator for $100.

http://www.elixa.com/silver/CS300.htm

Colloidal silver may be your best long-term water-disinfectant product, since you can make your own supply. It's non-toxic when used for water purification even with extended use, and is inexpensive. You can make all you need to purify your water indefinitely with two 0.999 pure silver wires or coins, a colloidal silver generator, rechargeable batteries, a solar battery charger and your own distilled water.

Water Pre-Treatment

No matter which water treatment method you select, it's important to pre-treat your water first, removing as many particles as possible before treatment. This decreases the amount of chemicals needed, and extends the life of your microfilter or purifier.

Pre-treat your water with *settling* and *prefiltering* techniques.

Settling

Allowing water to sit in a container for several hours permits the suspended particles to settle to the bottom of the container.

Let them settle for 24 hours if possible. Some solids will also float on top. Siphon off the water from 1 in. below the surface using a siphon with a foam flotation collar, leaving the lower cloudy layers to be discarded. This is especially important with murky or muddy water, or it will quickly plug up your filter, shortening its useful life.

Prefiltering

Next use coffee filters or layers of cloth to prefilter your water to remove as much particulate matter as possible before treating it with chemicals or running it through a microfilter. Any tightly woven fabric will work, such as a piece of felt or a denim pant leg.

With attention to detail and proper use of chemicals and equipment, you should be able to provide your family with the clean water they need during any Y2K disruptions.

WELLS

The ideal solution for emergency water supplies is to have your own independent water source and delivery system. The importance of a clean water supply is a big incentive for relocating to a rural location with its own well.

Before you establish a well on your property, check with the local authorities for rules and regulations. Unfortunately, zoning restrictions prohibit wells within most metropolitan areas.

Your well should not be dependent on electricity from the national electrical grid for pumping its water. You can put a manual well pump in line before the electric pump if the well is less than 260 ft. deep.

Alternatively, use a generator and continue pumping with the existing electric pump. A better solution is a solar-powered pump. Depending on its capacity, a well and pump can support the water needs of one or several families.

Have your well water tested for purity now, to be sure it's safe. The EPA lists State Officers which can refer you to certified water testing labs in your area.

http:/www.epa.gov/ogwdw/faq/sco.html

The book entitled *The Home Water Supply* deals with all major water supply problems. It explains how to locate and move water, outlines different purification methods, and provides plans for storing and distributing water to your home. *Cottage Water Systems: An Out-Of-The City Guide to Pumps, Plumbing, Water Purification, and Privies* by Max Burns is a how-to book on water supply issues as well as sanitation. Both have information on wells and are available from Amazon.com, 800-201-7575.

http:/www.amazon.com

The Jan./Feb. 1999 issue of *Countryside & Small Stock Journal* has an extensive 23-page primer on alternative water sources, called *Water On The Homestead*. It covers digging and driving wells, collecting rainwater, creating a sand filter, and creating your own well bucket for drilled wells. We recommend subscribing to this journal, as they are focusing on Y2K solutions throughout 1999. Annual subscription cost: $18; Jan./Feb. 1999 issue cost: $3. Contact them at 800-551-5691.

http://www.countrysidemag.com

Types of Wells

Hand Dug Well

A hand dug well is a shaft three to 20 ft. wide and rarely more than 50 ft. deep. It is dug into a shallow water table and is lined with walls to prevent it from collapsing. These wells are simple to construct, and can be dug manually.

The drawback is that hand-dug wells access primarily infiltrated surface water and aren't considered a true groundwater source. A high percentage are contaminated, and they frequently fail in dry periods.

Hand Dug Wells: Water With Limited Money and Materials covers this topic in detail. It includes general principals of ground water storage, preparatory work and actual construction of hand dug wells. Jade Mountain sells this book for $29.

Bored Well

This is a form of dug well, created with an auger. Bored wells can be up to 100 ft. deep. Clay is the best soil type; soil which tends to cave in or contain boulders is inappropriate.

Bored wells are lined with plastic, steel or fired clay tile. Be sure to seal off all surface water.

Driven Wells

The driven well is inexpensive and quick to install. Like the previous wells, it is relatively shallow and vulnerable to drying up if there are fluctuations in the water table's height. These wells are driven into the earth to depths of 25 to 100 ft., most obtaining water around 50 to 60 ft.

Driven wells can be used inside dug or bored wells which have gone dry, to extend them below the water table.

Washed or Jetted Wells

If the soil has a relatively consistent texture, a well can be dug by a pressurized water jet, digging into the ground and flushing the material before the well casing to the surface.

DeepRock, 800-333-7762, sells do-it-yourself jetted-well kits called *Hydra-Drills.* These may be appropriate in some cases for shallow wells with light soils.

http:/www.deeprock.com

In *The Home Water Supply,* author Stu Campbell cautions against this type of well drilling equipment. We recommend leaving well-drilling to the professionals.

Drilled Wells

These are the ultimate clean water wells. Drilled wells are deeper and less vulnerable to contamination. They are also the most expensive, due to depth.

With rock or rocky soils, drilled wells are the only way to penetrate down to the water table. Special equipment operated by professional well drillers is required for creating these wells, which may cost $2000 or more, and go down as deep as 2000 ft.

Pumps

Hand well pump: Be sure to have a hand pump in your water system. If your electric pump fails, you can still get your water. The book, *Water-Pumping Devices: A Handbook for Users and Choosers* by Peter Fraenkel, has a great section on human and animal-powered pumps.

If you have an existing well such as one in a basement, drill a hole in the pipe before the electric pump and thread the hole. Place a plug in the threaded hole. When you need to, remove the plug, screw in the manual pump or a short length of pipe to it and prime the pump. Presto! Water!

If you have a capped or unused well, remove and check the pump, drop lines, and point. Replace the point and any other defective parts and put the manual pump on top.

The Mark II hand pump from Jade Mountain, for $814 allows you to pump by hand from depths as low as 260 ft.

Also available from Jade Mountain, a Dempster hand pump will function at temperatures as low as 23° F and lift water from 100 ft. below ground. Contact Russell Groves at 303-449-6601, ext. 108, for more information.

Baker Manufacturing, 800-356-5130, makes hand pump water systems.

O'Brock Windmills, 330-584-4681, sells hand water pumps, windmills and books on Third World water systems. Their catalog costs $2. E-mail: windmill@cannet.com.

Manual well bucket: Jade Mountain sells a well bucket they describe in this way, "When the power goes out, your electric well pump is worthless. Pull the pump out of the well, tie a rope to the well bucket, and start lifting water out of the well. Bucket fills with water when you drop it, seals itself when you lift. More than 2 gal. with each filling. Requires a 5 in. minimum well diameter. The bucket is galvanized, solidly made, and sells for $45."

The Countryside magazine issue referenced above has plans for making your own well bucket for smaller diameter wells.

Solar-powered well pump: A solar-powered pump is not dependent on the electrical grid. Solar power has a large up-front cost for the collectors and battery storage capacity, but it gives you a simple electric supply.

Alternatively, if you used it only for water pumping, and were willing to provide water storage capacity for a gravity-fed system, you could pump during sunny days and use gravity-fed water from your water tank at other times. This eliminates the need for electrical storage batteries in your solar system. A good book on this subject is *Solar Pumping*. It sells for $27 from Jade Mountain.

A Shurflo submersible SubPump would be appropriate for single family use. It goes into the well shaft and delivers an average of 500 to 700 gal. per day. The pump and controller can be purchased for $820. It requires only one or two 75 watt photovoltaic (PV) panels which costs $400 to $800. Battery storage of extra solar energy production is an optional addition.

The SolarJack DC submersible pump and controller for $955 delivers from 970 to 1330 gal. per day with the use of 100 to 160 watts from 24 volt PV panels.

These surface pumps, other solar pumps, and good reference information, are found in the catalog from Jade Mountain.

Wind-powered well pump: Jade Mountain's Bowjon wind-powered water-lift system can be mounted in a windy area as far as 1/4 mile from your well, and can handle sandy or dirty water without any problems. Models pump as much as 400 to 600 gal. per hour and lift as high as 200 to 300 ft. Prices range from $1250 to $1550, respectively.

The book *Building a Domestic Windpump,* available from Jade Mountain for $23, gives step-by-step instructions for making your own water pumping wind machine from inexpensive, recycled materials. The design described would pump 200 gal. per day, raising it 10 ft.

O'Brock Windmills is a well-recommended windmill supplier of wind-powered water pumps.

Another water-pumping windmill supplier is Topper Co., 915-658-3277. Their catalog is $4.

Hydraulic-Powered Pumps: Hydraulic ram pumps use the force of water from a stream to pump water. The pressure of water flowing downhill when applied to a piston is used to lift a portion of the water up higher than the original source to a holding area or dwelling.

The Gravi-Chek motorless pump from Jade Mountain lifts water 30 ft. for every foot of fall in the water supply and works with as little as 2 ft. of fall. One to four in. sizes are capable of delivering from 5 to 137 gal. per minute and are available from $372 to $1681.

Jade Mountain's High Lifter gravity pump for $750 provides up to 1200 gal. per day and lifts water over 1000 ft. straight up.

The Ram Company, 800-227-8511, sells Fleming Hydro-Ram and solar water pumps.

A sling pump is anchored in a stream and uses the force of a river or creek to rotate the pump and produce up to 4000 gal. per day and lifts water 82 ft. Cost: $985 to $1300 from Jade Mountain.

Rife, 800-RIFERAM, sells sling and ram pumps.
http://www.riferam.com

In summary, if you can insure a stable supply of good water via your own clean well and manual well pump, do so. If not, be sure to secure at least 30 days of stored water and a good water filter and backup purification supplies.

It would be best to have the ability to purify at least 1000 gallons of water per person in your group. This capacity should safely take you through any future water distribution or purification problems.

Bottoms up!

WATER CHECKLIST

____ Store a one month supply of water for each family member

____ Store more water if possible

____ Use bottles, buckets, drums and/or tanks for water storage

____ Treat water for storage, using chlorine bleach

____ Protect water storage containers from freezing

____ Have buckets with resealable lids for transporting water

____ Be able to access alternative sources of water

Purchase water filtration and/or purification equipment from this list:

    ___ Handheld microfilters, such as Katadyn (our recommendation)

    ___ Pasteurization equipment

    ___ Boiling equipment

    ___ Distillation equipment

Purchase water disinfection chemicals from this list:

    ___ Chlorine

    ___ Iodine

    ___ Hydrogen peroxide (our recommendation)

    ___ Colloidal silver (our recommendation)

____ Store supplies of prefilter materials

____ Have alternate treatment supplies available

____ Have enough water treatment supplies to purify 1000 gallons of water per family member

____ Obtain your own dependable, clean water well

____ Obtain a reliable manual well pump

CHAPTER 4

Food

Until recently I hadn't thought very much about the connection between food on our tables and computers. But, as a new millennium approaches, that link is becoming all too clear....We are facing the potential of serious disruption because of this problem.

Dan Glickman
U.S. Secretary of Agriculture

The ready availability of food is taken for granted in our nation. At grocery stores and specialty markets, we can find a limitless variety of foods grown and produced around the world. What would we do if this easy access to food was lost? Few of us today have a self-sufficient food supply.

Our food distribution system is an efficient, computer controlled machine. However, there are only 16 days' worth of food in the distribution pipeline, five days' worth in cities at any given time, and typically three days' worth of food on grocery store shelves. If Y2K interrupts distribution, this food can disappear in hours as it's snapped up by concerned citizens.

With so few days' worth of food in the national distribution pipeline at any given time, a Year 2000 system failure could make it impossible to restock shelves. Y2K-induced food processing factory slowdowns or shutdowns could leave little processed food available for distribution. Compromised computer inventory and ordering systems could interrupt distribution. Should railroad and truck delivery fail, food couldn't move to processing plants and grocery stores.

Even more alarming is the possibility that the 2000 spring planting season could be missed. If farmers don't receive shipments of seeds and planting supplies, we could lose much of the year's harvest. There is no backup supply to feed our nation if that occurs.

STORED FOOD STRATEGIES

Your specific preparedness strategy regarding food will be determined by your level of concern that food supplies could be impaired by Y2K, and for how long.

Short-Term

Just as experts expect runs on banks due to projected cash shortages before Y2K, you can anticipate similar runs on the food stores. As early as mid 1999, you should plan on having at least 30 days of basic canned and storable food on hand in your home.

The core of your stored food supply should be built around foods similar to those you currently eat. These are foods your family will be comfortable with. Don't compound your Y2K stress by having on hand only unfamiliar food your kids refuse to eat, or that requires extensive preparation such as whole grains.

All such foods can be purchased inexpensively at your local supermarket. Starting now, buy double the amount of canned and dried storable food you currently purchase each week. After one month of buying twice as much as usual, you will have an additional month's worth of food in your home.

Mid-Term

If you feel that it could be as much as three months before

food supplies return to normal, then plan to have at least that much food stockpiled for each member of your family. First establish your one month supply of familiar supermarket foods. Then, use one of the following options to increase your stored food reserves until you have a three month supply.

To buy three months' worth of supermarket food, just multiply the pattern above. Double your food purchases for three months to accumulate three months of stored food.

Another option for a family of four is to buy a commercial one year package of storable food for one person. When divided among four people this equals three months of food for each.

Alternatively, you can inexpensively supplement your supermarket food by buying a 50 lb. bag of kidney beans and a 100 lb. bag of rice from a wholesaler or food co-op. This would compliment your other food purchases and significantly extend your food reserves by feeding a family of four for a month.

Long-Term

If you believe Y2K problems will impair the planting and growing seasons of 2000, causing food shortages, store at least one year's worth of food for each member of your family.

First, buy your core supply of familiar supermarket food as discussed above. Then you have some options as to how you put together your year's worth of food.

One option is to buy commercial one-year food storage packages for each individual in your group. They range in price, depending on content, from $750 to $3000 per person per year.

Another option is to buy commercially stored food ala carte and build your own package. It will cost about the same as a preselected food package, but you'll be able to select specific items your family will enjoy.

Finally, you can buy bulk food and store it yourself in appropriate containers. A basic diet of wheat, corn and beans to feed a person for one year can be purchased and stored for as little as $100, if you buy the food directly from the farmer and do the storage work yourself.

STOCK UP WITH SUPERMARKET FOOD

It's a simple matter to build a reserve food supply of items purchased from your local supermarket. Buy extra foods of the type that you already eat and those which will store well for several months.

Canned food from the grocery store is wet-packed. In contrast, canned food purchased from storage food suppliers is dehydrated or freeze dried. Wet-pack foods are ready to eat, and require no preparation beyond optional heating. They are not only convenient, but are also familiar foods we are used to eating.

If buying in bulk from the grocery store, try to get the larger #10 cans. These cans are about the size of a gallon of paint. They are more cost-efficient than the regular smaller size cans.

If you eat large amounts of fresh fruits and vegetables, you can easily substitute canned and dried varieties. If you enjoy meat products, buy a significant reserve of canned meats, poultry and fish. Crackers can substitute for bread products and pasta is always safe. Buy a variety of pasta sauces. Dry cereals are good to store and they can be eaten with milk packaged in ultra-pasteurized "retort" pouches or boxes, which last for months. Be sure to have lots of nut butters and fruit preserves. You can always fall back on peanut butter and jelly!

Buy a variety of spices and condiments for flavoring. Stock up on comfort foods such as favorite snacks. Likewise, store drinks or drink mixes which will be appealing.

Storage Life Of Wet-Pack Canned Foods

Wet-pack canned foods will last for years without spoiling, but the nutritional value will continue to deteriorate. Because they are processed at high temperatures, their food value is diminished. Buy a supply of inexpensive daily multivitamins to help compensate for the devitalized quality of canned foods.

Cans have a shelf life of two years or so. However, we have seen 10 year old wet-pack cans in cool storage which appear unchanged. A friend has been using 10 year old canned tuna from a storage program with no ill effects!

Store them where they won't freeze, as cans will rupture if frozen.

Rotating Canned Goods

Use an indelible marker to mark your canned goods with the date purchased. The main principle here is "first in, first out." Rotate the cans, putting the newest ones at the back of the row. Use the oldest container as indicated by the date and enter the newer ones to the storage pool.

Most canned goods are stamped with the date the item was canned. Unfortunately, these dates are usually recorded in a difficult to decipher code. Call the toll-free number on the label for expiration information. See also the websites below for information on canned food storage programs and deciphering coded can dates:

http://www.millennium-ark.net/News_Files/LTAH_Food_Store(6b).html

http://www.waltonfeed.com/self/lid.html

http://www.glitchproof.com/glitchproof/storlifofgro.html

http://www.ocweb.com/y2k/PFS.htm

http://www.aiusa.net/gary/expire.html

http://www.revelar.com/fsp.html

BUY A COMMERCIAL STORED FOOD PACKAGE

We recommend you provide your family members with at least one year of stored food and nutritional supplements. The easiest and most convenient way to get your food supplies is to call a commercial supplier and buy a stored food package.

These packages typically contain enough food to feed one person for one year. Some packages are basic and some are "deluxe." They range in price from $750 to $3000 per person per year depending on contents.

More than a dozen large companies and several dozen smaller ones sell storable food packages. Don't delay in placing your order. Some suppliers have back orders of several months.

Buy in bulk. Combine orders with your friends, to take advantage of large volume discounts. Compare the shipping costs of different providers. You may be able to buy closer to home, reducing the shipping expense.

Obtain a written guarantee on company letterhead as to when your purchase will be shipped to you. Place your order as soon as possible to guarantee delivery before 2000. Make obtaining your food reserves your highest priority. Take delivery of your food as soon as possible.

Package Contents

Older food storage programs were often variants of the Mormon "Basic Four" foods: wheat, powdered milk, sugar (or honey) and salt. These items all stored well and had long shelf lives. On the downside, they were dull, and without adequate supplementation could be seriously deficient in essential amino acids and vitamins.

Newer programs have a wider selection and contain dried mixes for a variety of pleasant meals. Many make extensive use of texturized vegetable protein as an inexpensive meat substitute.

Commercial stored food packages typically consist of dried or freeze dried food packed in cans or buckets.

Dried Food

Most dried food programs contain large quantities of whole bulk grains and beans. Other items included in the packages are flours, dried mixes, texturized vegetable protein and dehydrated vegetables and fruits. All these foods require rehydration with water to be edible. They store well and are space efficient because the water has been removed.

Freeze Dried Food

Freeze drying takes raw or cooked food, flash freezes it, then draws off the moisture by placing it in a vacuum chamber. Freeze dried food reconstitutes with the addition of boiling water. Fully prepared meals can even be reconstituted with room temperature water. It is of high quality, very tasty and has a great deal of variety.

Freeze dried products cost quite a bit more. Yet freeze dried food has the advantage of requiring little or no cooking to be edible. This feature could be important if you are unable to store large amounts of cooking fuel. The high price is partially offset by savings from decreased cooking fuel costs.

Caloric Intake

Stored food packages vary in the amount of calories provided per person per day. Most packages advertise their calorie counts in their descriptive literature. Look for a package delivering 2500-3000 calories per person per day. Packages delivering less do not contain sufficient quantities of food for hard working teens and adults, and need to be supplemented with additional food purchases.

Commercial Stored Food Suppliers

Before making a purchase decision, call several storage food distributors and shop around for prices. Ask questions, such as:

- What is the daily caloric level supplied by this package?
- Does this package need to be supplemented with additional bulk grains and beans?
- How much preparation and cooking is required to process the food for eating?
- When will I receive my order, and will you guarantee that in writing?

The following suppliers sell food storage programs as well as other preparedness items. This is a partial listing.

AlpineAire Foods/Gourmet Reserves, 800-FAB-MEAL
http://www.alpineairefoods.com
American Freedom Network, 800-205-6245
http://www.amerifree.com
B&A Products, 918-696-5998
http://www.baproducts.com
CSIN, 512-478-4922
http://www.csin.com
Emergency Essentials, 800 999-1863
http://www.beprepared.com
Future Foods, 800-949-3663
http://www.thepreparednesssource.com
Golden Eagle, 800-447-7911
Happy Hovel Storable Foods, 800-637-7772
http://www.wwmagic.com
Lakeridge Food Storage, 800-336-7127
http://www.lakeridge-food-storage.com
Major Surplus & Survival, 800-441-8855
http://www.majorsurplusnsurvival.com
Millennium Group, Inc., 800-500-9893
http://www.millenniumfoods.com

Millennium Market, 877-366-3200

http://www.food2000.com

Nitro-Pak Preparedness Center, 800-866-4876

http://www.nitro-pak.com

Out n' Back, 800-533-7415

http://www.citysearch.com/slc/outnback

Ready Made Resources, 800-627-3809

http://www.public.useit.net/robertg

SafeTrek Foods, 800-424-7870

http://www.safetrek.com

Sam Andy Foods, 800-331-0358

Special Op's Shop, 877-852-2486

http://www.compfxnet.com/opshop

The Survival Center, 800-321-2900

http://survivalcenter.com

UltraFood America, 406-333-4537

http://www.TLCalliance.com/food

Walton Feed, 800-269-8563

http://www.waltonfeed.com

Yellowstone River Trading Co., 800-585-5077

http://www.yellowstonetrading.com

In addition, an excellent list of preparedness provider's websites can be found in Appendix I of James Talmage Stevens' *Making the Best of Basics: Family Preparedness Handbook.*

CREATE A SELF-STORED FOOD PROGRAM

You may choose to create your own food storage program for several reasons. Chief among them is, it is significantly less expensive to create your own program than it is to purchase a commercial package. You cut out the costs from the processor, packager, and any middleman.

It will require a certain amount of effort to create your own program. When you buy a one-year commercial food package, you get all the food you need to eat for the year, delivered to your house in cans, boxes and buckets. If you create your own program, you have to decide what items you will buy, purchase each item separately, then package the food in appropriate containers that are suitable for storage.

By January 1999, orders at many commercial food package suppliers were backlogged by several months. Many predict a logjam by mid-1999. If and when this occurs, commercial packages may be impossible to purchase. If you don't place your order in time, your only option may be to create your own stored food program.

Sample Basic Storage Diet

In addition to their stored food packages, most commercial stored food suppliers also sell individual cans and buckets of stored products "ala carte." This allows you to choose the contents of your stored food package. If you were to put together a very basic food storage supply ala carte from a commercial cannery, one year's worth of basic food for one person would cost about $850 retail. An example is shown below.

- 250 lbs. high protein hard red winter wheat, 6 buckets, $160
- 250 lbs. yellow corn, 27 cans, $160
- 125 lbs. soybeans, 24 cans, $200
- 50 lbs. canola oil, $45
- 50 lbs. instant nonfat dry milk, 14 cans, $190
- 50 lbs. sugar, 5 cans, $45
- 25 lbs. salt, 3 cans, $25
- daily multivitamins, $25

If you purchase these items from a commercial cannery, they will be delivered to you packaged for storage. You can also purchase these items in bulk, and package them in appropriate containers yourself. Buying in bulk will decrease your cost.

As mentioned above, orders to canneries may jam up these supplies. It could become difficult or impossible to purchase commercially canned products from these distributors. In this case, you will have to buy items in bulk, and can, or package them yourself.

Foods to Buy in Bulk and Store Yourself

In his book *Making the Best of Basics: Family Preparedness Handbook,* James Talmage Stevens describes building blocks to a successful in-home storage program.

- Water—emergency stores and treatment supplies
- Whole grains, flours and beans
- Powdered milk, dried dairy products and eggs
- Sweeteners—honey, sugar and syrups
- Cooking catalysts—salt, oil and leaveners
- Sprouting seeds and supplies
- Canned and dried fruits, vegetables and soups—familiar foods in sufficient quantities
- Meats and seafoods—dried or canned
- Condiments and seasonings
- Vitamin, mineral and herbal supplements
- Pleasure foods—snacks, beverages, sweets and treats
- Cooking equipment—pots, stove and fuel

A brief list of suggested stored foodstuffs can be found at:

http://www.ionet.net/~rbrocato/FoodStuffs.html

The Federal Emergency Management Agency pamphlet entitled "Emergency Food and Water Supplies" has a clear, basic description of what you should do for your food preparations. Read it online at:

http://www.fema.gov/library/emfdwtr.htm

Some foods store better than others. Certain processing methods also produce foods which keep better. The following foods are recommended for a home storage program.

Grains

High protein hard red winter wheat, yellow corn, millet, sorghum, buckwheat, rye, barley, quinoa, amaranth, white rice and other food grains will provide a healthy diet, are inexpensive and store indefinitely. Rolled oats have a high fat content and don't keep as well. Brown rice has exposed oils on its surface which can go rancid. Some experts dispute that this is a problem. If you have a rice huller, you can store rice in the hull, called "paddy" rice, which will keep indefinitely. Otherwise, store white rice. Since it's just starch, it should last for decades.

Store a variety of grains to make your diet more interesting and palatable. Quinoa grain has the highest protein level, but is less common and more pricey. Hard red winter wheat (not soft red or white wheat) has a high 15% protein level due to the high gluten content. Be sure to buy grain which has been cleaned to USDA #1 standards.

The cheapest grain is hard red winter wheat. Purchased from a food co-op in 50 lb. bags, it costs $115 for 250 lbs. You can buy wheat for $2.90 per 60 lb. bushel direct from a grower; 250 lbs. costs only $12.

Purchased from a food co-op in 25 lb. bags, 250 lbs. of yellow corn costs $73. Direct from a grower, it costs $2 per 56 lb. bushel, or $9 for 250 lbs.

When purchased and prepared in quantity, a 5 gal. bucket of wheat weighing 36 lbs. can be home dry-packed for a total cost of $7. Corn is even less expensive.

Food storage cook books show you how to create a variety of meals from your stored grains. *Cookin' with Home Storage* by Peggy

Layton, *American Wholefoods Cuisine* by Nikki and David Goldbeck, or *Wheat For Man* by Rosenvall, Miller and Flack, are good choices.

Beans

Grains should be supplemented with beans at every meal to maximize the complimentary amino acids. Soybeans provide the highest protein amount per dollar invested. Red, kidney, turtle, garbanzo, pinto, navy, aduki, mung, northern, lima beans; peas; lentils; and any other common legumes gives a comparable supply and are easier to cook and digest. Beans store well for 10 or more years, peas for eight.

Buy 125 lbs. of a variety of beans for a one person/one year supply. At a food co-op, 125 lbs. of soybeans cost $76. Other beans in 25 lb. bags cost less. Soybeans are only $5.60 per 60 lb. bushel when purchased direct from a grower; 125 lbs. cost less than $12.

Rita Bingham's book *Country Beans* covers the topic of bean recipes well.

Flours

Eating a diet of whole cooked grains is possible, but requires a lot of chewing! Flours and the more coarsely ground meals are easier to eat and more efficiently digested, giving greater benefit for each unit of food eaten. Any grain mill will work to grind your dry grains and beans. As flour, the grains and beans require less fuel for cooking, because they cook more quickly. To further reduce cooking time, soak the meal first.

Once ground, flour has a shorter life span than whole grains. If possible, grind your grains and use them fresh or within a few days to minimize vitamin loss.

Dried Fruits and Vegetables

Store a wide variety of dried fruits and vegetables. This should make up nearly half of your stored food diet. Place bagged dried fruit in glass jars and seal them. Air dried food is less expensive than freeze dried. Items such as dried fruit take up less space than the fresh or canned form. Dried food takes up half the space of freeze-dried foods.

Dried foods need to be protected from vermin and water during storage. Once above a 10% water content, they mold easily. Dry-pack canning of air dried foods is a good way to insure their protection. Buy a canner if you want to do it yourself.

Sprouting Seeds

Store a supply of sprouting seeds such as alfalfa, mung beans, soy beans, garbanzo beans, lentils, buckwheat, radish, unhulled sunflower and rye. Fresh sprouts provide abundant enzymes and vitamins that are lacking in a stored food diet.

Any food seed or grain can be sprouted. Use intact seeds and soak them for six to eight hours. Rinse, then place in a wide-mouth glass jar with a piece of screen, netting or gauze secured with a rubber band or canning ring over the mouth. Rinse three to four times once or twice a day and drain well. Store the container in an inverted position. They can be eaten as soon as they sprout, or they will keep for a few days if well rinsed and drained. Before using, rinse off the loose hulls and enjoy live food!

Dried Dairy Products

Dried milk powder: Commercially canned nonfat dried milk costs $3.50/lb. and is a good protein source. Reconstituted with water it makes a serviceable beverage or ingredient. It stores for five to fifteen years. Once opened, if kept tightly sealed, it keeps for two months.

Instant nonfat dried milk is a form of dried milk powder which dissolves more readily than plain nonfat dried milk. You can buy 100 lbs. of bulk nonfat dried milk per person per year for $169 from North Farm Cooperative, 888-632-3276, and repackage it yourself. The instant form costs $183 for 100 lbs.

http://www.northfarm-coop.com

A good book on the uses of dried milk is Peggy Layton's *Cookin' with Powdered Milk.*

Dried butter powder: Commercially packed butter powder vacuum sealed in #10 cans costs $6.80/lb. It stores well and is a tasty product. Canned margarine powder costs $4.40/lb. Once opened, seal them with tight lids and the contents will last four months at room temperature, six months with refrigeration.

Dried cheese powder: Cheese powder costs $4.20/lb. in cans and will be a welcome item when you are trying to vary recipes with a high grain diet. Commercially canned, nitrogen-packed dried cheese powder will keep at full nutritional value for 5 to 15 years, and be edible for double that. Once opened, dried cheese powder will last for months, if kept tightly covered.

Dried Eggs

Canned dried whole egg powder is $6.00/lb. It makes a tasty high protein breakfast, or can be used as an ingredient in bread products. This topic is covered in detail in Peggy Layton's *Cookin with Dried Eggs.* Commercially canned, nitrogen-packed dried eggs will keep at full nutritional value for 5 to 15 years, and be edible for twice that time period.

Baby Food

If Y2K problems persist, a supply of baby food and vitamins would be critical for those with infant children. A day's emergency formula for a baby consists of 4 C. boiled water, 1 C. and 2 Tablespoons dried milk, 3 Tablespoons vegetable oil, 2 Tablespoons sugar and 1/3 crushed multivitamin.

Pureed solid foods can be obtained by squeezing a mixture of cooked ground grain and beans through a cloth, then bringing it to a boil once more to kill bacteria.

Emergency baby food and formula recipes as well as equipment and sterilization techniques are described on-line at:

http://www.geocities.com/Yosemite/2342/nwss_rpl.zip

Meats–Dried or Canned

Stock up on canned meats of all types, such as chicken and beef. A can of Spam may not seem too appealing today, but after being vegetarians for a week, it will taste great to many people.

Seafoods–Dried or Canned

A supply of canned fish such as sardines, tuna, and salmon is an important protein source to round out your supplies. Jack mackerel is the cheapest canned fish and is a good replacement in recipes.

Seaweeds were a food source used by the Vikings, and are used extensively by the Japanese today. Dried kelp is a prime source of balanced minerals. You can use it as a supplement, or mix small amounts in food. Kelp powder can be purchased at co-ops or health food stores for $4.10 per lb.

Canned and Dried Soups

Add some variety to your life with soup! Hot soup is a real comfort food. Children enjoy soup because it is flavorful and easy to eat. Buy cans as well as dried "ready to rehydrate and eat" soups.

Sweeteners

Sweeteners, though empty calories, add the important quality of a sweet taste to your recipes. Children and the elderly especially desire sweet foods and having an adequate supply of sweeteners will insure they eat sufficient calories. Choose from honey, maple syrup, white sugar, brown sugar, molasses, and corn syrup.

Buy your sweeteners at any supermarket or bulk supplier. If in bags, store in waterproof containers. They will keep forever as the hydrophilic action of the molecules prevents any life forms from retaining enough water to grow. Maple syrup has less density and should be kept sealed in the original sealed glass jar or it may mold. If this occurs, just scoop off the mold from the top and use the rest.

Store a minimum of 50 lbs. of sweetener per person per year. 50 lbs. of white sugar can be purchased for $27. At $1.24 per lb., a 60 lb. tub of honey costs $75. Molasses is $23 for a 60 lb., 5 gal. container.

Vegetable Oil

The emergency recommendation for fats is slightly over 1 oz. per day, or 2 lbs. per month. The typical American diet is composed of nearly 40% fat, so you'll want at least 2 oz. per day to help meet taste needs. Elderly people and children benefit from a tastier, higher fat content in food. Giving young children 1 oz. of fat daily (3 Tablespoons) or 10% of their caloric intake as fat is beneficial.

Monosaturated oils with a high oleic acid content, like sesame, olive and canola oils, have a naturally higher resistance to rancidity than other oils, and should last at least two years at room temperature. For greatest longevity, store oils in cans; away from light, heat and air.

Have 25 lbs. of vegetable oil per person per year at a minimum; 50 lbs. per person is better. Olive oil is the healthiest. It costs $179 for a 35 lb. pail, or $5.10 per lb. from North Farm. Sesame oil is $4.15 per lb. Canola oil is the cheapest. A 35 lb. pail costs $24, only 70¢ per lb., but it is highly refined and less healthy.

Salt

Salt is a vital food supplement. Sea salt is a better quality product with a balance of mineral salts, not just sodium chloride. Salt is important to maintain the palatability of otherwise bland grain diets. It is currently very inexpensive, but was once used as a cash equivalent. Store sea salt or iodized salt to insure sufficient iodine content and to prevent thyroid problems.

At minimum, have 10 lbs. per person per year available to maintain health. For food seasoning, and to approximate a typical American diet, have 25 lbs. or more of salt per person per year. Solar-dried sea salt is the best quality. Other types of salt are baked at very high temperatures to drive off moisture and prevent caking. This alters the minerals, making them harder for your body to use.

A 50 lb. bag of non-iodized sea salt costs $11 from North Farm. They also sell a 25 lb. bag of iodized mined land salt for $5.

Leaveners

Yeast, baking powder and baking soda are important cooking ingredients. Buy them from the supermarket and store them in waterproof containers. Packaged yeast has a shelf life of two years and lasts best under refrigeration. North Farm sells 5 lbs. of Red Star Baking Yeast for $11. Have at least 12 oz. per person.

Baking powder in #10 cans costs $16.70, and can be purchased from commercial storage food canners such as Sam Andy Foods. North Farm sells 5 lbs. of baking powder for $7. Once opened, it lasts for nine months. Store at least 2 lbs. per person. Alternatively, buy a case of 4 oz. cans from a grocery store. The smaller containers can be used up before going flat.

Baking soda lasts indefinitely if kept dry. It can be bought in bulk 50 lb. bags for $23 from North Farm. Have at a minimum 2 lbs. per person per year available.

One way to keep a ready supply of yeast alive is to start a sourdough culture. James Talmage Stevens' book, *Making the Best of Basics* describes how to dry and store this sourdough starter and has a section on sourdough recipes.

Condiments and Spices

Salt, black pepper, cinnamon, basil, mustard, etc. are inexpensive and should be kept on hand in sufficient quantity. Spices such as curry, onion and garlic powders will also make your stored food tastier and more pleasant to eat.

Where to Buy Bulk Food for Self-Storage

By buying locally, you reduce your shipping and transportation expenses. This can also reduce the long waiting times many are experiencing in receiving storage food orders. Bulk discounts are often given on whole case/whole bag purchases at your local supermarket or health food store.

A food co-op or buying club is an excellent source of inexpensive high quality bulk food suitable for storage. Most college towns have one. Co-ops may be listed in your Yellow Pages under "Food Co-ops", "Grain" or "Food, Wholesale." The following websites provide a listing of U.S. and Canadian co-ops. If you put down a deposit, co-ops will be glad to special order food and other items for you at below retail. Large bulk orders usually get an additional discount.

http://www.prairienet.org/co-op/directory
http://www.columbia.edu/~jw157/food.coop.html

Start a simple buying club with your friends and get the best prices. North Farm Cooperative in Madison, Wisconsin, is one of many distributors which sell to buying clubs. North Farm requires a $500 minimum order and will ship to your location. Call them for a price list. See phone number on page 153.

Your local co-op can direct you to the distributors serving your region, or you can join a buying club in your town.

Wholesalers such as Sam's Club often sell large bags of beans and grain such as white rice and wheat. You can buy 100 lbs. of pinto beans and 100 lbs. of rice from Sam's Club for $60. This will last an adult four months. Other bulk food wholesalers can be located under "Food, Wholesale" in the Yellow Pages.

If you are able, buy directly from a grower. Grain and bean growers have cooperative storage facilities in food producing regions. You may be able to buy grains and beans directly through a producer's co-op at a discount. Be sure they are cleaned to human consumption standards and dried to less than 10% moisture content. Contact local grower cooperatives for information. Producer cooperatives may also be listed in your Yellow Pages directory.

If you buy from an organic grower, your food will have a higher mineral content. Contact your State Land Grant College or Universities' Cooperative Extension Agent for listings of state certified organic farmers and producer's co-ops. Links to Extension Publications pages across the nation are at the following site:

http://www.oznet.ksu.edu/ext_f&n/HRAP/cespub.htm

How to Package Bulk Food for Storage

Once you have purchased your food, you'll need to prepare it for storage. Many dried bulk foods come in paper bags. They should be put into food-grade buckets, cans, or plastic bags. Before sealing, diatomaceous earth, desiccants and/or oxygen absorbers should be added to keep the food fresh; see pages 164 to 166.

The classic book, *Stocking Up III* by Hupping for $30, has 627 pages of complete step-by-step instructions for freezing, canning, drying, root cellaring and preparing all types of food for storage. A resource such as this helps you preserve your stored food with the least amount of loss.

Also review the storage suggestions on pages 43 to 52 of James Talmage Stevens' *Making the Best of Basics*.

Long Term Dry-Pack Food Storage Containers

We've ranked the following containers by order of preference:

Steel tins: Rectangular 5 gal. tin plated steel "squares" are the best for bulk grain storage. They're space efficient, rodent proof, airtight, easy to open and stack well. They are available for the retail price of $11 from the Freund Can Co. You may also be able to order them from a local bucket distributor.

Steel cans: Steel #10 cans are a great way to store your food. Most storage programs use these as the predominant container. #10 cans are space efficient, stack well in boxed cases of six and are easy to handle. They are less prone to waste food as only small volumes are exposed to air and moisture deterioration at any time when a container is opened. They permit true vacuum packing in carbon dioxide or nitrogen with proper equipment and are the most airtight. Empty #10 cans cost $2 each retail from Freund, but we've bought them in bulk for as little as 33¢ each.

Smaller cans such as the #2$^1/_2$ size are less practical for home storage dry-packing.

Manual #10 canners start at $520 from Freund. Lehman's sells a less expensive model for $475. Another supplier is Ives-Way Products, 847-740-0658.

Steel buckets: Steel 5 gal. buckets are painted on the outside, plain steel on the inside, air tight and rodent proof. The steel lids are one-piece. The drawbacks are, they are difficult to open and close. Once opened, a large volume of food is exposed to air and moisture deterioration. They are difficult to stack and they waste storage space, since they require 1/3 more space than square containers. But they are inexpensive, costing only $3 each including covers.

Drums: Galvanized steel drums are inexpensive and available in various sizes, from 10 to 55 gal. We don't recommend fiber and plastic drums for food storage since they're not rat-proof. See drum size and price information in Chapter 3, page 108.

We recommend using a plastic liner bag inside steel drums to establish food-safe container quality. Plastic liners let you reuse discarded buckets and drums. Even drums with small holes will work if the holes are sealed or lined with cardboard on the inside. Make sure toxic materials weren't previously stored in the drum, since liners are semipermeable and could permit contamination of the food. If you're not sure it's safe, don't use the drum.

Drums are very heavy and may have to be filled, sealed and used in place, due to their weight. However, if you purchase a drum hand cart, you could move your drums around freely. Drum hand carts have two heavy pins on the bottom which fit under the drum, and a clip which clamps on the top rim. They can carry 1000 lbs. and cost $160. See supplier info in Chapter 3, page 111.

Plastic buckets: 5 or 6 gal. HDPE plastic buckets come in a variety of sizes, don't rust, are readily available, and are inexpensive. Used and reconditioned food grade plastic buckets are available in some areas.

Plastic buckets are not rat-proof and are semipermeable to water and air over time. When used with dry ice to flush out oxygen, they absorb carbon dioxide and can eventually create a vacuum within the bucket. This sometimes causes the bucket to split and spill its contents. All buckets have stacking problems.

Used plastic buckets are suitable if the top lip is smooth and intact. Generic 5 or 6 gal. open-head round plastic buckets are available new for $3 to $4, reconditioned for $2.

Ro-Pak 4 gal. square plastic pails with resealable gasketed lids are best for space saving. They are available for as little as $2.20 each if purchased in lots of 240 from local bucket distributors. Freund also sells them as the #29500 square plastic pail series for $3.82 each when purchased in lots of 30.

Super Seal buckets with Life Latches are resealable round buckets with screw-on gasketed lids. They're available from Nutraceuticals 2000, 800-929-9972, in 3.5, 5 and 6.5 gal. sizes for $5.70, $5.95 and $6.85 respectively.

http://www.nutraceuticals2000.com

All buckets require new lids, since lids are damaged in the removal process. Lids are available from bucket distributors. Lids for certain manufacturer's buckets may not fit on other brands. Some lids have pull-out and pop-in plastic plugs, called Rieke Spouts, for easy pouring. Gamma Seal lids from Major Surplus and Survival are resealable and reusable. The outer ring seals on the top of a 5 or 6 gal. 12" bucket, and a screw-in airtight lid seats within it. They are $6.25 each.

Glass containers: Glass bottles and jars are small, susceptible to breakage, and admit light, which causes deterioration in some foods over time. When full, store them in a dark location, wrapped in paper and boxed. Glass containers can be reused after cleaning and are cheap, or free, if recycled.

Glass canning jars are the best container for short-term wet-pack canning. Store a supply of jars, rings and extra lids for future food storage needs. Mason jars, including lids and rings, cost about 50¢ each and are sold in cases by most discount retailers.

Liners

Mylar liners: 6 gal. Mylar bag liners for 5 or 6 gal. buckets are an excellent product. When lined with heat-sealed metalized Mylar bags, plastic bucket contents are airtight and watertight.

Mylar liners are composed of four layers; polypropylene, polyethylene, aluminum foil and polyethylene. They require a heat-sealer to make them airtight, which is available from Major Surplus and Survival for $25. Or, you can use a clothes iron with a piece of fabric over the Mylar.

The 4 mil. thick, 20 in. by 30 in. Mylar bags cost $1.65 each from Major Surplus and Survival.

Military Logmars Plus, 800-922-1717, sells 22 in. x 30 in. Mylar bags which fit 6 gal. buckets for $1.60 each.

http://www.oxygenabsorber.com

Clear instructions on sealing Mylar bag liners are available with other helpful info at Yonder Way's Food Storage Frequently Asked Questions (FAQs):

http://www.yonderway.com/rural/foodstorage/iv.htm

Plastic liners: Don't put food directly into steel buckets and drums, since they're not certified as food-safe. Inexpensive FDA-approved LDPE or HDPE bag liners work well in conjunction with steel buckets and drums for food storage. Some people even use them as an additional layer of protection inside plastic containers. Food-grade liner costs and suppliers are listed in Chapter 3, page 109.

Polyethylene plastic sheeting draped into the can, as long as it extends well above the sides and can be tied up or clamped between the lid and the can, is another alternative.

Plastic bags: Food-safe plastic bags are thinner than liners but can safely accomplish the same task for food storage.

12" x 8" x 30" gusseted 1.6 mil. HDPE bags for 4 to 6 gal. buckets cost $14 for 100 and are available from several Internet and many local suppliers.

Bags On The Net, 888-638-2247

http://www.bagsonthenet.com

Bags USA, 888-646-2247

http://www.bagsusa.com

RKS Plastics, 800-635-9959

http://www.allsizepolybags.com

Vacuum Pumps

Ideally, draw a vacuum on your containers before sealing them. Emergency Essentials sells the Pump 'n Seal hand vacuum pump for $20. 100 Pump 'n Seal Tabs for sealing the site after drawing the vacuum are $9.

The Vacu-Fresh Vacuum packer system contains a roll of bag material which allows you to make bags of any length. After filling, it then draws a vacuum on your bag before heat sealing it. The VacUpack operates on 110 VAC and costs $230. Available from Y2K Grub.

Container Suppliers

The above containers are available from commercial distributors. Look in the Yellow Pages under "Cans" or "Barrels and Drums." See the container supplier list in Chapter 3, page 110.

Other can and container suppliers are listed in Chapter 16 of James Talmage Stevens' *Don't Get Caught with Your Pantry Down!*

Oxygen Absorbers, Desiccants, Diatomaceous Earth

Oxygen, water and bugs can destroy your stored food supply. You can take simple steps to protect your food from their effects.

Oxygen absorbers: Add two or three oxygen absorber packets to a 5 gal. storage container before sealing to absorb any residual oxygen. This retards insect growth, prevents oxidation, and slows nutrient loss in the food. Major Surplus and Survival sells 50 of the "Fresh Pax" brand for 50¢ each.

Push all air out of the absorber packets' shipping package, and reseal it immediately after opening, to keep the remaining oxygen absorber packets fresh for future use.

Desiccare, 800-446-6650, sells 20 oxygen absorbers sized for 5 gal. buckets for $4.55, or 23¢ each.

http://www.desiccare.com

Other oxygen absorber suppliers include:

Military Logmars Plus

Multisorb Technologies, 800-445-9890

http://www.multisorb.com

Poly Lam Products Corp., 800-836-9648

http://www.foodsave.net

Clay desiccants: Clay desiccant packages work to absorb moisture in food containers. They will help remove residual moisture in food and keep the moisture level below 10%. Silica gel is another desiccant, but it isn't approved by the FDA for use in contact with food. You can buy 40 clay desiccant packets from Desiccare for $10. Use one in each 5 gal. bucket.

Other desiccant suppliers include:

Adsorbents & Desiccants Corp. of America, 800-228-4124

http://www.thomasregister.com/olc/adcoa/bagged.htm

AGM Container Controls, 800-995-5590

http://www.agmcontainer.com

Military Logmars Plus

Poly Lam Products Corp.

Diatomaceous earth: Dried food mixed with diatomaceous earth and stored in sealed containers is safe from insects. Diatomaceous earth (DE) is a mined deposit of microscopic *diatom skeletons*. These tiny skeletons have billions of sharp silica spines which mechanically scratch and puncture insects, causing them to dehydrate and die. It also plugs their breathing tubes.

Yet, diatomaceous earth is totally safe and even beneficial for people. The FDA has approved food grade DE to be mixed and eaten with grain products. It doesn't need to be removed before using the grains. It will contribute about 14 trace minerals, and won't change the taste or texture of the food.

One lb. of food-grade DE protects 250 lbs. of grain for $2.50. Simply mix the DE powder in with your stored grain, coating it well, and seal the container. The food will remain insect-free.

You can buy food-grade DE at many organic gardening product suppliers or at the following sources. Don't buy the DE processed for use in swimming pool filters, as it is dangerous to eat or inhale because of the high crystalline silica content.

Creative Solutions, 713-433-3182

Fossil Shell Supply Company, 800-355-9427

http://www.amaonline.com/fssc

Major Surplus & Survival

Perma-Guard, Inc., 800-813-9641, sells 5 lbs. of food-grade DE for $17, and 50 lbs. for $53.

http://www.permaguard.com

Basic Self-Storage Program on a Budget

For an inexpensive one person, one year self-storage program, buy 500 lbs. of grains and 125 lbs. of beans for each person, and a hand mill to grind them. Half the grain can be wheat and the other half yellow corn. The least expensive sources are commercial wheat, yellow corn, and soybeans. When eaten with 20% beans, this provides a healthy amino acid combination.

This quantity will provide one year of basic food, with a complete range of amino acids and abundant calories, sufficient for a hard working large adult. Smaller people will need less, so you'll have extra if you store this amount for everyone in your group.

 Store the beans and grains with DE, desiccants, and oxygen absorbers in sealed metal cans, buckets or drums; or in sealed food-grade-plastic liners inside metal containers.

Additionally, for each person in your group, buy 50 lbs. of sugar and/or honey as well as 5 gal. of oil and 25 lbs. of salt. Obtain a wide assortment of canned foods, including fruit, vegetables, fish and/or meats. Buy sealed spices, condiments and comfort foods. Also, store a supply of inexpensive multivitamins along with your food in your basement or other cool place.

 These foods can be purchased inexpensively from a co-op or discount warehouse and packaged at home. Additionally, buy a small Coleman camping cook stove and fuel, and you're all set!

SUPPLEMENTARY STORAGE ITEMS

Following is a list of supplementary items we recommend you include in your Y2K food reserves.

Comfort Foods

No matter which stored food option you select—supermarket canned goods, a commercial stored food package, or bulk foods you package yourself—be sure to store enough foods that are familiar to your family. The elderly and the young may not eat if served only unfamiliar foods they don't like. Children have literally starved, rather than eat foods that are foreign to them.

Seeds, nuts, pasta, granola, flour mixes, candy, bouillon cubes, beverage powders, pudding and dessert mixes, cold cereals, pretzels, crackers, peanut butter, jams or jellies and other familiar foods will be welcomed by your family. The comfort derived from eating them will give emotional support during Y2K-related challenges. Store enough so you will be able to include them often.

Pasta stores well and is cheap and tasty. An abundant supply of various noodles is a good idea.

Meals Ready to Eat (MREs)

"Meals Ready to Eat" are military surplus-type meals which were available in large amounts after Desert Storm. MREs contain from 810 to 990 calories per meal and include a variety of items from condiments and matches on down to toilet paper.

Y2K is likely to bring periods of stress and chaos. At these times, it would be great to have food you can eat without any preparation at all. MREs are also good for emergency travel. Just throw them in the car or your backpack, and you're ready to go. MREs are fully hydrated, but have a lot of preservatives and salt, so plan on consuming extra water when you eat these meals.

Irradiated with gamma rays and packed in heavy plastic and aluminum foil outer bags, MREs are designed to be good for 10 years without refrigeration—if stored at 60° F or below. At 120° F, they only last one month without loss of quality; at room temperature, they last six to eight years.

Check the expiration date on the package, and buy the freshest product available. Store MREs and all preparedness food supplies in your cool basement, not in your garage.

Current fresh supplies are selling for $5 to $7 each. Recently, military units have begun stockpiling these foods. While Military issue MREs are no longer available to the public, MRE manufacturers sell identical retail varieties.

Major Surplus & Survival and other suppliers sell the "Mil Spec" brand MRE, which is a civilian version made to the same military standards by one of the same manufacturers. Cost: $5 each when purchased in cases of 12.

Cheaper Than Dirt!, 888-625-3848, sells MREs for $50 a case with volume discounts.

http://www.cheaperthandirt.com

Emergency Essentials offers 90 MREs for $360 and MRE heaters for $1 each.

Long Life Food Depot, 800-601-2833, specializes in MREs and has the largest selection we've seen.

http://www.longlifefood.com

A list of MRE sources is available at:

http://www.millennium-ark.net/News_Files/INFO_Files/ MRE_Sources.html

Vitamin and Mineral Supplements

Be sure to stock up on Vitamin C and inexpensive multivitamins. Buy your multivitamins in bulk. They don't have to be high-potency; but you absolutely must have at least the Recommended Daily Allowance or RDA. A minimum level of supplementary nutritional support is vital since your stored food will be low in vitamins, especially as it gets older.

Bronson Pharmaceutical, 800-235-3200, sells bulk powdered vitamins at reasonable prices. You can purchase 1 lb. of Vitamin C in the calcium ascorbate form, which lasts indefinitely, for $19. All Insurance Multivitamin Powder costs $20 for 15.9 oz., and Vitamin and Mineral Dietary Supplement Powder is $9.50 for 8 oz.

Other discount vitamin suppliers are:

L&H Vitamins, 800-221-1152

http://www.bvital.com

Swanson Vitamin Discounts, 800-437-4148

http://www.healthy.net

The Vitamin Shoppe, 800-223-1216

http://www.vitaminshoppe.com

Storing high quality food supplements such as blue-green algae should also be considered. This is available from health food stores and Cell Tech, 800-800-1300.

http://www.celltech.com

Juicing: With a wheatgrass juicer, you can extract the chlorophyll and nutrition from any young grass or edible weed to be used as a food supplement. Wheatgrass juicers can be purchased from Major Surplus & Survival for $100, or for $58 from Kansas Wind Power.

STORING YOUR FOOD RESERVES

You'll need to decide where to store your food reserves. Whether supermarket canned goods, a commercial stored food package, or bulk foods you package yourself, take care that your food won't deteriorate during storage.

Exposure to high or freezing temperatures, moisture, oxygen, light and pests all degrade the quality of stored food. When storing food, avoid attics, garages, storage sheds and other outbuildings where temperatures fluctuate dramatically. Stable, cool storage temperatures are best, such as in a basement.

Dark or covered containers are best for preserving food as the light speeds up its breakdown. If you use glass jars, place the jars in a cardboard box or cover them with newspapers to block out the light. Black plastic bags can also be used as covers.

Store your metal cans, tins and fiber boxes on wooden boards or pallets to keep them off dirt or cement floors and protect them from moisture. Steel containers may rust and fiber containers may rot if they get wet. Don't push containers directly up against the walls, to prevent mold and mildew from forming.

Rodents can be a problem. Mice typically can't get into plastic buckets or drums, but rats can. Metal containers keep out rats.

Winter Storage of Wet-Pack Canned or Bottled Food

Wet-pack canned or bottled food is vulnerable to freezing and bursting. If you lose power, store your canned or bottled high moisture food in the area of your house you plan to keep warmest. As long as that or an adjacent room remains above 32° F, canned and bottled food won't freeze.

Underground Storage

A root cellar or buried storage pit safely below the frost line keeps stored items at the constant earth temperature of 45° to 55° F, depending on your location. This slows food deterioration to a minimum, and keeps food quality life expectancy high.

Root Cellar

An easy root cellar is a barrel buried below the frost line. Pile dirt on top and cover the root cellar with bales of hay or other insulating material for further protection. *Stocking Up III* covers root cellars well.

Buried Storage Pit

You can store your food reserves in underground pits. Select high ground on a slope where water won't collect. The weight of heavy machinery could split the containers, so choose a non-traffic area. Dig down five to six feet and line the pit with rock or sand for drainage.

Place your dry food inside plastic bags within waterproof containers. Cover the plastic or metal containers with plastic bags. Line the hole with plastic, pile the stored food no more than one or two feet high, and cover with more plastic. Place boards over the food to keep some of the weight from the dirt off the food.

Create a mound of dirt over the food to create a good slope for water drainage. Cover the area with plastic sheets extending well beyond the top of the pit, creating a domed waterproof plastic "roof" to direct water drainage away. Replace with two to three feet of insulating soil on top.

Mark the site by planting a bush on the spot. Or, measure and document exact distances to several nearby fixed landmarks. Make a map and be sure to keep it in a safe location.

FOOD PREPARATION
Grain Grinding

If you buy whole grains with your storage food package, you will want to grind them. Your food supplier may even include a mill with your order.

Grain mills can be purchased for as little as $45, but more expensive mills last longer with continued use. Be sure to buy a grinder that can handle whole kernels of corn, which is one of the largest and hardest grains to grind. Also buy spare millstones or grinding burrs.

The Country Living Grain Mill is one of the most durable, easiest to use grain mills available for small applications. Made of cast aluminum, it has a metal flywheel to assist in hand cranking. A built in V-belt is designed for motorized use. With an adapter, it can be powered by a bicycle. The mill sells for $310 and is guaranteed for 20 years. With a nut and bean auger and power bar for 40% easier grinding, the cost is $365 from Kansas Wind Power. Due to the demand for this product, be prepared for a four to five month back-order delay.

The Danish Diamant cast iron grain mill with similar features to the Country Living Mill is larger and sturdier. It also has the ability to grind finer flour. It costs $565 from Lehman's, or $540 from the Special Op's Shop.

The Corona Grain and Corn Mill has steel grinding plates. It costs $45 from Jade Mountain. A stone burr conversion kit is available for an additional $37, which works better on wheat.

The "Best, Low-Cost Grain Mill" has both steel and stone burrs and a 5-cup grain hopper. Jade Mountain sells it for $139.

Jade Mountain's Village Grinder is a high-quality, volume hand-mill with heavy-duty millstones, dust protected ball-bearings and a 24 in. flywheel. It grinds over 26 lbs. of flour per hour. The one-person model is sold for $529, a two-person model for $768.

The Special Op's Shop sells a Manual Grain Crusher for $85 which makes cereal flakes from whole grains to be used like rolled oats. Lehman's sells one for $80.

Meat grinders with small holes in the output plate will adequately grind soaked or sprouted grains for cooking or breads. They can be picked up for only a few dollars used, or purchased new from Lehman's or the Special Op's Shop for $45.

Dehydrating

You can dry your own vegetables, fruits and meat in your oven, or with a commercially sold food dehydrator. Food dehydrators can be purchased for as little as $50 from distributors such as Major Surplus & Survival and The Sausage Maker Inc., 888-490-8525, as well as manufacturers such as Excalibur. This is actually less than it would cost you to make one.

http://www.excaliburdehydrator.com

Instructions for drying fruits and vegetables are given in many books such as Greene, Hertzberg and Vaughn's *Putting Food By,* or Stevens' *Making the Best of Basics.*

Cooking

As explained in Chapter 2, it's a good idea to choose an alternative heating method that can double as a cooking source. In that chapter, we discussed several stoves that can both cook your food and heat your living quarters.

In this section, we'll look at a few specific cooking ideas that are handy for an emergency situation.

Solar Cookers

Solar cookers which will bake bread at 350° F without fuel can be easily built using cardboard, aluminum foil and a piece of glass. Cooking can even be done in the middle of winter on a sunny day. Solar ovens are currently used extensively in developing nations where fuel is at a premium.

Comprehensive books on this subject with recipes, diagrams, instructions and background information on how to build your own solar oven are available, such as *Heaven's Flame, A Guide to Solar Cookers,* by Joseph Radabaugh. 143 pages, cost: $18.

The following three books are sold by Jade Mountain.

How to Make and Use a Solar Box Cooker, cost: $9.

Cooking With the Sun, 122 pages, cost: $8.

The Expanding World of Solar Box Cookers is a definitive guide. With four sets of plans, it costs $10.

Other sources for solar cooker information are:

Solar Cookers International.

http://www.accessone.com/~sbcn

Humboldt College, Campus Center for Appropriate Technology

http://www.humboldt.edu/~ccat/sub/solovn.htm

Watch a solar oven being built at:

http://www.sunlightworks.com/page9.html

Some solar cookers for sale on the retail market are:

The Burns-Milwaukee Sun Oven, with a fiberglass case, tempered glass door, polished reflectors and silicone rubber gaskets, weighs 21 lbs. It reaches 400° F and is available from Off Line Independent Energy Systems for $260.

The Solar Chef is the highest performance solar oven. Its 16 high quality mirrored segments set on two separate angles create a dual focus. It bakes, browns, roasts and broils similar to a conventional oven, with temperatures reaching 500° F. The Solar Chef weighs 82 lbs., has a 39 in. diameter and 25 lb. capacity. It costs $385 plus $75 shipping, direct from Grain-Power Products, 612-545-7240 or from Solar Chef, 806-794-2150.

http://www.solarchef.com

Jade Mountain sells the Sun Toys Solar Cooker which folds to 2" x 14" x 14" and weighs 8 oz. for $19.

They also sell the Village Sun Oven which can bake hundreds of loaves of bread per day. It cooks any food in large volumes and generates temperatures of 500° F. Cost: $6950.

Hotbox Cooker

A hotbox cooker is nothing more than a well-insulated box. A pot of food is brought to a boil for five minutes, then placed in the hotbox. Insulating materials such as cloth, straw, crumpled paper, foam, or fiberglass are packed tightly around the pot. A minimum thickness of 4 in. of insulation must be packed around the sides of the pot, and more if possible on top. Due to the slow heat loss, the food is kept hot enough to continue cooking.

Most foods can be cooked by this method. If preparing beans in a hotbox, cook them for 20 minutes before placing them in the box.

The high tech Nissan Thermal Chef insulated cooker is used extensively in Japan due to the high cost of fuel. Bring food to a boil and seal it in the cooker, where it will continue cooking with no further heating. A real fuel saver! The Thermal Chef is distributed in the U.S. by Thermos. Grain-Power Products sells them at a discount, the 5 qt. model for $150 and the 9 qt. version for $200.

Pressure Cooker

A pressure cooker requires less fuel to heat the food inside and cooks in less time. They are great for rehydrating dehydrated foods. Buy only stainless steel, since aluminum leaches into food and has been linked to Alzheimer's Disease. Pressure cookers cost about $70 and can be purchased where cookware is sold.

Dutch Oven

A large cast iron dutch oven or stew pot with cover will come in handy for expedient emergency cooking. In addition, a dutch oven can be filled with stones, heated and placed on bricks to be safely used near your bed as a radiant heat source.

Many suppliers sell cast iron dutch ovens. Major Surplus and Survival's 12 qt. model costs $30, 8 qt. costs $20.

Enameled cast iron cookware such as the Le Creuset brand is more expensive, but easier to clean. The enamel prevents food discoloration caused from iron leaching into the food, but deprives you of the beneficial dietary effect of the extra iron.

Let's Cook Dutch: A Complete Guide for the Dutch Oven Chef by Robert Ririe contains recipes and instructions for cooking foods in dutch ovens.

Supplemental Oven

An add-on oven suitable for baking can be used with many of the heat sources listed in Chapter 2. These ovens concentrate the heat around the baking dish and cook like conventional ovens. Campmor sells "The Outback Oven" with a 10 in. pan for $50, and the "Coleman Camp Oven" for $40. A large cast iron dutch oven can do the same job plus many others.

Expedient Cooking Methods

Solid fuel tablets: One solid fuel tablet will boil 2.5 cups of water in five minutes, enough to warm one meal. This fuel source costs $3 for eight tablets. A simple stove in which to burn the tablets costs $5 from B&A Products.

Candles: Nuwick sells 120 hour candles which can be used with two wicks as a cooking heat source. The non-toxic slow burning wax is contained in a stable reusable and waterproof metal can. Major Surplus sells them for $12.50 each.

Refrigeration

If Y2K-induced power blackouts and brownouts continue for a long time, we won't be able to depend on our refrigerators and freezers. Preventing food from spoiling may prove difficult. During the first three months of 2000 in the northern climates, you can put your food outside to keep it cold. After that, an efficient solar, kerosene or LP gas powered refrigerator or freezer would preserve perishable foods.

Refrigerator/Freezers

Coolers designed to use 12 or 24 volt DC are common. Because the costs to produce solar electricity are so high, these alternative appliances are up to ten times as efficient as standard models. Despite the high initial costs, energy use is extremely low, requiring less power and fewer photovoltaic panels.

Solar Powered: Off Line Independent Energy Systems sells Sun Frost and Vestfrost solar powered refrigerators. A standard size 19 cu. ft. Sun Frost refrigerator/freezer costs $2800, but uses 85% less electricity. A 10 cu. ft. refrigerator costs $1600; and a 10 cu. ft. freezer costs $1700. The Vestfrost 7 cu. ft. refrigerator with built-in 3.5 cu. ft. freezer costs $1000. The Vestfrost 7 cu. ft. freezer costing $700, is sold by Jade Mountain for $675.

LP Gas: Off Line also sells LP gas refrigerator/freezers. A Danby 8 cu. ft. refrigerator with built-in 1 cu. ft. freezer costs $1100. A Servel brand refrigerator/freezer from Off Line has dual 120 volt AC and LP gas power, making it a good back-up model for $1300. It uses about 8 gal. of LP gas per month. Lehman's sells this model for $1150, and has the lowest prices on other models, as well. Both Lehman's and Off Line sell the FrosTek 8.5 cu. ft. chest freezer for $1835. It keeps food near 0° F.

Kerosene: Lehman's specializes in Servel brand LP gas and kerosene models. A portable 1.2 cu. ft. refrigerator which runs on either LP gas, 12 volts DC or 115 volts AC, sells for $435. It uses just 0.6 gal. of propane weekly. Jade Mountain sells it for $425. A 10 cu. ft. kerosene Servel brand refrigerator/freezer costs $1600. The kerosene model burns 1.75 gal. per week and the 2.5 gal. fuel tank holds enough for 10 days. The LP gas version uses 9.5 lbs. or 2.2 gal. of fuel weekly.

GROWING YOUR OWN FOOD

You may also want to make plans for growing some of your own food. Only a small percentage of U.S. citizens know how to produce their own food. You'll probably have to study if you want to do some serious gardening.

If you are relocating, try to select a temperate area with a long growing season, and adequate rainfall.

For information on small-scale farming, you can begin at the Alternative Farming Systems division of the U.S. Dept. of Agriculture, or the following sites:

http://www.nalusda.gov/afsic/sbjsmfrm.htm
http://www.farminfo.org
http://www.homestead.org

Some on-line agriculture books are available at:

http://www-cgi.cs.cmu.edu/cgi-bin/book/subjectstart?S

Seeds and Food Plants

Non-Hybrid Crop Seeds

Many food-crop seeds, sold both for large-scale farming and home gardening, are hybrid varieties. Hybrid seeds are designed to create large attractive crops for one generation, but the new seeds produced if planted, grow into inferior versions of their parents. You can't save seeds from hybrid crops to plant next season. With hybrids, you must purchase new seeds annually.

Non-hybrid seeds, on the other hand, produce crops containing seeds you can save and plant the following season. They grow into plants identical to their parents.

The large industrial farming operations which supply the bulk of our nation's food use hybrid seeds extensively. These farms rely on seed shipments each growing season. Transportation and distribution disruptions in 2000 could prevent farmers from receiving seed deliveries. The crops may not be planted.

We recommend you store a variety of non-hybrid seed, sealed in #10 cans. Several suppliers sell Y2K seed packages.

Out n' Back sells enough non-hybrid seeds to plant a garden the size of a basketball court, sealed in a #10 can, for $19.

The Ark Institute, 800-255-1912, sells a box of 49 different non-hybrid vegetable varieties in amounts sufficient for a family for three years. This package sells for $160 and includes the book *Build Your Ark! How to Prepare for Self-Reliance in Uncertain Times.*

http://www.arkinstitute.com/seeds.htm

Heirloom Seeds, 412-384-0852, sells two Y2K packages. One contains 136 separate vegetable varieties and 19 herbs for $200. The other has 233 vegetable and 38 herb varieties for $300.

http://www.heirloomseeds.com/y2k.htm

TLC Greenhouse, 970-527-3375, sells four $97 non-hybrid seed packages for different growing regions.

http://www.tlchub.com/seeds

We suggest you focus on purchasing varieties of crops and vegetables that have a short growing season and which store easily. Suppliers such as Denali and Johnny's Selected Seed provide these.

The following are further sources for non hybrid seed:

Baker Creek Heirloom Seed Co., 417-924-8917

solanums@yahoo.com

Burpee, 800-888-1447

http://www.burpee.com

Denali Seed Co., 907-344-0347

http://www.denaliseed.com

Johnny's Selected Seeds, 207-437-4301

http://www.johnnyseeds.com

J.W. Seed Co., 800-297-3123

http://www.jungseed.com

Matthew's Old Time Seed Co., 612-974-0955

http://seed.bioreagent.com

Pinetree Garden Seeds, 207-926-3400

http://www.superseeds.com

Planet Tonasket, 509-486-1047

http://www.planettonasket.com/GoodSeed

Seed Saver's Exchange, 319-382-5990 (Seeds are traded.)

Seeds of Change, 888-762-7333

http://www.seedsofchange.com

For good links to non-hybrid seed suppliers, go to:

http://www.millennium-ark.net

Plan on saving your own seeds from all crops and plants, for future use. The books *Seed To Seed* by Suzanne Ashworth for $21 and *Saving Seeds* by Mark Rogers for $13, both describe this process in detail. Plan on holding back the seed from the best specimens of your plants for an ongoing seed supply. Each species may have special requirements for germination. Seed selection is a skill.

Tree Suppliers

If you want to establish perennial crops such as berries or an orchard, you can purchase stock from the following suppliers:

Miller Nurseries, 800-836-9630

http://www.millernurseries.com

Stark Brothers, 800-775-6415

http://www.starkbros.com

The Northern Nut Growers Association provides an excellent informational service regarding tree crops.

http://www.icserv.com/nnga/

Books on growing perennial plants, shrubs and trees are:

Plant Propagation: Principles and Practices by Hartmann and Kester, and *Seeds of Woody Plants in the United States* by the USDA Forest Service, Agriculture Handbook #450.

Mushroom Spawn Supplier

Mushrooms have significant food value. Grow your own with spawn from Gourmet Mushroom Products, 800-789-9121.

http://www.gmushrooms.com

Farming and Gardening

Farming is hard work. It's rewarding physically and emotionally, but it hasn't been financially rewarding for decades. That may change if there are Y2K-induced food shortages.

Gardening is something which can be done on a small or large scale. Everyone can grow a few vegetables to compliment their diet.

If you'd like to produce your own food, there is a wealth of information available to assist you. A basic organic gardening book is *How To Grow More Vegetables* by John Jeavons. High on your list should be Carla Emery's *Encyclopedia Of Country Living*.

The *Countryside & Small Stock Journal* is an excellent resource for small-scale farming, gardening, and Y2K topics. See Chapter 3, page 133, for subscription information.

Topics such as animal husbandry, draft animals, orcharding and perennial crops can be researched if they interest you. Publishers of small-scale farming books include:

Diamond Farm Book Publishers, 800-481-1353
http://www.diamondfarm.com
Rodale Press, 800-914-9363
http://www.rodalestore.com
Storey Books, 800-441-5700
http://www.storeybooks.com

Soil Preparation

Following are some considerations for soil preparation, to get you ready for food production.

If possible, select a garden site which has rich soils, such as a clay loam or sandy loam. Locate your garden next to a permanent source of irrigation water such as a stream, river, pond or lake. Buy and spread mineral and animal fertilizers. Till your soil in 1999. Hire a local farmer to plow it and later disc it to cover the sod and hasten its decomposition. Any soil turning you do with power equipment now will save you time and effort later. If possible, stockpile fuel for a small tractor to pull a disc or single bottom plow. You may opt for a rototiller if your plot is small.

Gardening Tools

Buy a supply of high-quality hand gardening tools, including contractor-grade fiberglass or steel handled shovels, rakes and hoes. Human powered equipment such as a hand-held broadcast seeder, pushed wheel plow, garden planter and cultivator will make gardening easier.

Sources for low-tech and homesteading machinery and equipment are Cumberland General Store and Lehman's Hardware.

WILD FOOD COLLECTION

Wild foods can extend your stored food reserves and provide vitamins, minerals, high quality protein and variety which may otherwise be lacking in your emergency food supply.

Gathering

The collection of native plants for food is an excellent strategy to provide fresh, vital food for your diet. Many wild foods or weeds are actually more nutritious than cultivated varieties, and are quite tasty. Wild amaranth or pigweed, lambs quarters and purslane are much more nutritious than commonly cultivated vegetables. They all make excellent greens when cooked. White oak acorns can be processed into a healthy flour. Get a book with photos and drawings to identify wild edible plants in your region, and begin to familiarize yourself with the food around you.

Good books include the *Peterson Guide #23, Field Guide to Edible Wild Plants*; *Identifying and Harvesting Edible and Medicinal Plants* by Steve Brill; *Guide to Wild Foods* by Christopher Nyerges; and *Edible Wild Plants* by Elias and Dykeman.

A source of information about wild foods is the Self Reliance Institute in California.

http://www.self-reliance.net/

Hunting

There are many good books on hunting wild game for food, Amazon.com has 285 listings for books on hunting. We recommend you get one and review their suggestions. But don't plan to "live off the land" exclusively. Its not as easy as you might think, and others will have the same idea. During the Great Depression of the 1930s, populations of wild animals dropped to record lows due to excessive hunting.

Fishing

Store fishing supplies such as a spool of 10 lb. test line, a variety of hooks, leads, split lead weights, and bobbers. A fishing pole and reel is needed for casting. A fishing spear or trident is a helpful tool, but the most efficient piece of fishing equipment is a net. Consider buying a net, but be sure to always obey the hunting and fishing laws in your state!

In summary, store at least 30 to 90 days of food reserves, cooking supplies and fuel for each family member. Buy a supply of food production books, supplies and equipment. Also buy some hunting and gathering books and equipment.

Good eating!

FOOD CHECKLIST

_____ Store a 30 to 90 day supply of food for each family member

_____ Consider storing a year's worth of food for each family member

_____ Stock up with canned and dried supermarket food

_____ Buy a commercial stored food package

_____ Create your own food storage program

_____ Buy foods in bulk and store them yourself

_____ Use cans, tins, buckets and/or drums for food storage

_____ Use vacuums, absorbers and desiccants for food storage

_____ Use diatomaceous earth for grain storage

_____ Buy MREs

_____ Buy comfort foods

_____ Buy vitamin supplements

_____ Buy a grain grinder

_____ Buy a cooking stove

_____ Store enough cooking fuel for 90 days

_____ Buy a solar cooker

_____ Buy a hotbox cooker

_____ Buy a dutch oven

_____ Obtain alternative refrigeration

_____ Buy a supply of non-hybrid garden seeds

_____ Buy a supply of gardening tools

_____ Establish a food-production library

_____ Establish a wild food-collection library

_____ Buy hunting and fishing supplies

CHAPTER 5

Safety

*It is increasingly evident that an appreciable part of the nation's
infrastructure could be adversely affected...by...Y2K...Considering
the possibilities of a large-scale disruption of governmental, commercial and other routine daily activities, it is certain the National
Guard will be among the first organizations activated to assist.*

Maj. Gen. Edward Philbin
Executive Director, National Guard Association

Fire and police protection as well as emergency medical services have been provided throughout our lives. Place an emergency call to 911, and the police, fire department or paramedics
quickly arrive.

However, the services we depend on may be overloaded or
inaccessible during a Y2K crisis. We may not be able to rely on
having prompt emergency response.

Given these possibilities, we should plan to be more independent of city-supplied emergency services. By preparing, we should
be better able to weather Y2K.

COORDINATED 911 EMERGENCY SERVICE

The 911 system requires functional software, computer systems
and an intact telephone network to feed it correct information. In
the event of a Year 2000 crisis, the telephone system may not function properly, if at all. Therefore, it's essential that municipalities

insure that their 911 software and equipment as well as their telephone network is Y2K compliant.

Yet, in late 1998, a survey by the National Association of Counties found that 50% of the nation's 3069 counties were without a comprehensive strategic plan to deal with potential computer failure caused by the Y2K problem. Our 911 systems are clearly at risk.

National Safety

Lack of 911 services, combined with the infrastructure failures Y2K is likely to cause, could lead to societal unrest. Several nations have announced plans to mobilize their national guard or military forces in response to these potential problems.

Under a plan dubbed *Operation Abacus,* Canadian Forces will pre-position emergency supplies and equipment prior to 2000. The British Home Office is drawing up emergency plans for the Armed Forces to help maintain vital services in such key infrastructure areas as hospitals, electric power, and water supplies.

In the U.S., the National Guard is preparing for mobilization as needed to assist the civilian population and maintain law and order. As of this writing, the National Guard is planning *Communications CPX,* an exercise to practice full mobilization of all 480,000 Guard members, using a new high-frequency radio system. Scheduled for May 1, 1999, the exercise will take place without the use of conventional phones, TV or radio. It is designed to prepare for a possible mobilization in the event of Y2K-induced disruptions to power, telecommunications, transportation and banking.

Emergency Communications

Coordinated 911 emergency services are life savers. The speed with which highly trained emergency workers arrive on the scene of an emergency is often the deciding factor between life and death.

In an emergency, two or three minutes often makes the difference.

There are alternatives for contacting emergency help if the telephones are out of commission. Police monitor radio frequencies such as Citizen's Band channel 9 and the General Mobile Radio Service "emergency channel" of 462.675 MHz. These methods are covered further in Chapter 8, Communications.

Emergency medical services: In a Y2K emergency situation, EMS/paramedic aid may be unavailable. We recommend you acquire first aid training, to cope with situations that may arise. See Chapter 9, pages 292 to 293, for details.

FIRE SERVICES

The local fire department is one of our most critical public services. The key to a successful fire department is quick notification and response to fires. In our town of 35,000 citizens, we have two fire stations one mile apart. The International Association of Fire Chiefs estimates there are 32,000 fire departments in the U.S. How many of them will be prepared for the Year 2000 date change?

Fire vehicles require a water supply; water pressure is dependent upon electrical power. Even if the 911 system relays the emergency call, will water be available at the hydrant?

It's not possible to predict exactly how Y2K will impact your city and its fire department. Therefore, we recommend you prepare to deal with fire emergencies in case outside aid is unavailable. Knowledge of fire prevention is an important first step.

Fire Prevention

Fire prevention is an important aspect of fire protection. Prevent fires before they start by inspecting your surroundings and setting up a fire-hazard-free environment.

A fire requires three things to start; heat, fuel and oxygen. These are referred to as the *fire triangle*. Remove one or more of the three sides, and a fire can't be supported. Prevent fires by keeping these three factors from co-existing.

Eliminate Fire Hazards

Always store gasoline, kerosene, and other flammable substances outside of the house, in a properly vented storage facility.

Eliminate all excess trash, newspapers, oily rags, and all other flammable materials.

Inspect Your Surroundings

Always adhere to manufacturer's guidelines for safe operation of heat sources. Check your furnace, wood stove, kerosene heater or propane heater. Inspect your electrical wiring. Look for loose, frayed, or exposed wiring. Check all cords and switches on appliances.

Turn Off Power and Gas

If a problem develops in the electrical or natural gas delivery system, it may become necessary to shut off the electricity or gas to your home. Familiarize yourself with the location of the shut off valves for each of the utilities.

For electric power, locate your electric service panel. The "main" shut off should be clearly marked in your panel. If you have fuses, disconnect the electric power by removing the cartridges in the center of the panel. If you have breakers, turn off the "main" breaker toward the top of the panel. To be safe, turn off all other breakers as well.

A gas leak will require shutting off the incoming gas at the meter. This is usually found outside the building along the wall. Sometimes it is in the basement. All you need is a pipe wrench or crescent wrench to turn the valve 90 degrees, a quarter turn, in either direction.

If you need further instruction or assistance, contact your utility company or certified professionals.

Pre-Fire Planning

Planning

Establish a strategy for your escape in the event of a fire. Locate all exit doors and have at least two ways out of each room. Decide on a safe place for family members to meet outside of your home. Make sure the children know exactly where to meet.

Drilling

Fire drills are overlooked by most people, yet this is one area that can't be over-done! A fire at any time, especially in the middle of the night, can create panic. Panic makes for mistakes, knowledge overcomes fear. So, practice fire drills at least once a month. Practice according to your pre-fire plan and time drills to see how long it takes to make a safe and orderly escape.

Your local fire department is equipped to answer any questions you may have concerning pre-fire planning, fire safety in your home, or preparing fire drills.

Fire Safety Products

During Y2K, the 911 system, telephones and fire departments could be overburdened or compromised. You should be ready to fight a fire yourself. However, if the fire is large or threatening your escape route, it's better to escape than risk being injured.

There are three types of fires you may see in your home:
• Class A: Caused by ordinary combustibles—paper, wood, trash, cloth, and all other ordinary combustibles.
• Class B: Caused by flammable liquids & gases—gasoline, paint lacquer and tar, and oils.
• Class C: Caused by live electrical equipment.

Fire Extinguishers

Position fire extinguishers in your home, garage and automobile. In the event your neighborhood lost water pressure due to Y2K, you would have the ability to suppress a fire by yourself if caught in time.

Class ABC fire extinguishers generally meet all of your home fire safety needs. We purchased a Kidde Full Home Fire Extinguisher at Home Depot for $12. It's a Class ABC fire extinguisher containing monoammonium phosphate, a dry chemical extinguishing agent. The agent is non-toxic, less costly and more effective than carbon dioxide extinguishers. Fire extinguishers are sold at department stores such as K-Mart, Home Depot, and all hardware stores.

The next question is "How many fire extinguishers do I need and where do I put them?" Kidde Safety, 800-880-6788, a manufacturer of fire safety products, recommends having one fire extinguisher for every 600 square feet of living space. This is dependent upon the size and layout of your home. Main areas of concern would be: basements, laundry rooms, sleeping areas, garages, etc. When determining how many fire extinguishers to have, remember—it's better to have too many, than not enough.

http://www.kidde.com

It is also recommended you carry a fire extinguisher in your automobile. Auto fire extinguishers can be mounted in the trunk. The Kidde Auto Fire Extinguisher is compact in design, and can be attached to uncarpeted surfaces by using the included Velcro adhesive strips, or stored in a bracket mounted with screws.

No matter which fire extinguisher you purchase, read the owner's manual.

Using a fire extinguisher: The extinguisher's label contains all necessary information on how to use it. You should be familiar with any extinguisher you plan on using.

There are three steps to follow when using a fire extinguisher:

1. Hold the extinguisher upright and pull out the safety pin.

2. Stand about six feet back from the fire and aim the nozzle at the base of the fire.

3. Squeeze the lever and sweep the nozzle from side to side.

Smoke and Carbon Monoxide Detectors

A smoke detector is a good investment, considering the increased possibility of fire, coupled with the potential loss of services, chiefly fire protection, during the Y2K dilemma.

While smoke can be readily noticed, carbon monoxide is an invisible, odorless, and lethal gas. Therefore, it would be prudent to also install a carbon monoxide detector in your living quarters. This is especially important if you will be burning fuel to power your generator, wood in your fireplace or wood burning stove, or kerosene in a heater.

Make sure the smoke and carbon monoxide detectors you purchase are battery operated. Devices powered by AC are useless in a power outage situation. Carbon monoxide and smoke detectors can be purchased at hardware stores, department stores, and various other outlets.

K-mart sells a battery-operated First Alert extra sensitive model #FCD1 for $40. The First Alert model has a 10 year warranty, 2 years on the module. Smoke detectors start at $10, and can be found in a variety of outlets.

Take precautions to establish adequate ventilation with the use of any space heater. If you elect to use propane as your main source of fuel, note that the by-product of burning propane is CO_2, carbon dioxide. CO_2 is not nearly as dangerous as carbon monoxide or smoke inhalation can be in close quarters. Yet, high levels of CO_2 have been known to cause headaches, nausea and unconsciousness.

Fire Escape Ladders

If you have a multi-level home, purchase fire escape ladders. Kidde offers a variety of escape ladders. Model #KEL-15, a 15 ft. ladder, easily attaches to a window sill, is strong, lightweight and tangle-free. Model #KEL-25 has the same features and is 25 ft. long.

Other companies which sell fire safety related products:

Code Three Fire and Safety, 707-429-5323

http://www.quickpage.com/c/code

General Fire Equipment Co., 800-293-6641

http://www.generalfire.thomasregister.com

Fire Blankets

Fire blankets are wrapped around a person who is on fire to extinguish the flames. Fire safety suppliers sell them.

POLICE SERVICES

In case police services are less available during Y2K, take steps to reduce your potential need for police protection.

If Y2K leaves us without working telephones, we won't be able to call the police via 911. Police could be overloaded by multiple problems and emergencies. We may be left on our own. How many of us are prepared for such a scenario?

Consider the following real life situation:

In July of 1977, parts of New York City lost power for from 5 to 25 hours. During that time, 2000 stores were looted, hundreds more were torched and 3700 vandals were arrested.

What would happen if your city lost power for 5 to 25 days, or longer! Bear in mind that in the example above, power was down in only one city. If Y2K induces power outages, they will probably be widespread. Areas experiencing problems rely on outside assistance in emergencies. Y2K consequences may be global, making outside assistance unavailable.

Community Planning

A good course of action to ensure that your area will be safe for you and your family is to make efforts to strengthen your existing neighborhood watch program, or begin one if one does not already exist in your neighborhood. Invite a local law enforcement officer to attend and to explain when citizens' arrests are and are not allowed, and to explain when the use of force, including deadly force is justified. Remember, the law provides citizens with the right of self defense.

Know Your Neighbor

In today's world, many of us are not familiar with our neighbors. We may not even know their first names. It was different when we were growing up. We knew our neighbors, and borrowed things like milk or eggs from them.

Now is a good time to establish positive relations with your neighbors. During the possible Year 2000 crisis ahead, these neighbors will be your greatest allies.

No man is an island. By pooling assets, talents, strengths, etc. we can all do a lot better. From a psychological standpoint it is less stressful in larger groups as opposed to smaller ones. For more detailed information on this topic, refer to Chapter 11, on Community.

Personal Security

Most of us are generous and compassionate people. We want to help and assist others who are in need. Yet, in a Y2K emergency situation, such generosity could have negative repercussions. Remember, your first obligation is to provide for your dependants.

When faced with only enough food for your immediate family, do you turn others away? Do you turn away friends and neighbors, who have nothing to eat?

Mull this over for a few minutes—ask other family members for their opinions. Chances are you'll get many different answers, and you may even change your own mind a few times. It will be best to store extra food and water with the understanding that it is dedicated to feeding the hungry.

During the Great Depression, the needy knocked at doors with empty hands, asking for handouts. After Y2K, we may be faced with armed visitors demanding to be fed! There are any number of possibilities that may arise during the emergencies we may face in the aftermath of Y2K.

Hopefully such social disruptions will not be the case. Yet, it is better to be ready than sorry. It is prudent to plan now for these situations, rather than being forced to make difficult decisions under pressure. A possible plan of action includes:

- Think twice before accommodating strangers.
- If alone, never let more than one person approach your door.
- Be ready to defend yourself.
- Don't wear jewelry.
- Never feed the same person two days in a row—to encourage them to find other sources.
- Forbid those you feed to tell others of your generosity.
- Require labor in return for each meal.
- Do not feed strangers inside your home.
- Make exceptions to these rules for the elderly and infirm.

These are suggestions. Create your own guide. Talk over your plan with your immediate family, and come up with your own list of rules. If carefully thought out, it will cover most situations.

HOME SECURITY

Securing your home is important even when there is sufficient police protection. What if you didn't have the police services you are accustomed to? Would you feel secure in your home? Due to power outages, Y2K may limit communications for a time. Ask yourself, "Is my home adequately protected and secure as it stands?" Probably not. The answer will become clearer as you continue.

Home security doesn't happen by chance. Adequate home security takes time and effort, requires cooperation of all family members, and requires some investment.

The first step in any successful security program is to conduct a careful and thorough security survey of your premises. Make sure your home is not easy pickings for a burglar.

The following five elements make up a successful home security program:
- Adequate barriers to entry
- A security room for family retreat
- An alarm system or watch dog
- Avoiding attracting the attention of burglars
- Keeping in close contact with neighbors

Good locks are the key to home security. Evaluate the protection afforded by your current locks. Are there any noticeable gaps between the jamb and the door? A noticeable gap allows a would-be thief to pry open your door!

Home Fortification

Prepare a security plan by assessing your home and surrounding environment looking for vulnerable points of entry. Remove any bushes or trees which might provide cover for anyone attempting to break in. Make sure basement windows are protected with gratings or metal guards. If you have a sliding patio door, secure it with a charley bar or extra throw bolt.

Install peephole viewers in all entry doors so that you can see visitors without them seeing you. We particularly like the Door

Scope which allows for a 132° field of horizontal view. It projects a true image, and comes in plastic or aluminum. We purchased one from a local locksmith for $33. A similar product called the Security Door Viewer retails for $20. It fits door sizes of 3/4 in. to 2 in., has a field of view of 136°, and gives you a clear image of your visitor from up to 7 ft. away. It can be purchased through D-Mail at 800-686-1722, or on the Internet at:

http://www.d-mail.com

For dog lovers, a reliable watchdog is good to have. Watchdogs alert you that strangers are present, keep away unwanted guests, and can even keep you warm on cold nights.

In summary, your home will be relatively safe in an emergency if all of your doors have been inspected and have dead-bolt locks; all windows are secured and latched at night; there is adequate exterior lighting, especially in the rear; all glass panel doors and basement windows are protected with metal guards; and there is an effective burglar alarm system, 24 hour watch (family member), or a dependable watchdog. Develop a routine and these things will become an established habit.

Personal Defense

Self-defense is our right. It is something guaranteed to us through the law. We depend on our system of laws, through our local police protection, to see to it that our rights are not violated.

Y2K infrastructure problems could be catastrophic. These disruptions could create social unrest, even chaos. Power outages and other disasters have caused panic in the past, and we can expect the same from Y2K. These possibilities continue to be evaluated by the governments of many nations. Martial law is even being considered as an emergency means of maintaining law and order during Y2K.

With the possible loss of communications and contact with police through 911 calls, we must plan for our personal protection.

Firearms

Firearms are one of many self-defense options available. This is an area of great controversy. Whether or not to have them is a decision which only you can make, according to your conscience. Discuss the topic with your spouse and family. There are very good arguments which are made on both sides of gun ownership.

For those opting to acquire firearms, become well versed in their proper maintenance and safe storage. Purchase a gun locker or safe and always utilize gun trigger locks. Safely store ammunition in locked containers. Get professional training in the proper use of firearms.

Karen Anderson's website "Y2K Women" provides a balanced perspective on gun ownership.

http://www.y2kwomen.com

Non-Lethal Defenses

There are a variety of non-lethal self defense options available.

Martial arts: Consider taking some basic classes in the art of self-defense. Many colleges and community centers such as the YMCA offer classes on basic self-defense or various martial arts such as Karate, Tae Kwon Do, Judo, Jui Jitsu, Tai Chi or Kung Fu.

Aikido is a martial art which strives to defend without causing any harm. Aikido demonstrates the ideal defensive strategy and goal, to render your attacker helpless without killing or injuring him, but keeping yourself and others safe.

Certain protective devices are designed to protect you without permanently injuring an attacker. Before purchasing any self-defense product, ask the manufacturer if it is legal in your state.

Stun guns: Stun guns render an assailant temporarily incapacitated by overriding the nervous system. Neuromuscular control is lost for about 1/2 hour, but no permanent harm is caused. Stun guns are relatively inexpensive.

The Stun Master, touted as one of the most powerful stun guns on the market, powered by two 9-volt batteries to deliver 300,000 volts, is safe, effective, and non lethal. The Stun Master sells for $36.

The Muscle Man 400K Super Stun Gun delivers 400,000 volts and costs $60.

Both are available from Freeman Marketing, 888-GO-STUNGUN, which sells a variety of non-lethal self defense products at inexpensive prices.

http://www.freeman-mkt.com/toc.htm

Air Tasers: A form of remote stun-gun is the Air Taser. It eliminates the need to be in direct contact with an assailant. Such proximity may not be healthy.

The Air Taser is available from Freeman Marketing for $125 after rebate. It requires a supply of compressed air cartridges.

Pepper spray: Large aerosol cans of oleoresin capsicum pepper spray are available which are big enough to stop a grizzily bear. Pepper spray is more effective than Mace, and would be helpful in close encounters of the defensive kind. Available from Freemen Marketing starting at $10.

Shomer-Tec, 360-733-6214, supplies law-enforcement and military equipment. They sell a variety of self-defense items.

U.S. Cavalry, 888-88USCAV, also sells self-defense items.

http://www.uscav.com

Loompanics Unlimited Publishing Co., 800-380-2230, offers a website catalog with many books addressing self-defense.

http://www.olympus.net/egi-form

Asset Protection

The protection of personal property will present greater challenges during a period of Y2K disruptions than we would normally face. As stated, we may not have reliable police protection. People not normally inclined to theft might be pressured by necessity into seeking out others' goods. Finally, valuable assets usually stored in banks and safe deposit boxes are likely to be found in private homes during Y2K.

Asset Storage Strategies

Your safety and security depends on several factors; the foremost is, "Tell no man!" Don't discuss your purchases. However, be sure someone knows what and where your assets are in case you are incapacitated. This information should be limited to your inner circle and family. Make a list of your assets with their location and keep the list in a separate, secured area.

Second, make it difficult to locate your assets and remove them. Here are three strategies for storing your valuables:

1. Keep them in a bank vault or private repository. This is very secure. However, there is a monthly or annual storage fee and your belongings are not always available when you want them.

Bank vaults have timers which open on set schedules. If Y2K knocks out the microprocessor controlling the timer, the door won't open. If the power goes out, the bank or repository won't open. If there are runs on the banks and they close or are closed by the government, you are out of luck.

2. Keep your commodities in a safe owned by a friend, a business associate, or your lawyer.

3. Store your hard cash on your own property in a safe or secure hiding spot. There are many relatively secure areas in your home. A burglar will usually only stay in your home for from 10 to 30 minutes, as the risk of his detection rises with his length of stay.

Make it difficult for a robber to find your cache. Valuables such as jewelry, rare coins, gold and silver coins and bullion, cash, etc., should not be stored solely in a safe. That might sound foolish, but if burglars break into your home, that would be the first place they'll look.

There are myriad hiding places in the average home. They may be any place that is out of the way and difficult to access. For example, good hiding places are:

- Air returns in a forced air heating system, if the valuables are out of sight within them, and they don't excessively block the passage of air back to the furnace
- Fake air intakes which may be cut into the wall and covered with an additional wall plate; if located behind or under furniture, they are especially inconspicuous
- Fake electrical outlets cut into the drywall and covered with plugs and a wall plate. Be sure not to use or modify a live outlet due to the risk of electrocution (Nitro-Pak sells a Hidden Wall Outlet safe for $9)
- Behind the kickboards under cabinets
- In the dead space under furniture, such as under a heavy bookcase or the entertainment center
- Behind baseboards
- Under floorboards or stair treads
- Inside a furnace cabinet
- Underneath a refrigerator or washing machine
- Inside a water heater which has been cut open for access and appears to be in use
- Behind a false rear wall in your closet which is covered over with wallpaper
- Behind a false front covering the space under the bottom steps of your stairwell

- Inside hollowed-out furniture or other items
- Coins taped individually underneath furniture with heavy duct tape

Another idea is to bury your valuables in PVC pipe sections. Use a section of 4 in. PVC pipe no longer than 24 in. Affix a cap to one end with PVC cement. Attach a screw-top cap to the other end and cement it in place. Take the threaded portion of the cap out and place the pipe section in an oven set to the lowest setting for about 15 minutes, to dry out the air within it. When dry, add the valuables, cover the threads with Teflon thread tape, and screw in the threaded cap.

This sealed time capsule will withstand moisture and keep the contents safe. Bury it about 3 ft. down and plant a bush over it for concealment and to mark its location. Be sure to mark the exact spot as measured from known landmarks in the area. Keep a copy of the location information with your list of valuables in a secure place. Those searching for your cache may use a metal detector, so bury an old alternator or similar junk metal over it, to deter them. Several similar junk metal deposits in the surrounding area helps to discourage detection.

The possibilities are endless. Call 800-BUY-COIN and Swiss America will send you a copy of their "Y2K CPR" newsletter. This outlines a list of strategies for keeping your belongings safe and secured on your property. A book which further details this issue is *How To Hide Anything* by Michael Connor for $12.

Safes

If you feel safer having your valuables in your home rather than in a bank's safety deposit box, consider acquiring the ultimate protection, a safe. Safes can be bolted to a wall or to the floor. Or, they can be hidden by burying them in a cement floor. Professional concealment construction builders are available in some metropolitan areas, who can make any size safe disappear in your home.

Safes are of two general types, those which are fire-resistant and those which are burglary-resistant. Composite safes combine both fire and burglary resistance in one unit.

Fire-resistant containers: Underwriters Laboratories tests and rates safes as being able to withstand a fire without letting the contents of the safe get hot enough to be damaged, or above 350° F. This generally means the safe can endure temperatures of an average house fire or 1200° F and keep the contents safe. Some fire safes are rated as being able to withstand temperatures up to 1850° F.

U.L. Class 350° F ratings for fire resistance are for durations of 30 minutes, 1 hour and 2 hours. Buy a safe rated for one hour or more if possible. Normally, house fires are put out quickly by municipal fire departments. Fire departments' response times may be delayed by Y2K communications problems, or their effectiveness diminished by loss of municipal water pressure.

Safes are also U.L. listed as having an impact rating and ability to withstand falls if floors collapse during a fire.

Lockable fire-resistant containers are sold by Sentry and other manufacturers. They can be purchased for as little as $30 from department stores. It's a good idea to store all valuable personal papers in a fire resistant box or safe.

Electronic Media Safes: Computer diskettes, CDs, cartridges and cassettes have a critical environment of 125° F and 80% humidity. Electronic media safes maintain that environment during a fire. Media coolers are insulated inserts which fit inside fire safes to further protect the contents.

Burglary-Resistant Safes: Underwriters Laboratories also lists safes as being burglary-resistant. Tool-resistant safes can withstand cutting with high-power drills and saws for periods of time before being breached. U.L. Ratings include Residential Security

Container (RSC), or being tool resistant for 15 minutes (TL-15) or 30 minutes (TL-30).

Floor safes are constructed to be buried in a solid floor. If buried in a basement floor and cemented in place, they become a permanent part of the home. They can be hidden as they are flush with the floor. Floor safes offer a measure of fire protection because of the concrete they are buried in. This fire protection factor can be increased by covering the top with bricks or concrete blocks.

Consider having a visible "decoy" safe containing some valuables, combined with a hidden floor safe containing most of your assets. This strategy will throw off many burglars, especially if the floor safe is well hidden and difficult to access.

Composite Safes: Safes which combine both fire and burglary resistance in one unit are called *composite safes*. Normal fire safes are thin-walled containers which can be broken with a sledge hammer. Composite safes have heavy, thick walls of dense metals.

Gun safes: A measure of burglary and fire protection is of fered by manufacturers of gun safes for the storage of rifles, handguns and ammunition. It is important to keep these items from children and criminals.

Cannon, Browning and American Security Products Co. sell gun safes. Many gun manufacturers offer a line of gun safes. Check with your local gun shop.

Safes typically cost several hundred dollars and weigh hundreds of pounds. A typical small composite safe costs about $1000 and weighs half a ton.

Safes can be purchased used, but they hold their value and the resale price is very near the cost of a new safe. Sometimes a safe can be purchased from an owner who is moving. We recently saw a used half-ton residential safe advertised for $300.

Some safe manufacturers are:

American Security Products Co., 800-421-6142
http://www.wbmkt.com/amsec/
Meilink, 800-MEILINK
http://www.fireking.com
Sentry, 800-828-1438
http://www.sentry-grp.com

In conclusion, establish alternatives for providing family safety in the areas of emergency communications, fire protection, self defense and valuables. Anticipate problem areas, and put responsive strategies in place. Practice emergency responses, so that you can act quickly and correctly in an emergency.

Being prepared will provide comfort to your family members. You will be glad that you took safety steps.

SAFETY CHECKLIST

Fire protection:

____ Prevent fires by eliminating fire hazards

____ Establish pre-fire planning

____ Conduct regular fire drills

____ Buy fire extinguishers

____ Buy battery-powered smoke and carbon monoxide detectors

____ Buy fire-escape ladders

Security planning:

____ Develop community safety and security plans

____ Develop personal security plans

____ Develop home security plans

Self defense:

____ Establish personal self-defense strategies

____ Get self-defense training

____ Buy non-lethal self-defense products

Home security:

____ Fortify your home

____ Store your assets safely

____ Cache valuables near your home

____ Buy a fire-resistant safe for paper assets

CHAPTER 6

Finances

A few months ago people were talking about seeing the light at the end of the tunnel. Now the only hope is keeping the world economy from total deterioration.

Jeffrey Garten
Dean, Yale School of Management

To get your assets safely through the troubled waters of Y2K, it's advisable to allocate your funds into diverse areas that are not vulnerable to computer or economic system failures. Because of its great dependency on computers, the financial infrastructure, including banks and the securities industry, is highly vulnerable to Year 2000 problems.

Daily, over $3 trillion in electronic payments is moved worldwide in millions of separate computerized transactions. Peter Miller, Chief Information Officer of the J.P. Morgan Company, testifying before the Senate Special Y2K Committee, said "The financial industry offers a perfect illustration of the enormous size, scope, and complexity of the problem. Finance today is a global business, where almost unimaginable sums of money are in a constant state of electronic flux, and interdependency is particularly acute given the networked nature of market participants."

As we've seen, computer glitches in one section of the industry can cascade to others. Assets held in banking institutions, invested in the stock market, or otherwise locked in the system could become temporarily inaccessible. In a worst-case scenario, some of these assets could be permanently lost. Consider the possibility that *your* funds might get locked-up or lost within the system.

HOW TO PREPARE YOUR FINANCES FOR Y2K

Most Y2K-savvy analysts agree that the first key to preserving your assets through the year 2000 and beyond is to increase your financial liquidity. *Liquidity* refers to how quickly your investments can be converted into cash.

How many steps does it take you to get access to the money you have invested in the financial system? The more steps there are between you and your cash, the greater chance a Year 2000 glitch will swallow up your assets.

If your money is in a bank account, it's a 1-step process:

1. You go to your bank, present a check or withdrawal slip to the teller, and receive your cash.

If your money is in a money market fund, it's a 3-step process:

1. You call the money market fund and ask it to mail a check to you or wire the money to your bank.

2. The money market fund sends your check or wire transfer.

3. You get the currency from your bank.

If your money is in the stock market or mutual fund, it's a 5-step process:

1. You call your stock market/mutual fund, tell the agent to sell shares and mail a check to you or wire the money to your bank.

2. The shares are sold.

3. Money from the sale is deposited to the brokerage account.

4. The brokerage sends your check or wire transfer.

5. You get the currency from your bank.

Y2K may erect obstacles between you and whatever cash you have locked up in the system after 1-1-2000. If we lose power, the phone lines shut down or the computers shut down, you may not be able to get your money.

If you go to your bank on January 3, 2000, and they say, "I'm sorry, but the computers are down, we can't access your account," that means you won't be able to get your cash out. No matter how long the computers are down—days, weeks, or months—that is how long you may have to wait for your money.

Experts agree, we may experience a temporary inability to access cash after December 31, 1999. Recommendations to withdraw extra money at the end of 1999 in preparation for this are so prevalent, the Federal Reserve has printed an additional $50 billion to meet the expected demand for cash. For many people, advice to have extra cash on hand before the New Year translates into concern for the ongoing safety of their funds in the system.

This leads us to the second key to preserve assets in the midst of possible Y2K-induced problems—*minimize financial risk.* As global economic turmoil increases and the Y2K deadline draws nearer, financial risk evolves. What was financially secure yesterday may not be so today or tomorrow.

Today, investments in the stock market are being looked at as too risky for comfort. The threat of possible Y2K computer glitches, plus collapsing world markets, intensifies this risk.

The stock market is not the only investment vehicle which assumes an aura of risk. To a growing number of people studying the Year 2000 problem, even banks look suspect. Recent surveys show that the possibility of inaccessibility to or loss of funds is causing some depositors to consider pulling their money from bank accounts prior to 2000.

We agree with many financial analysts who recommend decreased exposure to the stock market and real estate, and increased holdings of short-term treasury bills, precious metals, and cash.

FOUR Y2K ASSET ALLOCATION PORTFOLIOS

Let's first look at the Y2K portfolio recommendations of four financial analysts, then examine practical steps to implement these recommendations. Their views represent different perspectives on protecting your assets from Y2K-induced disruptions.

Portfolio #1: Dr. Edward Yardeni

Dr. Yardeni, the Chief Economist and a Managing Director of Deutsche Morgan Grenfell Securities, North America, is widely regarded as the most knowledgeable of all Wall Street economists on the Y2K issue. At his popular web site, you can download free copies of his *Y2K Netbook,* and other valuable information.

      http://www.yardeni.com

Dr. Yardeni calls himself an optimist, but also an alarmist on the Y2K problem. He predicts a Y2K-induced global recession with a 30% drop in stock prices. His recommended portfolio, at the time of this writing, includes the least amount of liquidity of the four. Yardeni believes there will be a great economic recovery starting in 2001, and that the Dow could reach a record 15,000 by 2005.

Cash *(currency, multiple deposits, money market, gold coins)* 25%
Government Securities *(1-10 year maturities)* 40%
Equities *(U.S. and Europe, blue chip stocks)* 15%
Speculative Assets *(equity puts, zero-coupon bonds,*
              commodity shorts) 20%
Risky Assets *(emerging markets, real estate, commodities)* 0%

Dr. Yardeni states that this is just one of many possible model portfolios. It is based on a 70% chance of a global recession in 2000. No assurances about performance are given.

Details about Dr. Yardeni's financial recommendations can be obtained at his website, listed above.

Portfolio #2: Thomas Cloud

Thomas Cloud is Chairman of the Board of Cloud and Associates Consulting, Inc., established in 1977. Under Cloud's direction, this financial planning and tangible assets firm pays close attention to developments on the Y2K front.

As of this writing, this is their recommended asset allocation model.

Stocks *(U.S.)* .... 15% to 20%
Gold Mining Stocks 5%
Fixed Income *(bonds and annuities)* .... 40% to 50%
Foreign Currency *(foreign bonds, Swiss Annuities,*
        and global CD's) ....5% to 15%
Tangible Assets *(precious metals, gemstones,*
        and historical documents) .... 15% to 20%
Cash .... 10% to 20%
Real Estate 0%

While the above asset allocation model is designed to help balance risk and give investors security, C&A strongly recommends you consult with your personal financial advisor before making any type of change to your financial portfolio.

For specific information regarding the above portfolio allocation model, contact Cloud and Associates by phone at 770-642-6702, or by e-mail at cloudtgl@mindspring.com.

Portfolio #3: Randy Flink

Randy Flink founded Championship Financial Advisors in 1991. His is one of the elite corps of Y2K-aware financial planning firms able to assist clients to position their assets for the Year 2000.

Flink's Y2K financial recommendations can be found in articles on the *Y2KWatch* website.

http://y2kwatch.com

For details on Flink's Year 2000 asset allocation model, see his Internet article "Y2K Personal Insurance, Part A: Financial Assets."

http://y2kwatch.comshowart.php3?idx=81&rtn=y2kman.htm

Flink can be reached via e-mail at clientservices@championshipfinancial.com, or by fax at 214-365-6016.

Heaviest Weighting
• **U.S. Treasuries** *(emphasize short-term, then intermediate-term)*

Modest Weighting
• **Precious metals bullion** *(larger denominations; emphasize gold, then platinum)*
• **Short positions in individual stocks or indices**
• **Numismatic Mint State gold and silver coins**

Smaller Weightings
• **U.S. banknotes** *($10, $20, $50, $100 bills)*
• **Precious metals bullion** *(smaller denominations; emphasize gold, then silver)*
• **Semi-numismatic U.S. gold coins** *($20 Saint-Gaudens and $20 Liberty gold pieces)*
• **Semi-numismatic foreign gold coins** *(British Sovereigns and Swiss Helvetias)*
• **Long positions in recession-resistant stocks or commodities** *(avoid mutual funds)*

Portfolio #4: Donald McAlvany

For the past 20 years, Donald McAlvany has edited the *McAlvany Intelligence Advisor,* a monthly geopolitical financial intelligence newsletter. McAlvany is president and owner of International Collector's Associates, a 24 year securities, precious metals brokerage, and consultation firm serving clients in over 20 countries.

McAlvany's Y2K asset portfolio recommends the highest degree of liquidity of the four models. In his November 1998 newsletter, he advocated getting 100% out of the stock market, including U.S. and foreign stocks as well as equity mutual funds, "unless you are a speculator who is shorting the market on rallies or are speculating in a fund that shorts the market." His only exception is holding a 5% to 10% position in gold stocks.

Semi-Numismatic Gold Coins 25-35%
Bags of Junk Silver .... at your discretion
Cash .... 3-6 months supply
Short Term T-Bills or T-Bill Money Market Funds
    (180 days or less) .... at your discretion
Real Estate .... reduce to no more than 25% of portfolio
Barterable Goods .... at your discretion
Stocks *(U.S. and foreign, equity mutual funds)* 0%
Out of Debt .... *(reduce debt to zero, or as close as possible ASAP)*

For more information on McAlvany's economic news and information, call 800-528-0559, e-mail mcalvany@indirect.com, or visit his web site.

http://www.mcalvaney.com

HOW LIQUID SHOULD YOUR FINANCES BE?

After looking at these four sample portfolios, you may be wondering how to reconfigure your own finances in preparation for Y2K. What changes should you make to your current asset allocation model, to increase its odds of surviving the economic upheavals ahead?

As we saw in the earlier chapter on planning, all such decisions are based on your personal assessment of the level of risk from the Year 2000 problem you're likely to face. Having weighed all the evidence, do you feel the computers will be fixed in time? Are you confident the phones will stay in service? Do you believe your money will be safe where it is? Should you make some changes to your investments, just in case?

The above sample portfolios reflect varying levels of assessed risk. For example, Ed Yardeni predicts a 70% chance of a global recession. His recommended portfolio continues to be heavily weighted in government securities, equities, and speculative assets which he believes will survive a recession.

On the other hand, Don McAlvany expects a global financial meltdown. He advises total escape from the stock market, with minimal holdings in short term treasury bills as his most illiquid recommendation.

A clear illustration of the impact of risk assessment upon a Y2K financial portfolio was given in the *Y2K Weatherman Report #65,* a posting from the free Y2K-News e-mail service provided by:

http://y2kwatch.com

In this report, finance consultant and Y2K news columnist Randy Flink was asked, "If banks and communications are disrupted, how do you convert treasury bills into cash?"

Flink responded: "The Y2K Personal Insurance Plan does not assume that Y2K disruptions will result in the total collapse of our financial system. Rather, the Y2K Personal Insurance Plan is designed to give you a balance of safety and liquidity in anticipation of a serious recession or depression triggered (or prolonged) by Y2K disruptions.

"The task of converting your entire portfolio of financial assets to banknotes, precious metals bullion and/or an array of barter items is gargantuan," Flink continued, "but is something you should undertake if you think Y2K will collapse the present financial system."

Flink explained further, no matter what the various financial analysts recommend, your personal assessment of the level of risk posed by Y2K is the determining factor in deciding how to position your funds for the eventualities ahead.

If you believe Y2K will be only a bump in the road, leave your money right where it is, with minor adjustments. But if you believe the Year 2000 may precipitate a total collapse in global markets, including the United States, your comfort zone might demand you cash in your chips on Wall Street and hunker down with hard assets in hand.

The information in this chapter is designed to help you make the necessary decisions to position your finances to survive whatever economic instability may come. We recommend you seriously ponder these strategies, and contact financial professionals for any additional advice you may need. When all is said and done, you alone must decide how to position yourself financially for Y2K.

DEFENSIVE FINANCIAL POSITIONING FOR Y2K

The most important financial considerations for Y2K have to do with protecting your assets. This we call *defensive financial posturing*. Defensive posturing is not designed to make additional money. It is designed to protect and sustain the assets you currently own. Y2K also creates opportunity for return on investments. This will be considered later in this chapter.

For on-line information on defensive asset allocation strategies in preparation for Y2K, see Jim Lord's Westergaard 2000 *Y2K Tip of the Week* articles #25, 26, 27, 28, 31, 32, 42, and 55:

http://www.y2ktimebomb.com/Tip/Lord/index.htm

The Y2K-aware investment professionals listed in this chapter can provide you with information to assist in making your personal asset allocation decisions.

We'll begin our look at defensive positioning by discussing what to do about stock market investments.

Stocks and Mutual Funds

To cash in your chips, or not to cash in your chips, that is the question. In November 1998, a friend confided to us he'd lost $40,000 in the stock market in the preceding few months. Shocked, we told him, "Thank God you got out before you lost everything!" "Oh, I'm not getting out now," he said. "I'm staying in to recoup what I lost!"

Obviously, he's not alone in his strategy. As of this writing, the market is rallying. On November 23, the Dow hit a record 9374.27. The Detroit News reported, "Market surges 214.72 points as mergers, megadeals sweep away summer slump."

The debate is on as to what the stock market will do. Is a bear market growling around the corner, or are we just experiencing temporary market corrections?

In a July poll, 55 of 55 economists surveyed said the odds of a recession or that the stock market would enter a bearish phase are slim. The public remains bullish. *Time* magazine reported that even if the boom is over, "stocks remain your best bet for long-term security." *U.S. News* stated in its September 14 issue that a bear market might be in the works, but emphasized "the danger of abandoning buy and hold."

On the other side of the fence, by late fall, several respected financial analysts were convinced we'd entered a bear market. Historical cycles prove it can take up to a year to break the bullish sentiment after a new bear market commences. In his November 1998 newsletter, Don McAlvany noted "today's investors, who have been pampered in the sheltering arms of a 24-year bull market, have no respect for the speed at which a bear market can ravage one's savings."

It's your choice to stay in or get out of the market. Your decision should be based on your personal assessment of the level of risk. Y2K brings yet another dimension of risk to the stock market equation. Jim Lord addressed this added Y2K dynamic in his book, *A Survival Guide For the Year 2000 Problem.* "The real problem with leaving your money in the stock market...is the fact that the marketplace itself could collapse or experience terrible disruptions due to Y2K-related problems in the vast computer systems used to operate the market."

Today's stock market volumes often exceed 500 million shares daily. Each transaction involves several computer systems, including that of the buyer, the stockbroker, the stock exchange, the buyer's bank, the stockbroker's bank, and the stock exchange's bank. Alan Greenspan, head of the Federal Reserve, admits that in the financial sector, there must be 100 percent accuracy to prevent collapse. It's hard to believe Y2K could come and go without serious disruptions to the stock market.

Most Year 2000 analysts recommend limiting your exposure to the stock market. Of our four sample portfolios, three suggest holding a small to modest amount of stocks as we approach the new millennium; the fourth advises no exposure to the market.

Admittedly, getting out of stocks is a difficult concept to grapple with. If you are heavily invested in the stock market, and have made substantial money over the past several years, you may be reluctant to give up this earning potential. You may also be reluctant to incur the capital gains tax.

You have to weigh the risk, and decide if it's worth the reward. Are you willing to risk losing part or all of your investment by taking the chance to reap whatever gains might be in store?

Bonds

There are four major types of bonds, or fixed-income securities: corporate bonds, municipal bonds, government agency securities, and U.S. Treasury issues. Issues of the U.S. Treasury are considered the safest of any investment because they are backed by the "full faith and credit" of the U.S. Government. If you are positioning your assets for greatest survivability through the year 2000 and beyond, many believe it is best to hold no other bonds but U.S. Treasury issues.

Of the three forms of Treasury issues—T-bills, notes, and bonds—T-bills are the safest and most liquid. In fact, they are deemed to be the safest and most liquid investment vehicle in the world. Because of this, T-bills are often recommended to those preparing their finances for Y2K.

Two of our sample investment portfolios, those of Randy Flink and Don McAlvany, emphasize T-bills for Y2K asset allocation. In his November newsletter, McAlvany advised: "Put conservative funds in short-term Treasury bills or T-bill money market funds—180 days or less...very short-term T-bills are your safest bet—unless the Fed/Treasury bailout ignites a super or hyperinflation—in which case, exit the T-bills."

Purchased at a minimum face value of $10,000, these short-term securities are issued in maturities of three, six, and twelve months. T-bills offer an alternative investment vehicle for those getting out of the stock market, who don't feel comfortable putting their assets in First Federal Mattress.

While they are the safest and most liquid of all forms of bonds, redeeming T-bills for cash still entails multiple steps relying on functioning phones, computers, banks, and possibly the postal system as well. All of these are vulnerable to Y2K glitches.

To liquidate T-bills, you must first contact either the Federal Reserve or the brokerage firm holding them. After placing your redemption order, normally there is a three-day turn-around time to receive your money. You will be mailed a check, or your bank account will be credited with the cash value of the liquidated securities. Finally, you'll go to your financial institution and cash the check you received, or withdraw the cash deposited to your account.

In the event Y2K glitches cause disruptions to the infrastructure or the financial sector, it might be difficult or impossible to redeem your T-bills—at least temporarily. Also keep in mind the Treasury Department, issuer of these securities, is one of the Federal agencies consistently rated behind schedule in pursuing its Y2K repairs. Of the four report cards issued by Senator Horn this year, grading 24 U.S. agencies' Y2K efforts, Treasury received two "Ds" and two "Cs."

If you consider this an unacceptable level of risk, you might want to opt for a more liquid investment vehicle.

Real Estate Holdings

The value of real estate in the form of homes and property is presently at an all-time high in this country. This value is determined by what home buyers are currently willing to pay. In a financial downturn, the value of real estate will drop. As the market weakens, there will be fewer people willing and able to buy. David Elliott discusses this in his book, *Everyone's Guide to Making a Million Dollars on the Year 2000 Crash:* "The market collapse of 1929 and the market correction of 1987 taught many valuable lessons about real estate: any large correction in the stock market reflects negatively on the real estate market."

Many Y2K analysts advise selling all real estate except for your home. Some recommend selling all urban real estate, and holding only a rural retreat. Their strategy is—since property values will likely plunge, take the money now and reallocate it to a more secure position.

None of our sample portfolios recommend holding any real estate beyond your own home.

Bank/Credit Union Accounts, Certificates of Deposit

The question of whether or not to leave your money in your local bank or credit union goes to the heart of the Y2K issue. There is nothing inherently risky about these financial institutions. Millions of people keep some or all of their assets on deposit in them. You probably do too. And until Y2K came along, you probably never gave it a second thought.

What is making a growing number of people begin to think twice about the safety of their accounts in the face of Y2K? Recently, we sat down with the branch manager of our local credit union, where we have our own checking and savings accounts. We were surprised at how frank and open he was. He admitted that while he and his colleagues were doing all in their power to bring the credit union into Y2K-compliance, there were simply no guarantees of success. If even one of his vendors didn't complete their own repair work, the credit union could be brought to its knees.

Banking is one of the most computerized industries in the world today. On its Year 2000 web site, the Federal Reserve Board states "90% of all bank assets are electronic entries in data bases and virtually all bank transactions involve electronic processing." As Fed Chairman Alan Greenspan said, "in the financial services industry, 99% readiness for the Year 2000 will not be enough. It must be 100%."

Quite simply, it's a roll of the dice. Without a crystal ball, we just can't know what will happen. While many industry spokesmen claim that the financial sector is on track with their Y2K repairs, no institution to date has issued a written statement guaranteeing its computers will continue to function error-free, and its doors will remain open into the new millennium.

Some people are deciding that the level of risk involved in leaving their money in the bank is higher than they can tolerate. A number of surveys taken in 1998 showed that many people are giving serious thought to withdrawing their funds. In one study, 25% of those polled said they plan to withdraw most or all of their cash sometime in 1999; 52% said they will "move their money around." Another poll revealed seven out of ten people plan to take their cash out before 2000.

Later, we'll discuss withdrawing cash from the bank.

Money Market Mutual Funds

A money market mutual fund is similar to the money market account available through your bank. Here again, you have to remember that your money is tied up within a computer network, and liquidating your funds to cash relies upon functional computers and banking institutions. Whether or not to leave your assets in a money market mutual fund is a personal decision.

Precious Metals

You're probably not as familiar with trading in gold, silver, and platinum as you are with stocks, bonds, and mutual funds. Our own crash course in precious metals began when we started to prepare for Y2K.

There are several ways to invest in precious metals, such as owning individual mining stocks, precious metals mutual funds, precious metals bullion, and jewelry. In this section, we'll discuss the purchase of bullion, specifically gold and silver coins.

Financial experts have long recommended precious metals as an excellent way to diversify your financial portfolio. Historically, precious metal bullion maintains its purchasing power in hard times. Both gold and silver coins are good choices for Y2K asset reallocation, as they will hold their value when stocks, bonds, and other assets decline. And, if the financial transaction system breaks down, gold and silver coins are a natural choice for use as money.

For straight investment purposes, you can purchase bulk gold and silver bullion coins, coin-like "rounds," and bars. For use as an alternative form of money to purchase small items on a day to day basis, you need small denomination bullion coins and rounds.

Ordinary bullion coins are minted in mass quantities, and are priced at slightly over the spot, or current precious metal price, to cover the cost of minting. Numismatic and semi-numismatic coins are older, limited quantity coins. These are priced according to their condition of wear. We recommend buying ordinary bullion coin rather than numismatics. In a barter situation, people will care about the bullion value of the precious metal coins, not their rarity or mint condition.

At current gold prices just under $300 per ounce at the time of this writing, a 1 oz. gold coin costs about $23 over the spot price. Smaller fractional coins are a bit higher due to additional minting costs. For example, a 1/2 oz. gold coin represents just over $150, 1/4 oz. just over $75, and a 1/10 oz. coin about $35.

At current spot price just over $5 per ounce, a 1 oz. silver Eagle coin, priced about $1.75 over spot, is worth $7. Junk silver coins—pre-1965 previously circulated 90% silver dimes, quarters, and half dollars—are currently worth about five times their face value. At the current spot price, a bag of junk silver coins, consisting of coins totalling $1000 face value—approximately 720 oz. of silver—sells for about $5000.

Silver is much bulkier than gold. An amount of silver coins worth $10,000 fills three large shoeboxes and weighs almost 100 lbs. Gold coins valued at $10,000 fit in the palm of your hand. However, smaller denomination silver coins will buy a loaf of bread or a quart of milk more easily. Gold stores more efficiently, silver spends more conveniently.

If the present financial transaction system breaks down, gold and silver coins could easily supplement our currency supply. Therefore we feel it's advisable to have a supply on hand. In the December 1998 Market Update newsletter from Cloud and Associates Consulting, Thomas Cloud wrote,

"C&A recommends investors hold somewhere between two to six months of barter coins in an amount equal to what it costs your family to live monthly. I believe the first round of barter protection will be physical cash and I recommend holding cash to meet short term needs (i.e., from two to six weeks) if there are interruptions in the banking, telecommunication, or brokerage communities. If there are interruptions with check cashing or credit card use, physical cash will be mandatory. If problems persist for any long term, the shift will go to precious metals. This was the case during the 1990's for Chili, Argentina, Bolivia, and Brazil."

Gold and silver bullion coins are considered the best insurance against a Y2K-ignited economic catastrophe. With an eye on using your precious metals bullion as an alternative form of money, Randy Flink advises sticking to "highly familiar" gold and silver coins. For those of us in North America, that means coins minted in the U.S. and Canada.

The best gold coins for us to use as money would be American Eagles and Canadian Maple Leafs in the 1 oz. and fractional denominations of 1/2 oz., 1/4 oz., and 1/10 oz. Recommended silver bullion coins include 1 oz. American Eagles and Canadian Maple Leafs, or generic 1 oz. silver rounds printed by private mints. These cost about $1 per coin less to purchase. You should also buy bags of junk silver coins to serve as fractional denominations since silver coins smaller than 1 oz. are not currently minted.

If you can afford it, we recommend holding $5,000 (purchase value) in coins, half in gold and half in silver, for each member of your family. Buy 3/4 bag of junk silver and 35 1/10 oz. gold American Eagle coins per person. For a family of four, purchase three bags of junk silver and 140 1/10 oz. gold American Eagles. This would cost approximately $20,000 at current spot prices.

If you can't afford this, don't despair. The most important thing is to begin preparing, however you are able. As discussed in Chapter 1, prioritize your Y2K preparations as your finances allow. First budget for stored food, water, warm clothing, and vital medications. If you are able, next concentrate on accumulating a three-month reserve of cash on hand. Then, if your resources allow, begin purchasing precious metal coins.

On a smaller precious metals budget, start buying gold and silver coins as your finances allow. As stated, 1 oz. silver Eagles or silver rounds cost $7; 1/10 oz. gold Eagles cost about $35. Split your investment equally between gold and silver coins.

If you have more than $20,000 to convert to precious metals, consider 1 oz. Krugerrands, Maple Leafs, or American Eagles. At current spot price, these sell for about $330 each. When converting large amounts of money, focus on gold rather than silver. Remember, $10,000 in gold coins can be carried and stored easily.

To purchase bullion coins, look in your Yellow Pages under

"Coin Dealers." Out-of-state suppliers, if they don't reside in a bordering state, won't charge you sales tax. The shipping fees will be a small fraction of the amount you'd spend on taxes. A bag of junk silver can be shipped for $55. One oz. to 15 oz. of gold can be shipped for $10.00, and is insured by the seller.

We recommend you contact precious metals dealers who understand the Y2K equation. If you use a local bullion coin distributor, be sure to use a wholesaler, not a retailer; retail prices are higher. Call several dealers for quotes. Compare prices and go with the lowest. Join with others and buy in bulk for volume discounts.

Following is a list of precious metals distributors; the contact individuals have expertise in Y2K financial preparations. Tell them you got their number from *Y2K—It's Not Too Late.*

Blanchard, contact Paul Thurber
888-332-4653, http://www.blanchardonline.com
Franklin Sanders
901-853-6136, http://www.the-moneychanger.com
Golden Eagle, contact Pat Wojahn
800-447-7911
Investment Rarities Inc., ask for Dept. C
800-328-1860, http://www.investmentrarities.com
Jefferson Coin and Bullion
800-593-2584, http://www.jeffinc.com
McAlvany's International Collectors Associates
800-525-9556, http://www.mcalvany.com
Monex, contact Arthur Levine
800-949-gold, ext. 2854, http://www.monex.com
North American Investment Services, contact Ron Brown
800-595-0561, naia@highfiber.com
SafeTrek Outfitters
800-424-7870, http://www.safetrek.com

Swiss America, contact Craig Sallas
800-BUY-COIN, http://www.buycoin.com

Cash on Hand

Experts advise having cash on hand December 31, 1999, in case Y2K glitches shut down ATMs and bank computers. No one knows how long the financial system could be disabled.

We recommend having three to six months' worth of cash readily available. This would allow you to pay bills and purchase goods even if you are unable to access money in your bank account, cash paychecks, or use credit cards.

Fractional reserve system, potential for bank runs

The U.S. banking system is called a *fractional reserve system.* This means that only a fraction of the actual cash value of the money supply is in circulation or on reserve. Think about your local bank account. Perhaps you've got $500 in your checking account, and $1000 in savings.

To take your money out of the bank, you present your withdrawal slip and receive cash. That doesn't mean the cash you previously deposited was sitting in the vault waiting for you. Neither are there little piles of cash for all the other bank depositors.

No bank—or any other type of financial institution—has in its vault the total amount of cash on deposit in its accounts. *For every $100 on deposit in our nation's banks, there is only $1.27 of actual cash on hand in the vaults.*

Customer deposits in U.S. bank accounts total $3.7 trillion. Individual banks hold about $47 billion in total reserves. What happens if all the people demanded their $3.7 trillion?

If all depositors decided to withdraw their money at once, only 1.27 percent of the people would get their cash, or each bank customer would get only $1.27 for every $100 on deposit.

The Fractional Reserve System

(U.S. dollars, rounded to nearest billion)

Total bank deposits .... $3,700 B
Total bank reserves .... $ 47 B

System Reserve Requirement
$47 B (reserves) ÷ $3,700 B (deposits) = 1.27%

- The system reserve requirement is 1.27%.

- If every depositor lined up at all the banks tomorrow and demanded all of their money, **1.27% of the people could get their money.**

- Alternatively, **all the people could get $1.27 for every $100 they have on deposit.**

Adapted from "The Weird Wonderful World of Fractional Reserve Banking" by Franklin Sanders, http://www.the-moneychanger.com/html/it_s_funny_money.html

The fractional reserve system works as long as people believe their money is safe in the banks. The Board of Governors of the Federal Reserve System—the Fed, America's central bank—agree "Trust, at the consumer level, is the foundation of the banking system."

A bank run occurs when people become worried their money is not safe in the bank, and withdraw so much money that the bank reserves can't meet the demand. If the lines at the teller windows and at the ATM machines get too long, the government could step in and impose a moratorium on withdrawals, and close the banks, as it did in 1933.

In an attempt to avoid this scenario, the Fed announced it's printed an extra $50 billion in cash, on top of the $150 billion it usually keeps on reserve for emergencies. If the banking system's on-hand reserves of $47 billion is not enough to meet withdrawal demand, the Fed will release their additional $200 billion reserve to meet the need.

This is the first time the Fed has planned for a nationwide demand for extra cash. They're not the only central bank doing so—the governments of Australia, New Zealand, England, and Canada are also printing extra cash to meet expected heavy pre-Y2K demand within their countries.

Yet this extra printed currency may be only a drop in the bucket. Analysts have shown there is only one month's supply of currency per household available in our nation's vaults, even with the extra money being printed. If enough people try to draw out more than their one month's share of the total reserve, it could empty the vaults.

$2,470 Available Per Household
(U.S. dollars, rounded to nearest billion)

Bank reserve ....$ 47 B
FED reserve (includes extra $50 B) ....$200 B
Total bank reserves ....$247 B

Total U.S. households .... 100 million

Bank Reserves Available Per Household
$247 B ÷ 100 million = $2,470 per household

Since the average household income in the U.S. is $34,000 per year, this reserve will provide one month's spending.

Adapted from Gary North's website, http://www.garynorthcom/y2k/detail_.cfm/2367 and http://www.garynorthcom/y2k/detail_.cfm/2694

As you can see, the probability of bank runs is quite real. As public awareness of Y2K spreads, more and more people will grasp the potential for problems in the financial services industry, and consider withdrawing part or all their money from the banks.

At this point, you're thinking, "But what about the Federal Deposit Insurance Corporation? Since my money is in an FDIC-insured bank, even if bank runs do occur, my money is guaranteed safe. Isn't it?"

Indeed, of the $3.7 trillion on deposit with U.S. banks, $2.7 trillion is insured through the FDIC. But what does this mean? Will the federal government reimburse a potential $2.7 trillion lost during Y2K-precipitated bank closings?

Not exactly. According to the FDIC's Internet web page, as of the second quarter 1998, reserve ratios stood at 1.40 percent. Thus for every $100 you deposit in the bank, the FDIC has one dollar and forty cents to reimburse your potential loss.

The FDIC was set up to handle the failure of individual banks. It wasn't designed to bail out an overall system failure. It's predicted that 5% to 20% of U.S. banks could fail because of Y2K. That's more than 2,000 of the nation's 11,000 banks. *If banks containing 1.40% of total deposits fail, this could bankrupt the FDIC.*

Federal Deposit Insurance Corporation Reserves

Deposits insured by FDIC .... $2,700 B
FDIC total reserves *(as of 2nd quarter 1998)* .... $ 38 B

$38 B (reserves) ÷ $2,700 B (deposits) = 1.40% Reserve Ratio

- **For every $100 in the bank, the FDIC insures $1.40.**
- **If banks containing 1.40% of total deposits fail, the FDIC will be bankrupt.**

Adapted from "Y2KSupply.com Banking Chart," http://www.y2ksupply.com/fdicchart.htm. and "The FDIC Quarterly Banking Profile," http://www2.fdic.gov/qbp/1998jun/qbpall.html

The bottom line is, in today's financial system, there is a great disproportion between actual physical cash—dollars you can hold in your hand—and entries in the record books. This disproportion is comprised of money that exists in computer data bases but has no corresponding physical monetary counterpart.

Surveys revealing the plans of an increasing number of people to withdraw cash before 2000 have industry officials worried. Spokesmen in the financial sector seek to allay the public's fears that their money is unsafe by claiming the financial services industry is the farthest ahead of any in Y2K repair work. Others cite the tremendous potential for cascading failures throughout the system.

While the withdrawal of large quantities of cash could precipitate a bank run, the alternative for those who see the handwriting on the wall is to leave their cash in the system and lose it if Y2K failures occur. Most of us find it difficult to be this altruistic, given the facts as outlined in this chapter. As Dr. Reynolds Griffith, professor of finance, Stephen F. Austin University, Texas, stated, "I don't think that as individuals we should refrain from taking precautions just because there would be adverse effects if everyone did."

The final decision is yours. How much cash, if any, will you withdraw before the new year? If you decide to build a cash reserve, keep the following tips in mind.

Be aware of the reporting rules on currency withdrawals. A $10,000 withdrawal, or two or more withdrawals totalling $10,000 within a time span of six months, will put you on the IRS watch list. Reporting requirements are getting stricter. For more information on cash transaction reporting relative to Y2K, see Jim Lord's excellent on-line article:

http://y2ktimebomb.com/Tip/Lord/lord9849.htm

Also remember, sometime in 1999, Y2K awareness will begin to spread, and may turn into Y2K panic. Once panic occurs, bank

runs may not be far behind. With bank runs may come govern-
ment-mandated banknote rationing. If you plan to withdraw cash
in preparation for Y2K, start doing it now—before the lines form
at the ATMs.

Non-Financial Assets

Financial advisor Randy Flink believes "A portion of one's Financial Assets should be reinvested in Non-Financial Assets as a
means to insure survival and relative stability in a Y2K-battered
economy. The choice of Non-Financial Assets is a matter of personal perception, the amount invested dependent on one's level
of Y2K discomfort." The greater your perception of risk regarding Y2K, the more you may want to reallocate your assets.

Preparedness supplies: The money you spend purchasing
preparedness supplies—stored food, water purification equipment, heating and cooking stoves and fuels, and other goods—is
an investment in non-financial assets. Presently we value the equity in our homes, cars, and other consumer goods. In an emergency situation, preparedness supplies will have utmost worth.

Barterable goods: It's often said in Y2K circles, "hope for
the best, but plan for the worst." If the millennium bug impacts
checking accounts, credit cards, ATMs and financial institutions,
you could be in trouble. The value of the dollar could crash, and
there may not be enough money in circulation. In this worst case,
we would need an alternative exchange system. People will still
need to procure things they don't have, and not everyone will have
silver and gold as an alternative money supply

In this situation, barter—the exchange of goods and services
without using money—will emerge. Throughout history, the barter system has flourished. In 1600, the colonists in Massachusetts
used corn as legal tender. We've all heard the expression, "worth

his salt," which harks back to when salt was a precious barter item. To this day, the barter system is alive and well. It is commonly reported that 50% of Russia's economy is based on barter.

If there is a cash shortage, commodities will take on new value. People will start to trade for the goods and services they need.

Y2K analysts recommend stocking up on supplies which may take on value as barter items. Some of these are toilet paper, matches, Bic lighters, coffee, tea, sugar, salt, and ammunition, especially .22 caliber. Ideas for barter items can be found at:

http://www.ionet.net/~rbrocato.InventoryAndBarter Items.html

Y2K expert Paloma O'Riley of the Cassandra Project recommends the following web sites as source material on barter:

'Les French' (one of the oldest bartering networks)
http://www.lesfrench.com/html/tutorial.htm
'Trade World'
http://www.thetradeworld.com:80/flyer4.html
'The Barter Station' (provides barter services at no charge)
http://www.solutions-4u.com/barter/aboutbs.htm

Complete Financial Liquidity

The most radical asset allocation model is *complete financial liquidity.* You may want to consider this if your personal Y2K risk assessment makes it difficult for you to sleep at night as long as any part of your financial portfolio is locked in the electronic money system as we head into the year 2000.

Converting your entire financial portfolio to banknotes, precious metals, Y2K preparedness supplies, and barter items may be a big job, but it is possible. The most challenging part is deciding whether to cash out of CDs, 401(k) plans, IRAs, Keoghs, and other investments which impose a penalty for early withdrawal.

You'll have to decide if the cash in hand is worth the loss of some percentage of the funds.

If you plan to pursue complete financial liquidity, begin immediately. The closer we approach to the December 31, 1999 deadline date, the more difficult it might be to liquidate your assets. For assistance, contact the financial advisors listed in this chapter or seek other Y2K-aware financial consultants.

Caching Your Liquid Assets

If you choose to liquefy part or all of your assets, and acquire such valuable commodities as precious metals and extra amounts of cash, consider a method of safe storage. See Chapter 5, page 199 to 204, for information on safe storage of your liquid assets.

OPPORTUNITIES FOR RETURN ON INVESTMENTS

Y2K potentially threatens the global economy, but this crisis can be turned into an opportunity. Experts can make money regardless of whether the economy is going up or down, by employing different strategies for the different environments. You can too.

There are investment strategies which can make money from the Y2K situation, including Y2K and mining stocks, commodities futures, futures options, and leveraged precious metals purchases. But, for most of them, you have to be willing to take a chance. You could lose money.

Money invested in these or other strategies after 2000 is potentially at risk. If the phones are down, you won't be able to liquidate investments and take possession of your cash. We don't recommend leaving funds in high-risk investments after late 1999.

Y2K Stocks

If you plan to continue investing in the stock market, you may want to shift your investments to Y2K-related stocks. These are stocks in companies actively involved in repairing the Y2K problem, providing products and services to correct the software code vulnerable to the century date change problem.

A $600 billion market for Year 2000 conversions has been created practically overnight. As demand for their services has increased, stock in these companies has risen in value far beyond the national average. This demand for repairs will increase as we approach the Year 2000.

In his book *Everyone's Guide to Making a Million Dollars on the Year 2000 Crash*, David Elliott lists 44 Y2K stocks to watch. *The Year 2000 Crisis—An Investor's Survival Guide* by Tony Keyes lists 27. These companies are intensely traded and fluctuate like all stocks. They are also vulnerable to being pulled down in massive stock market "corrections" which can be expected in 1999.

There are two excellent web sites with information for the serious Y2K investor. Author Tony Keyes' site is located at:

http:/www.y2kinvestor.com/intro.html

Keyes and other investment analysts post on-line articles at the Westergaard Year 2000 website:

http:/www.y2ktimebomb.com/Investing/index.htm

Mining Stocks

Of the previously mentioned financial experts, McCloud and McAlvany both recommend investing from 5% to 10% of your assets in gold stocks. Gold stocks are equity shares in gold mining companies.

Invest in mining stocks by researching individual companies, or by investing in precious metal mutual funds. The precious metal funds invest broadly in gold, silver and platinum mining companies as well as the metals themselves. Both Keyes and Elliott list some precious metal mutual funds in their books.

Gold stocks are tied directly to the price of gold bullion and will jump if there is a financial panic or scramble for gold and other precious metals. This could begin as early as the second quarter of 1999, but could be delayed until as late as the last quarter of 1999. Gold stocks involve delayed gratification!

Commodities Futures

Raw materials futures contracts have been traded by producers and manufacturers on the commodities market for 150 years. Speculators, including many mutual funds, also use this market for profit.

All transactions in commodities futures are amplified. Investments of thousands of dollars can be parlayed into hundreds of thousands of dollars. The downside is, these markets are extremely volatile and require significant understanding and capital investment. You could just as easily lose all you've ventured, even go into debt due to your contractual agreements. If you choose to pursue commodities futures, be sure to study the subject and secure the services of an excellent broker.

Y2K dynamics will create driving forces for commodity prices. However, just when those forces will begin to impact the markets is unclear.

As long as there is deflation, the prices for precious metals and other raw materials will fluctuate within a narrow band with prices at near record lows. When shortages appear, there may be prolonged and significant pressure driving commodity prices up.

You might consider that the proper time to get into commodities purchases.

Futures Options

Options on futures are another layer of investing in commodities. They basically track the futures market and are bets that commodities will rise or fall by a certain amount. They are somewhat less volatile than the futures markets, but have a smaller profit potential. The commodities markets also offer futures and options on non-raw material items such as foreign currencies, bonds and indexes of bonds and stocks.

Puts and calls are purchases of commodity futures options. When buying calls, you are betting the future of a particular commodity or index will increase. With puts, you are betting value will fall. You can use put and call options with specific commodities such as silver, or with broad indicators like the Dow Jones Stock Index. Recently, for example, many investors have bought puts on the Dow Index, betting it will go down. If you think they will go up, buy call options on Y2K stock indexes or gold futures.

Just remember, futures and options are a zero sum game; for you to win, someone has to lose. This is a form of competitive gambling with experienced players. If you haven't done your homework, and even if you have, you may be the one who loses.

A reputable, professional commodity brokerage is Fox Investments in Chicago. Call 800-621-0265 and ask for their booklet entitled *Short Course in Futures and Options*.

Leveraged Precious Metals Purchases

If metals are increasing in price or you are confident they will in the near future, a leveraged precious metals purchase could earn you a significant gain.

Companies such as Monex can help you multiply your investment in precious metals by providing leverage in the form of loans. Their promotional material states, "Experienced investors know that the results of their investments can be amplified by using leverage. For example, if you were to invest only 20 percent of the full value of the metal and finance the remainder, the results of a price change relative to your investment is multiplied five times the equivalent of an all-cash purchase."

Broker Arthur Levine understands Y2K dynamics and can help you develop a Y2K strategy. He can be reached at the Monex Company, 800-949-GOLD, ext. 2854.

http://www.monex.com

The downside of this strategy is, you have to pay monthly repository storage and interest fees. To realize a profit, there must be a significant rise in the price of your commodity; if the price drops, you can end up owing money.

Leveraged precious metal purchases present an investment risk. We had a contract with Monex before deflation pulled the rug out from under precious metal prices, and were lucky to get our original investment back!

However, if the commodity you choose to leverage such as silver, gold or platinum jumps in price, your profits multiply dramatically. When the Y2K problem and related potential cash shortages become an issue for the average citizen, the price of silver and gold may shoot up.

By all logic, precious metals should do well in a Y2K scenario. But, only time will tell.

In summary, our financial assets underpin our sense of security. The threat of losing our monetary worth is among the most unsettling of thoughts. Many people have worked hard building up a nest egg, the loss of which would be catastrophic.

Consider the information outlined in this chapter, and take any steps you deem necessary to secure your financial stability during the potentially challenging times ahead.

FINANCE CHECKLIST

Diversify your assets, minimize your financial risk, and increase your financial liquidity by the following means:

_____ Limit your exposure to the stock market
_____ Consider short term T-bills
_____ Sell real estate holdings, aside from your Y2K location
_____ Evaluate the safety of your funds in bank accounts/CDs
_____ Evaluate the safety of money market mutual funds
_____ Buy gold and silver coins
_____ Have 1-3 months' or more worth of cash on hand
_____ Invest in barter items
_____ Invest in preparedness supplies
_____ Consider complete financial liquidity

Protect your liquid assets:

_____ Study Chapter 5, pages 199 to 204, for ideas on where to store your liquid assets
_____ Store your cash and precious metals in secure locations

Consider investments which may prosper due to Y2K:

_____ Y2K stocks
_____ Mining stocks
_____ Commodities futures
_____ Futures options
_____ Leveraged precious metal purchases

CHAPTER 7

Power

The "party line" of the industry remains: everything's OK, this isn't a big deal, we'll get it fixed. However, anyone in the industry who understands the total scope of the problem, and who will speak off the record, is scared to death.

Rick Cowles
Author, "Electric Utilities and Y2K"

Our nation is diligently attacking the Y2K problem, utilizing a virtual army of skilled professionals. In some areas, progress is being made. In others, given the time constraints of the immovable 1-1-2000 deadline, we have cause for concern. Our greatest concern is electric power generation and distribution. Will the electric grid continue to function?

Most of us take electrical power for granted. We assume we will always have an adequate, if not infinite, supply of electricity at the flick of a switch. Electric power is behind nearly everything we use. If we were to lose all electric power on a scale affecting our entire city or state, major disruptions would ensue.

Think of all the amenities in life we take for granted; they are all dependent on electrical power. Water pressure to flush our toilets; heating and air conditioning; our lighting and all other appliances require electricity. We depend on electric power in nearly every facet of our lives. If we lose the ability to generate and distribute electricity, it won't matter whether the computer networks are Y2K ready or not. Nothing will work!

The power grid supplying our nation is a large interconnected system. It is separated into four electrical grids, powering the eastern states, the midwestern states, the northwestern states, and Texas. These grids all interconnect in Nebraska.

The built-in computerized security of the electric grid is designed to anticipate and handle up to two disruptions concurrently. In the event a primary line goes down, power would be shut down to a specific section, while electricity is rerouted around the trouble area. If the grid encounters another problem it is designed to shut down completely.

As realists, we can't be certain that we'll have an uninterrupted supply of power on January 1, 2000. If we lose electrical power, we won't be able to run any electrical appliances without an alternative power source. Depending on what you foresee as the potential duration of Y2K problems, you may want to have short or long-term electrical power generation equipment.

First, let's consider the necessity of an alternative power source.

DO YOU NEED ALTERNATIVE ELECTRICAL POWER?

Today, electricity is integral to all the systems in our homes. Heating, air conditioning, refrigeration, cooking—all of our appliances require electricity to run. Even natural gas furnaces require electricity to power their fans. The only non-electrically dependent appliances are certain models of gas stoves.

Of all our appliances and devices, most are wants, not needs. While our washing machines, TVs, and electric can openers make life more comfortable, they aren't necessities.

However, losing heat in the middle of winter in northern areas could be life-threatening. The ability to cook our food is also a need. While not a necessity, living without light for any period of time would be difficult to tolerate.

Securing a continuous source of heat to warm your home and cook your food is not dependent upon electrical power. Neither is a continuous source of light. As we saw in Chapter 2, you can accomplish these purposes with fuels such as wood, propane, and kerosene.

Why, then, do you need an alternative electrical power source?

You may be content with fuel-powered heating and lighting. Waiting out the Y2K problem until uninterrupted electrical power is restored may suit you fine. In this case, you don't need to consider generators or solar power systems.

On the other hand, if you believe Y2K will be a short-term problem and you'd like a bridge to provide some electricity over a few weeks or months, a fossil fuel generator can meet your needs.

If you believe Y2K will be a long term disruption and you want to have the convenience of electrical power in your home, investing in a renewable or sustainable electrical generating system may be for you.

We'll look at both options in this chapter.

FOSSIL FUEL GENERATORS

If you want a bridge to get you over a brief period of some weeks when you may experience electrical brown-outs and black-outs following Y2K, consider buying an electrical generator and storing sufficient fuel to run it. Generators allow us to produce our own electricity independent of the electric power companies. A generator serves as an efficient short-term solution in a power outage situation.

It's not a long-term solution, since generators are an expensive source of power, consuming a lot of fuel to produce electricity.

Fossil fuel generators run on gasoline, diesel or propane. The larger the generator in watts, the greater the fuel consumption.

Our 5000 watt gasoline generator consumes 3/4 to 1 gal. of gasoline per hour of run time. Running it seven hours a day requires about 7 gal. daily, or about 49 gal. weekly.

As you can see, a month's supply of gasoline requires a considerable storage area. For most of us, storage of large quantities of fuel is impractical and dangerous.

As a short-term solution however, a generator is invaluable. During any Y2K-induced electrical blackout, we plan to use our generator to power up our household. Once electricity is restored, we can concentrate on setting up the rest of the emergency equipment—propane heater, kerosene lantern, communication devices, etc.—in relative comfort.

When the rest of the equipment is in place, we don't have to use the generator to power the furnace and the lights. We can conserve fuel, running the generator intermittently to keep the refrigerator cold and the sump pump running as needed. Our generator serves as a temporary emergency backup power source.

If you plan on purchasing a generator, we recommend you place your order as soon as possible. Demand is beginning to exceed supply.

Calculating Power Requirements

Most of us have never needed a generator, and are unfamiliar with its use. Some basic information will help clarify how a generator is used.

The first consideration in purchasing a generator is your total power requirement. What devices are you going to power with the generator? Figure out how much power you need, then you can decide what size generator to buy.

Power is expressed in watts, or kilowatts (watts x 1000). The power in watts is determined by multiplying the line voltage (source of voltage for the device) times the amperage (current used by the device).

To determine your overall power requirements, decide what items requiring electricity you are going to use. Next, determine each item's power usage, in watts. Finally, add all of the items' individual power consumption, again in watts.

Wattage for a particular device can be determined by multiplying the voltage times the amperage. For example, a hair dryer using 120 volts at 12.5 amps consumes 1500 watts. While a hair dryer is not a priority item in an emergency, it is a familiar illustration.

There are two types of electrical devices you can power with your generator, those that are *resistive loads* and those that are *inductive loads.*

Appliances that have moving parts, like a compressor in a freezer or refrigerator, are inductive loads. They require more power to start them than they require to keep them running. This extra startup power is called *surge power.* This additional load is necessary to overcome friction and get the parts in motion, and lasts only a few seconds on start-up. Other appliances requiring surge power are washers and dryers, blenders, and circular saws.

Devices like radios, light bulbs, and televisions are resistive loads. They do not require surge power. Their starting or surge wattage, and running or rated wattage, are the same.

Surge power for starting these devices is generally 2.5 times the listed watts. You must include surge power wattage when you calculate your overall power requirements. Look in your appliance instruction book or on the appliance itself, usually on a silver metal tag on the back, for the rated wattage and surge requirements.

Some appliance wattage requirements are as follows:

	Rated Watts	**Surge Watts**
Furnace fan	1100	2100
Refrigerator	500	800-2000
Freezer	400	1000
Sump pump	800	600-2000
Light bulb	100	100
Totals:	**2900**	**7200**

Let's do a little calculating. We have a 5000 watt generator, which can power our household. We want to run all the items listed above. The rated watts equal 2900, but the surge watts, at the high end, equal 7200 watts. Your power requirement calculations must be made using the surge watts.

The first thing to do is prioritize our device usage. Since the generator is 5000 watts, and the surge watts for our selected devices total 7200 watts, we can't run everything at once. But this is easily remedied.

The sump pump only has to be run when the water level reaches a critical height, so it can be temporarily disconnected until needed. The refrigerator and freezer can be run intermittently; they will remain cold inside for hours if closed, even with the power shut off.

The furnace can also be run intermittently, just enough to keep the house comfortable. So, we can alternate between running the furnace, freezer, refrigerator, and sump pump. Even if we run the furnace and minimal lighting continuously, we'll still have excess wattage available.

Our 5000 watt generator works out fine, giving us all the power we need to run these devices. Depending on your situation and needs, you can elect to go with a higher or lower output generator.

How to Power Your Home With a Generator

There are basically three ways to use your generator to supply power to your devices. They are:

1. Extension cords
2. Back feeding
3. Double Pole Double Throw Switch

The first method is simple. Using extension cords, plug the desired device into the generator.

Extension cords are an inexpensive and easy method of utilizing the electricity furnished by your generator. Extension cords come in a variety of sizes. This refers to gauge, not length. We recommend you use heavier gauge cords, #10 and larger.

Be sure to use the proper capacity rated in amps, as required by your generator. Number 10 and larger gauge cords will have lower resistance than the smaller gauges. Lower resistance means less voltage drop between the device and the generator. A large voltage drop can damage the device.

When using extension cords always adhere to the following safety practices:

• Don't use damaged or frayed cords
• Don't exceed the cord's power rating
• Don't use extension cords in wet areas
• Don't run extension cords under rugs or carpeting
• Pull out by the plug, not the wire

You can purchase extension cords from your local hardware store or building supplier stores such as Home Depot, Builders Square, etc. Or, you can custom-make cords according to your needs. You can purchase lengths of three or four conductor extension cord off the spool from any of these stores, and with connectors produce the exact length of cord you need.

The second method of using a generator is called *back feeding*. This method powers your household by "plugging in" your generator to an electrical socket in the house, via a plug-to-plug cable. Power is fed from the generator through a wall plug to the device plugged into another wall plug. If you use backfeeding, you must turn off the main breaker. Otherwise, an unsuspecting lineman could be injured or even killed.

The third method of generator installation utilizes the *Double Pole Double Throw* switch. This is the only safe way to connect a generator to your home wiring, and is the method we recommend.

The DPDT is installed at your main breaker box. When in the normal position, regular utility power is allowed into the house. When moved to "generator power" it cuts the utility power, allowing your generator to power the house. When the utility power is restored, it is isolated and will not damage your house or your generator. The DPDT should be installed by a licensed electrician.

Protection from Inclement Weather

Generators are not designed to be operated indoors, even in a garage. But, the more moderately priced generator models are not designed for outside operation during wet weather. What do you do, then, during a rain or snowstorm?

The solution is, build a "dog house" to protect your generator from inclement weather. This can be a simple structure, with the following features:

Install an air intake vent in the peak on one side and a louvered, electric exhaust fan on the other side. Generators create a large amount of heat, even in winter, which must be vented. Vent the exhaust outside with a flexible exhaust coupling and some plumbing if possible. Don't use more than one right-angle bend in the exhaust or you'll increase the exhaust system back-pressure and damage the engine.

If you insulate the dog house with fiberglass, you have the additional advantage of lowering the noise created by the generator.

In summary, if you elect to use a generator, follow these steps:

1. Assess your wattage needs and determine what size generator you need to purchase.
2. Choose your connection method. Our recommended method is to install a double pole double throw switch.
3. Ground the generator to prevent electric shock.
4. Locate and label all circuits in your power panel.
5. When you are ready to use the generator, turn off all breakers in the panel or remove fuses. Flip the DPDT switch to the generator-powered position, and start the generator. Then, one by one, turn on the circuits that you want to use.
6. When using a generator, always start your largest electric motor first, then power up the remaining items one at a time.

Always follow all manufacturer's guidelines for safe usage.

Generator Options

Wattage

You can purchase generators with an output rating from 500 to 10,000 watts and more. What size generator is right for you? As discussed earlier, it depends on what you plan to power with it, and how much you can afford to spend.

An 8500 watt generator can completely power an average-sized three bedroom home. In his book *Electric Utilities and Y2K,* Rick Cowles recommends the Generac 5500XL, a 5500 watt generator, for emergency backup power. Home Depot sells this for $1000.

We found the 5000 watt Generac PP5000T at a local discount warehouse for $469. This is a suitable substitute, only 500 watts smaller, at a savings of $500! We recommend you determine your individual needs and your level of affordability, and then shop around for the best deal.

Generator manufacturers include Coleman Powermate, Dyna, Generac, Homelite, Honda, Northern Hydraulics, Northern Pro, and NorthStar Generators. Northern Tool and Equipment carries a wide selection of generators.

For further generator manufacturer links, see:

http://209.52.183.182/Generator/generator_manufacturer _links.htm

Features

Features and options available with different generator models vary. Some boast quiet engines, others run on multiple fuels, and some come with wheels. Fuel economy and run time per full tank vary among manufacturers. Most generators come equipped with a low oil shut-off sensor, which is important to have. If the generator runs low on oil the motor could be permanently damaged.

Your decision on which model to purchase is dependent on your individual power consumption needs, plus whatever extras you can afford within your budget. We recommend you look for the following features in a generator:

- Overhead valve (OHV) engine for longer life, quieter operation
- Auto idle control to reduce noise and fuel consumption
- Large fuel tank—5 gal. tank may last 5 to 10 hours
- Low oil shut-off feature to prevent engine damage
- Wheel kit, to make it easy to move around

Gasoline Generators

Gasoline fueled generators are a short term solution, as it is impractical to store large enough quantities of fuel for long duration use. A couple of 55 gal. drums with a hand pump to transfer fuel to a 1 or 5 gal. can would only allow for about three weeks of moderate usage.

In a gasoline generator, use fresh unleaded gasoline with a minimum octane rating of 85. When the generator is in storage, the gasoline in it should be treated with Stabil gas treatment, which can be found in automotive or hardware stores. Alternatively, the gasoline can be drained from the gas tank and carburetor bowl.

Gasoline generators range in price from $250 for the smallest, on up to $4000 for 8000 watts and greater sizes. The gasoline models offered by Northern start at $450 for a NorthStar 5 HP Honda-Powered Generator. This model claims 2900 watts surge, 2600 watts continuous use, and produces 21.7 amps at 120 volts.

At the high end, Northern offers an 8000 Watt, 16 HP Dyna Standby Generator for $4200. The Dyna produces 8 KW of continuous power when fueled by propane, and 7.2 KW continuously when powered by natural gas. The Dyna has a Briggs electric start OHV engine.

In their January 1999 catalog, Northern offers a 5500 watt, 4500 continuous watt 9 HP Honda Industrial OHV engine on sale for $1000. This is a savings of $900 off the normal price of $1900.

Propane Generators

Methods are available to convert a gasoline powered generator to propane. The advantages of using propane over gasoline are longer engine life, easier cold weather starting, and greater fuel storage safety. We recommend propane conversion.

For information on converting your generator to propane contact US Carburetion, Inc., 800-553-5608. They offer $160 conversion kits for most gasoline generators. They also offer the book *Generators Buyer's Guide* for $15, with information on choosing a generator and fuel supply.

http://www.uscarb.qpg.com

Winco Trifuel Portable Generators from Jade Mountain run on gasoline, natural gas or propane. The 6000 watt model costs

$2100 and the 9000 watt version is $3100.

Winco also offers a Packaged Standby System which automatically transfers your home's power demands to the generator when power failure occurs and back to the utility when power is restored. Everything is covered in a weather protective enclosure. The 8000 watt model runs on propane or natural gas and costs $5600.

Northern Tool and Equipment sells a similar propane 8000 watt Dyna Standby Generator for $4200, battery not included.

Portable Onan Commercial Gensets from Jade Mountain carry a two year/2000 hour limited warranty. They have electronic ignition, commercial grade electronic components, low 1800 rpm operating speed and automatic low oil pressure shutdown. The 4500 watt propane model costs $3235, the 6500 watt is $4500.

Diesel Generators

Diesel generators have triple the life and double the fuel savings of gasoline models, but are also significantly more expensive. If you feel your generator may need to last longer than a year or two of frequent use, consider buying a commercial diesel model initially rather than having to rebuild or replace your gasoline model later. For use in an alternative power system, if you expect to run the generator more than 300 hours per year to back-up your solar collectors, buy a diesel genset.

Diesel fuel is more stable than gasoline. When treated with Stabil-D to prevent algae growth, it will last for years. Since you'll need half as much diesel, your storage requirements will also be less.

Jade Mountain sells portable Commercial Diesel Gensets. They have glowplugs for easy starting, variable speeds and are liquid cooled like cars. A 7500 watt model costs $6800—as much as a car!

Northern Tool and Equipment sells an air-cooled Northern Pro 10 HP, 6000 watt portable genset for $2760. It runs for nearly nine hours on 5 gal. of diesel fuel when at 75% of capacity.

Harbor Freight Tools sells a Chicago Electric Power Tools 10,000 watt diesel generator for $3500.

China Diesel Imports, 800-341-7027 is another supplier. **http://www.chinadiesel.com**

Steam Engines

A steam engine is the ultimate Y2K power solution—producing electrical power, heat and hot water! This is the only fueled generator which can run with a renewable fuel—wood.

Residential steam engines take the place of conventional gensets run on fossil fuels. With an alternative power system, you can use it as a back-up generator for cloudy days without wind. A steam engine can also be used as a sole power source.

In addition to producing electrical power for a home, steam engines can produce residential hot water, space heating and your own steam sauna! The boiler can be fueled with wood, natural gas or propane. The 5 horsepower Liberty produces up to 2000 watts for $2900 from Jade Mountain. A 10 HP model is also available for $5700. The boiler should last for 50 years and the engine for 20 years. Jade Mountain reports that they are easy to set up and use and are provided with a comprehensive set of instructions.

Fuel Use and Storage

Fuel Life Extenders

Untreated gasoline loses octane after six months and can be worthless after a year. Buy high octane fuel for storage, as it has a longer life before the octane deteriorates below operational levels for combustion engines. After treatment, gasoline should maintain its octane and last for at least a year.

Sta-Bil from Goldeagle is a standard for gasoline and diesel fuel treatment. It is sold by any automotive parts supplier, and is also available at WalMart.

Another product that claims better results is PRI. Major Surplus sells PRI-G for gasoline preservation. One pint costs $20, and treats 250 gal. It claims to keep fuel fresh for 10 years or more.

Nitro-Pak sells Fuel Saver Plus, designed to keep gasoline good for three years. It costs $28 per quart, and will treat 500 gal.

You can also treat diesel fuel, to extend its life. Algae can grow in diesel and degrade the fuel's value. In order to keep it from breaking down, there are a number of products available, including PRI-D from Major Surplus.

Links to websites of several fuel life extenders are online at:

http://209.52.183.182/generator/oilfuel_treatment.htm

Fossil Fuel Alternatives

Besides gasoline, propane and diesel, there are other fuels that can be used in some generator models.

Biogas: One of our families used a methane digester to produce natural gas from the fermentation of animal and plant wastes on their farm. This gas was used to cook food and help heat the house. The use of biogas is very popular in developing countries.

China has seven million local biogas systems in place. Like natural gas, biogas can be used for cooking, heating, electrical generation and fueling trucks. *A Chinese Biogas Manual* priced at $21, is one of five books which detail biogas processes available from Jade Mountain. Another is a $12 construction manual for a *Three Cubic Meter Biogas Plant* used in thousands of Indian locations.

Gasohol: Brian Horne's $16 book *Power Plants: Biofuels Made Simple* discusses sustainable energy sources which can substitute for conventional sources. Ethyl alcohol from plant carbohydrates can extend or replace gasoline as a fuel. Jade Mountain sells this book. Another book on ethanol is available for $12 at:

http://www.geocities.com/heartland/lane/5515/index.html

Gasohol can't be used in all generators, as it burns hotter than gasoline. Check with your generator manufacture to see if it can be used in your model.

Liquid Fuel Storage Containers

Your method of liquid fuel storage depends on which fuel you're dealing with—gasoline, diesel, or kerosene; on how much you want to store, based on your usage assessment; on where you will store the fuel; and on what your local codes will allow. While kerosene is not a generator fuel, it is stored the same.

Gasoline is highly explosive. It should be stored in a well-ventilated area, outside of your home. Diesel and kerosene are not explosive, which makes them safer to store.

Liquid fuel storage containers smaller than 300 gal. must be painted to indicate the fuel contents. Gasoline is indicated by red, diesel by green and kerosene by blue.

Liquid fuels should be stored in closed-head HDPE plastic or steel containers. The 5 gal. containers are the most common; but 1 and 3 gal. containers are also available, and are easier to handle. You can also use plastic or steel 55 gal. closed-head drums for fuel storage. See the suppliers listed in Chapter 2, page 108.

The Sportsman's Guide has a good deal on reconditioned like-new 5 gal. French Military Issue Jerry Cans. They are priced at $12 each, and the optional metal nozzle is $7. Purchase the Jerry Can and the nozzle together for only $14. Consider buying more than one, for use as a good barter item.

Major Surplus & Survival also sells fuel cans and hand pumps. They sell a 5 gal. metal fuel can for $10, and the accompanying flex nozzle for $7. A $17 hand fuel pump lets you transfer fuel from drums to buckets.

Another fuel storage alternative for gasoline, diesel and kerosene is steel tanks. The 250 gal. fuel oil tanks used to store home heating fuel for oil furnaces are ideal. Any fuel oil distributor will sell them for around $240. You may be able to get a permit to have one installed even in the city.

Home heating oil and #2 grade diesel fuel are exactly the same thing. While municipal zoning may restrict fuel tanks, they are commonly used on farms. If you don't have zoning restrictions, they would be your best solution for large volume fuel storage.

Above ground steel fuel storage tanks are available from:

Turner Tanks, 800-672-4770

http://www.turnertanks.com

Eaton Metal Sales, 303-296-4800

http://www.eatonmetalsales.com

Omega Systems offers polyethylene fuel storage tanks. The 300 gal. tank costs $600 and the 500 gal. tank is $750.

Container suppliers can help you make your fuel storage container selections. For more links to fuel container suppliers plus further information on treating and storing fuel, see:

http://209.52.183.182/Generator/oilfuel_treatment.htm

Propane Storage Containers

Of the three common generator fuels, propane is the easiest to store. It doesn't deteriorate over time and lasts indefinitely since it is sealed in a pressurized tank. The pressurized white cylinders or tanks in 1 lb., 20 lb., 40 lb., and 100 lb. sizes can be purchased from a propane supplier. If your zoning allows, you can rent larger tanks ranging in size from 120 lb. to 1000 lb. for the back of your house.

Propane is safer to store than gasoline, but it is heavier than air and thus pools if there is any leakage. It should be stored outside or where it can be vented to the outside at floor level, to prevent an explosive accumulation if there is a leak.

The safest place to store your propane tanks is outside. If security is a problem, chain the tanks to a secure object. If you have more than one tank, chain them together. Propane is not affected

by cold weather, and will vaporize even in sub-zero temperatures.
See pages 75 to 76 for cylinder and gas prices and suppliers.

Safety Considerations

Whatever source of fuel you choose for powering your generator, keep safety in mind at all times. Be aware of the importance of proper fuel transfer and fire safety. We recommend keeping one or more fire extinguishers, suitable for fuel fires, near your fuel storage. Never attempt to fuel your generator when it is running or after you have turned it off and it is still hot.

Adhere to all manufacturer's guidelines with regard to safe operation and fuel storage. Purchase carbon monoxide and smoke detectors, fire extinguishers, fire blankets, and any other necessary safety equipment. See Chapter 5 for more information. See also the following website for tips on generator safety:

http://209.52.183.182/Generator/safety.htm

LONG TERM ALTERNATIVE POWER SYSTEMS

If you believe Y2K puts you at risk of being without dependable electrical power for an extended period of time, and you have sufficient resources to invest in renewable power, consider establishing an off-the-grid alternative electrical power system. These systems are generally composed of solar, wind, or hydroelectric components which produce electricity and store it in batteries until needed. A comprehensive reference work on alternative power is the 1160-page *Renewable Energy: Sources for Fuel and Electricity* from Island Press sold by Off Line for $45.

Alternative electrical power systems are pricey when initially established, but are effective long-term investments since they last for years. An alternative system delivering continuous access to the amount of power typically consumed in a suburban American home could easily cost as much as $20,000 to install. However, most people scale back their energy consumption and utilize energy-efficient appliances to permit comfortable life-styles for significantly less investment.

In order to keep alternative electrical systems smaller and costs lower, decrease electrical demands through conservation. Typical alternative appliances may include high-efficiency electrical, natural gas or kerosene refrigeration; fluorescent or LED lighting systems; gas or wood stoves and water heaters; and wood-burning furnaces. Passive solar design elements in a home's architecture also utilize the sun's energy by receiving the sun's heat through windows during the winter and shading the home during the summer.

System Components

Stand-alone alternative power systems typically utilize the following components:

Power Sources

These are solar photovoltaic panels, wind generators or hydroelectric generators used singly or in combination. A fossil fuel powered generator may be added as a backup system for periods when other sources aren't producing enough electricity, such as extended periods with little sunshine or wind.

Battery Power Storage

The most crucial element of alternative power systems is the storage of electricity for the times when it is needed. Wet cell batteries provide storage of the energy in chemical form. This power is available whenever electricity is needed.

The use of batteries arranged in banks is how electrical power is stored. Alternative power systems are specifically designed to most efficiently utilize the Direct Current from batteries to power household appliances. That is why most "off-the grid" systems use DC for lighting and water pumping.

Batteries which combine deep cycle, wet cell and lead-acid characteristics are the best for efficient storage of solar power. They come in both sealed and refillable types.

Certain types will last longer than others. In general, the more you pay, the longer they will last. Automobile batteries may only last a few months or a golf cart battery for 2-3 years. Gel Cell batteries will last 3-5 years and Trojan L-16s sold by Jade Mountain will last 8-12 years. Chloride industrial strength batteries last 20 years and the Lineage 2000 brand up to 70 years!

Trojan L-16s cost $190 each from Jade Mountain and are state of the art for home storage systems.

Deep cycle lead-acid batteries are also available anywhere boats are sold or serviced, as they are used in marine electrical systems.

Battery Charger

These devices convert alternating current from wind, hydro-electric and fossil fuel generators into direct current which is used to charge the battery bank. The suppliers listed here sell models which range in price from $150 on up.

Charge Controller

Charge controllers or voltage regulators protect the battery systems by only charging them to safe levels and at safe rates. They range in price depending on capacity from $40 to $300 and are sold by all the alternative power system suppliers listed here. Be cautious with the models employing embedded chips. Get written manufacturer assurances that the chips are not date sensitive and won't be impacted by the century date change.

Inverter

Inverters take DC power and turn it into useful AC voltage for use in conventional 110 volt AC appliances such as televisions and power tools. During Y2K, you can use an inverter with a car battery or any DC system to generate AC power. This can be used to power small appliances, such as a lap-top computer or a radio.

Some inverters are designed to be used in automobiles, drawing power from the car's electrical system. We purchased a factory refurbished 300 watt power inverter from Damark International for $40. The product performs better than expected. We have recharged power tools, powered a portable television, and other small appliances. A handy feature is the built-in sensor which monitors the battery and automatically shuts down the inverter when the car battery gets low. Since it is self-monitoring, you don't have to worry about a dead battery and your car not starting.

Heartland America, 800-229-2901, offers the following array of power inverters:

Rated Watt	Peak Watt	Price
140	250	$ 29.99
300	600	$ 49.00
500	800	$ 99.99
1000	2000	$249.99
1500	3000	$349.99

http://www.heartlandamerica.com

Portawattz is another good brand of inverter. They are manufactured by Statpower, 800-994-STAT. They also offer refurbished inverters at good prices, a 1000 watt inverter costs $170.

http://www.statpower.com/

Solar Power

Solar power is a unique and fascinating source of energy. Through the use of photovoltaic (PV) cells in panels we can harvest the energy given freely by the sun.

PV panels are banks of solar cells, which are semiconductors

made of materials similar to those of computer chips. When pho-
tons from sunlight strike the semiconductor, electrons are released.
These electrons then do work in electrical systems.

PV panels are warranted for 20 years if protected from breakage, such as from hail.

The size of a solar system will depend on three variables: the
amount of power required as measured in watts; the amount of
time it is used in a day, measured in hours; and the amount of
energy which a particular location has available from the sun,
which is measured in sun hours per day. You can't do anything
about your region's amount of sunshine except relocate. But you
can control the watts and hours you require.

Mr. Solar offers an Internet solar course for $100.

Complete Residential Systems

Suppliers such as Off Line Independent Energy Systems sell
complete, engineered solar power systems for remote off-the-grid
homes which range in price from $13,500 to $32,000.

Golden Genesis, 800-544-6466, sells solar system components
as well as complete stand-alone Residential Solar Electric Systems.
A system which can handle a small home or cabin costs $4900.
One which can power most household appliances in a region
which has optimal solar exposure costs $16,900.

http://www.goldengenesis.com

Jade Mountain sells Home Power Systems priced from $750
to $12,500, on up. Their $5 *PV Design & Sizing* booklet will help
you determine what components you need and their capabilities.

Backup Systems

Simple backup systems, such as those designed for solar lighting or running a few small appliances, can be set up with a single
PV panel, a battery, a charge controller and a DC light bulb. These
systems cost less than $700.

One such solar reserve power system consisting of a soft solar panel, marine battery and inverter is $600 from W.L. Greene:

http://www.y2k-links.com/solar/

Another is the SunRunner 75/30S sold by Off Line for recreational vehicles at $800. It requires the addition of a battery if not used with an RV's battery.

Other solar equipment suppliers include:

Solar Extreme, 805-299-9365

http://www.solarextreme.com

Millennium Power Systems, 410-686-6658

http://www.offgrid.com

PV arrays can be combined with a generator and a battery charger; the generator takes over when the PV array falls short. The generator handles the AC loads and charges the batteries.

Research the subject of solar power by reading *The Solar Electric House* by Steven Strong for $22 or the 694-page *Solar Living Sourcebook* by John Schaeffer for $25.

Wind Power

Wind power generators can be cost effective if the average wind speed is nine miles per hour or more at the location of the wind generator. They can provide power for a DC system and can charge batteries during good wind conditions. You can test your specific wind velocity with a number of devices. Off Line sells the Kestrel 1000 Pocket Wind Meter for $89 and the Dwyer Mark II Wind Speed Indicator for $50. They also sell wind generators.

Kansas Wind Power has the best prices on wind generators. They sell the Southwest Windpower Wind Turbines' AIR Wind Module for $485. This small 300 watt generator can be mounted directly onto a roof. Larger ones must be mounted on a tower. Towers start at $200.

Jade Mountain sells the higher-tech World Power Wind Generators which begin at $1200 for the 600 watt Whisper. These offer the lowest cost per watt in the industry. Jade Mountain also offers complete wind power systems with the Whisper which includes: Easy-Wire System Center which connects, controls and monitors the entire system; batteries; cables; and inverter for $2020.

For more information, join the American Wind Energy Association, 202-383-2500 for $35 and get their newsletter. Or, buy *Wind Power For Home And Business* by Paul Gipe for $26 from Kansas Wind Power.

Hydroelectric Power

If you have a dependable stream during at least a portion of the year, you can enjoy free power with moderately priced and very low maintenance equipment.

Hydroelectric Generators

To produce enough hydroelectric power to run a small household, you need approximately 100 Gallons Per Minute (GPM) of water falling 10 ft. through a pipe, or about 5 gal. per minute falling approximately 200 ft. through a pipe.

The amount of power you can generate depends on:
1. The dynamic head, measured in feet
2. The amount of water flow, in gallons per minute
3. The efficiencies of the turbine (18%) and generator (30%)

To get a better understanding of available power in watts use the following formula:

Head (in ft.) x Flow (in GPM) x 0.18 x 0.3

Hydroelectric turbines coupled with car alternators can charge batteries 24 hours a day, and you can draw power from the battery as needed. Any power generated will help to supplement your

DC system. Off Line sells Harris Pelton Turbines starting at $760. Jade Mountain has models which begin at $490.

If your stream is a distance away from your home, use a High Voltage Turgo from Jade Mountain to prevent power loss while traveling over the wire. These begin at $1000.

Micro-Hydropower for $31 from Jade Mountain is a definitive source book on hydroelectric power. Or, get the video *Residential Microhydro Power* with Don Harris for $40 from Off Line or Jade Mountain.

Hydropower information and system plans are available at: **http://www.public.usit.net/pinecrst/text/hplans2.htm**
Submersible Generator

If you are near a fast flowing stream that is at least 13 in. deep, you can install a submersible generator without having to construct a dam or install piping. The Aquair Submersible Generator from Off Line or Jade Mountain costs $1100 and produces 1.5 kilowatt hours per day in a stream flowing 6 mph.

DRY CELL BATTERIES

Store extra batteries for your small appliances. Standard, alkaline and rechargeable batteries should be purchased in quantity in the sizes you anticipate using. AAA, AA, C, D and 9 volt are the standard sizes.

Start off by making a thorough assessment of all devices you now have in your possession, or plan to acquire. Next, as best you can, estimate the daily use in hours of each device. Then, based on the battery life in each device, you'll be well on your way to determining your overall battery needs. Don't worry about over buying, extra batteries can be an excellent barter item.

Warehouse clubs like Sam's Club and Costco, 800-774-2678, have the best deals available. We recently purchased a 24-pack of

Duracell alkaline AA batteries at Costco at a price of $11 with a shelf life good until March of 2003. That's a very affordable 46¢ each. We also purchased from Costco, a 40-pack of Kirkland Alkaline AA batteries. The shelf life of the Kirkland batteries matches the Duracell brand. The Kirkland batteries only cost $8.50 for the 40-pack, that's only 21¢ each! We tried both brands, and both work well. The only difference is the price.

http://www.costco.com

Industrial strength Powersonic rechargeable nickel-cadmium (NiCad) batteries are available from Jade Mountain. They have much higher capacity and longer life, so deliver more power for your investment than other brands. NiCads can be used up to 1000 times, so are a good investment. AAAs and AAs cost $2.75 each. Ds are $11.50 and 9 volts sell for $12.25 each.

Nickel Metal Hydride (NiMH) batteries have a 50% to 100% higher capacity per volume and weight than NiCads. Ham Radio Outlet, 800-644-4476, sells "AA" type rechargeable NiMH cells for $3 each.

http://www.hamradio.com

D-Mail sells a portable, sealed 5 amp alkaline battery called the Auto Starter. Designed to help boost car batteries, it can also power communication devices and laptop computers. The Auto Starter sells for $50. See page 321 for more information.

Solar Dry-Cell Battery Charger

For Y2K use, solar energy is the ideal power source for recharging batteries. Disposable batteries are great—until you run out. An important, inexpensive option is a solar-powered battery charger.

Solar battery chargers enable you to recharge AAA, AA, C, D and 9-volt rechargeable dry cell batteries. Some chargers even successfully trickle charge so-called non-rechargeable standard, carbon zinc and alkaline batteries.

Off Line's Solar AA Battery Charger is a pocket sized charger which takes 5 hours in full sun to charge four AA batteries. It or a version handling two Cs or two Ds cost $28.

A solar Button Battery Charger from Off Line revitalizes used mercury batteries from watches and hearing aids which are normally not rechargeable. It costs $15.

Real Goods offers a Solar Super Charger that fits AAA, AA, C, or D size batteries. They claim it's waterproof and nearly unbreakable. It's economically priced at $30.

We recommend the Keep It Simple Systems' Jupiter solar battery charger. This model uses a large flexible solar panel to recharges standard, alkaline, Ni-Cad or NiMH AAA, AA, C or D batteries! A safety features prevents overcharging of batteries. The unit comes with a power cord, allowing it to double for AC use. Available from Jade Mountain for $190.

In summary, decide if you need an alternative power source. If you want to run standard electrical appliances during Y2K power outages, you'll need a backup power source.

Portable home generators are a short-term option. For a long-term renewable alternative energy source, consider solar, wind, or hydroelectric systems. To power small devices, store quantities of conventional dry-cell batteries, and purchase a solar dry-cell battery charger.

POWER CHECKLIST

_____ Decide on an alternative source of power

_____ Buy a suitable electrical generator that meets all your short-term power requirements

    ___ Determine installation and connection methods for your generator

    ___ Purchase heavy gauge extension cords

    ___ Purchase sufficient fuel for the generator

    ___ Investigate alternative fuels

    ___ Use fuel life extenders if planning on longer-term use

    ___ Purchase appropriate containers for fuel storage

_____ Purchase fire safety equipment

    ___ Smoke detectors

    ___ Carbon monoxide detectors

    ___ Fire extinguishers

_____ Consider a long-term alternative power system

_____ Investigate solar, wind and hydroelectric systems

_____ Store a varied supply of batteries

    ___ Alkaline batteries

    ___ Rechargable batteries

_____ Buy a solar battery charger

CHAPTER 8

Communications

The consequences of not resolving Year 2000 problems in the telecommunications infrastructure are broad-based and potentially disastrous.

Joel Willemssen
Director, Civil Agencies Information Systems,
General Accounting Office

Communication, like electric power and other conveniences, is something Americans take for granted. For a small fee, we can be reached, or reach anybody, anywhere, at almost any time. We use a variety of telephones—land lines, pay phones, cordless, cellular, digital, as well as cell phones with built in two-way radios. We use facsimile (fax) machines. We correspond over the Internet by e-mail and search the worldwide web for all types of information. We send letters and packages via the U.S. Postal Service, UPS and myriad overnight mail services.

A multitude of newspapers and magazines inform us of nearly everything that is going on anywhere on the planet. In addition, radio and television receivers give us audio and visual information.

Yet, all this could be threatened by the Year 2000 problem. Global telecommunications failures or compromises could create havoc. Telephone networks are completely computerized and dependent on embedded microprocessors in the circuit switching networks. The cumulative effect of Y2K-induced failures in the telecommunications networks could compromise or eliminate our telephone and Internet service. People would be cut off from one another. Our local radio and television broadcasting stations are likewise not immune to extended disruptions in electrical power, which could silence them.

If we suddenly lost our ability to communicate as a result of Y2K-induced failures, what alternative methods of communication could we use? How would we obtain accurate information about what is happening around the world, or around the corner? This chapter describes many alternative communication methods you can select from, based on your estimated duration of disruptions, individual need and finances.

COMMUNICATION OPTIONS

If conventional communication networks are not functioning reliably, you could use alternative techniques to stay "in the know." There are many options available.

One group which has prepared an alternative communications system in anticipation of Y2K failures is the Rogue Valley Y2K Task Force in Oregon. They plan to use Citizens Band radios to relay messages around their region. Check out their website:

http://www.rv-y2k.org/rvcecom.htm

A forum where you can chat with radio experts as well as novices on Y2K communications options as well as other Y2K topics and read their archived comments is:

http://206.67.59.5/forum.htm

A word of caution about any electronic equipment. Be sure that the component microchips are Year 2000 compliant! Take the time to contact the manufacturer and ask for a written guarantee on company letterhead stating that the specific model of equipment you are buying will work after 2000.

Another strategy is to buy simple, older equipment which is not as dependent on microprocessors. For example, older ham radio equipment uses vacuum tubes, which are totally Y2K compliant!

As you decide what form of communication equipment to have on hand during Y2K, there are two primary considerations to keep in mind.

Receivers vs. Transceivers

First, do you need equipment that lets you merely listen to broadcast information, or do you also want to have the ability to exchange information?

Some communication devices, such as traditional radios, allow you to listen only. These are called *receivers*. If you want to engage in two-way communication, you need a radio *transceiver* which both receives and broadcasts radio messages. With a transceiver you can send information, enabling you to enter into a conversation, ask questions and get answers!

In this chapter, we will look at a variety of radio receiver and radio transceiver options.

Range: Local vs. Long Distance

Second, over how great a distance do you want to be able to communicate? If you want to communicate within your neighborhood, you can get by with short-range devices. On the other hand, if you have friends or relatives in another state, you might want to establish the means to keep in touch in case normal communications are lost.

Depending on your needs, you can opt for inexpensive radios with limited ranges, or invest more money in radios capable of long distance or worldwide communication. Some of the equipment covered in this chapter has local capabilities, and some is capable of long distance communication.

RADIO RECEIVERS—ONE-WAY COMMUNICATION

If your information needs will be met by listening only, meaning you don't require two-way communication, all you'll need is a radio receiver. An inexpensive receiver will allow you to monitor many radio frequency bands.

Not all radio stations will be silent at any given time during an extended Y2K scenario. All have some backup electrical power generating capability; some more than others. A good radio receiver with AM/FM and shortwave frequency reception will let you find a variety of stations which will give you national and international news updates.

AM/FM Radios

We're all familiar with Amplitude Modulated (AM) and Frequency Modulated (FM) radios. AM and FM bands are short-range local frequencies. Most people already have inexpensive AM/FM radios. These can be used during Y2K just as they are now, to pick up news and other broadcasts.

Y2K problems could disrupt or eventually terminate many commercial radio broadcasts. Therefore, it would be a good idea to have a backup information receiver, in addition to an AM/FM radio.

Shortwave Radios

If we lost radio and TV news stations as well as newspapers due to Y2K, we'd be totally out of touch with the local and world situation. To address this problem, we recommend you purchase a shortwave radio. In an emergency situation, information from shortwave radio could provide security and comfort to you and your family.

Shortwave Reception

Shortwave radio provides daily access to world news, and all types of long-range communications from the shortwave bands of 1.7 to 30 MHz. Most shortwave radios also have the ability to receive AM and FM signals. Shortwave frequencies are utilized by churches, the military and other services. With a shortwave radio, you can access the world through the touch of a dial! Best of all, you don't need a license to receive shortwave transmissions.

Every major country in the world, as well as many other countries, transmit their English language programs directly to North America. Some of these signals can be heard clearly on an inexpensive shortwave radio.

Some of the easiest stations to pick up are the high-powered international broadcasters, like BBC London, Radio Moscow, and The Voice of America. Just below this level are hundreds of other broadcasters in many countries, such as RNE Spain, Radio Japan, and Vatican Radio.

A variety of transmission modes are used on shortwave. Single sideband is used by military services, ham radio operators, aircraft and ships. AM is typically used by international broadcast stations. Morse code is used with Amateur Radio activities. Fax transmissions are used for sending weather pictures; teletype transmissions are used by news services throughout the world.

We recommend you purchase a guide to shortwave radio, such as the *Shortwave Listener's Handbook* by Andre R. Yoder, available for $24 from Amazon.com. This book helps you select and use your equipment, gives lists of SW stations, and provides simple, inexpensive ways to improve your reception.

Shortwave Antennas

Some portable shortwave receivers on the market come with a retractable, built-in antenna. While convenient, they are often incapable of receiving anything but the signals from the stronger stations. If you want to optimize the range and reception of your shortwave radio, upgrade the antenna. See your radio equipment supplier for information.

For good, consistent long-range reception of the average to weaker signals, consider using an outdoor horizontal single wire antenna of from 30 to 70 ft. in length. Building one yourself is described in Dave Ingram's book, *Guide To Emergency Survival Communications.*

D-Mail sells a device developed by the military that boosts reception on any type of radio. The Powertip Signal Enhancer slides onto the tip of your present antenna, helping your radio pull in distant signals. Cost is just $10.

Shortwave Radio Options

Shopping for a shortwave radio is like shopping for a television or stereo system. Some of the better portable models are Grundig and Sony. Higher performance receivers include Kenwood, Drake and Lowe.

There are many suppliers in the shortwave receiver market. Radio Shack, 800-843-7422, is a convenient starting point. They recently had a sale on four shortwave receivers priced from $40 to $200, and also offered a 32 ft. retractable SW antenna for $9.

http://www.radioshack.com

Specialty ham radio shops are also a good source of knowledgeable salespeople. The trick is to find someone able to help you find what you're searching for and explain the product.

We were fortunate to find a factory serviced Grundig Yacht Boy 400 Shortwave Radio in the DAMARK catalog, 800-827-6767, for only $117! The Yacht Boy comes complete with reception from 1.6 to 30 MHZ, single side band, 40 preset memory locations, built in clock and alarm, a shortwave listening guide, telescopic

FM/shortwave antenna, built-in ferrite AM/LW antenna, a carry case, and an external retractable wire antenna. It is powered by 6 AA batteries with an optional plug-in 9 volt adapter.

http://www.damark.com

Scanners

If we lose access to commercial communications, another means of staying in the know is to purchase a handheld scanner. Scanners automatically surf the police, emergency, fire, aircraft, marine, and weather radio channels, allowing you to listen in. Many scanners offer pre-programmed services with the ability to toggle through the above mentioned frequencies.

Some scanners offer "trunk tracking" which allows you to follow police and emergency medical service transmissions which shift from channel to channel. Trunk tracking provides uninterrupted monitoring of these transmissions. Without trunk tracking, you will only hear partial transmissions.

Reception of the frequencies covered by a standard scanner is chiefly "line of sight," which means you will not normally be able to receive those stations beyond the horizon.

Scanner Options

Handheld models are preferable to table top models because of their portability. Scanners sell for from $80 to $500. You can purchase a good model for $220 to $300.

Scanners can be purchased through a variety of retailers—sporting goods stores, catalogs, department stores, and electronics stores. Radio Shack carries a wide selection.

DAMARK offers two scanners by Uniden. One is a Base Scanner, a 300 channel Trunk Tracker home model that can track both sides of a conversation even if the channel switches between replies! It warns of approaching severe weather and has a RS232C port for connection to a computer for recording. It costs $300.

The other scanner offered by DAMARK is a handheld model, powered by rechargeable batteries which are included. It has trunk tracking, and sells for $250. We bought a comparable model from Radio Shack on sale for $169.

Before purchasing a scanner, give careful consideration to the power source. Scanners powered only by conventional 120 volt Alternating Current won't be too useful during a power outage! Many home models will work with either AC or DC power.

Consider buying a solar battery charger; see Chapter 7, pages 262 to 263, for information. NiCad batteries can be recharged with a solar battery charger and used to power your scanner.

We recommend scanners that operate on AA batteries. They are portable and compact. While it may take as many as 8 to 10 batteries to power the unit, you can inexpensively stock up on quite a few batteries at a discount retailer such as Costco or Sam's Club, where packages of 40 Alkaline AA batteries cost $8.

Scanner Frequency Guide Book

To receive the maximum benefit from your scanner, we recommend purchasing a copy of Radio Shack's *Police Call*. This book is a comprehensive source of scanner frequencies listed by state, with nationwide listings, and more. Included are listings of police frequencies and their call signs, fire departments, military, and much more—all in alphabetical order. The price is $13.

Self-Powered Radios

These radios avoid power supply problems entirely!

Kinetic Radio Receivers

Kinetic radios contain internal generators, powered by a hand-cranked spring mechanism. Some have solar power capabilities, or are dual-purpose radio flashlights or radio lanterns.

The BayGen Freeplay Radio from South Africa has become a favorite of Y2K customers. Hand cranking for 20 seconds provides 30 minutes of reception. It receives AM and FM as well as SW bands between 3 and 18 MHz and costs $100. A separate portable SW antenna costs $20.

The BayGen Freeplay Solar Radio receives just AM and FM, but runs directly off of sunlight and/or the kinetic spring as sunlight decreases. It costs $80.

BayGen radios are sold by various solar, preparedness and radio suppliers. Jade Mountain and Amateur Electronic Supply, 800-558-0411, sell them at the prices listed above.

http://www.aesham.com

The AM-FM Dynamo & Solar Radio receiver gives you 20 minutes of playing time for about 40 cranks. It's also solar-powered, or runs on two AA batteries. This handy product is available through The Sportsman's Guide, priced under $25.

Jade Mountain also sells a kinetic-powered cassette player for $125!

Crystal Radio Receivers

These receivers, the original radios, are powered by radio waves and require no additional power source. They receive AM broadcast band stations and can be modified to receive higher power SW stations. Buy a kit and a set of 4000 ohm headphones and you are all set to be power-free! Antique Electronic Supply Co., 602-820-5411, sells crystal set kits.

NON-LICENSED TWO-WAY COMMUNICATION

Transceivers are sending and receiving radios—two-way radios—and can take the place of telephones in an emergency. They are used daily by many professions such as the police, fire and emergency medical services. Some transceivers such as the

Amateur, Business and Marine bands require an FCC license. Others such as the following do not.

Communicators, Citizens Band, General Mobile Radio Service and Family Band radios are all two-way radios with limited power and range. They don't require any training or an operator's license. The General Mobile Radio Service radios require an equipment license, but have no operator's training or licensure requirement. All are useful for communications within your local community or while traveling with a group.

We recommend you purchase a pair of two-way radios from those described in the following sections. In an emergency situation when family members are separated, two-way radios provide constant communications, thus alleviating anxieties.

Communicators

Hobbyist-type "walkie-talkies" or communicators operate on the 49-MHz frequency "free band" and are used for a combination of very low power, unlicensed communication. Due to the low power, the effective range of the signal is only 1/8 to 1/4 mile. Wireless baby monitors, motorcycle communicators and children's walkie-talkies are examples.

Communicators have up to 5 channels. Voice activated transmission (VOX) and all-in-one mike/earphone configurations make them good for hands-free use. Maxon, Midland and Radio Shack are all good brands. Communicators can be purchased at local sporting goods stores, motorcycle dealerships, or through catalogs such as Amateur Electronic Supply. They sell a single channel Maxon MX-49SX for $30. The 5-channel Maxon MX-49FX sells for $50.

Citizens Band Radios

The Citizens Band is a two-way service for personal or business use with a total of 40 channels. CB functions like a giant intercom or old-fashioned telephone party line on the nation's highways! Anyone tuned to the same channel can listen in on your conversation. It's still a useful tool, despite the lack of privacy.

CB signals are limited by law to 5 watts. They can reach out 20 miles if a channel is clear, but if the channel is congested, they may only go 4 miles. CB also has a nationwide emergency monitoring network, the Radio Emergency Associated Citizens Team (REACT) on Channel 9, which is also monitored by the police.

There are plenty of CB radios to select from and they are reasonably priced. You can purchase handheld or base model CB radios at sporting goods stores, Radio Shack and department stores.

Many handheld CB radios start at about $100 a pair. However, we recently purchased a pair of General Electric 40 channel handheld CBs for $40 on sale at a discount electronics store. Handhelds normally come with a car adapter which plugs into the cigarette lighter jack, or run on up to 8 AA batteries.

Mobile CB radios are designed to be mounted in your car like cassette players. They start in price at about $70 and have higher power outputs. They use a permanent or magnetically attached car antenna.

Some of the major CB radio manufacturers are as follows:

Cobra is one of the best known and respected manufacturers of CB equipment. Their prices range to meet anyone's budget. Cobra has been researching and developing CB radio for over 30 years.

Maxon produces a quality product at a fair cost.

Uniden is well known for both their scanners and CB radios.

Radio Shack is one of the most well-known brand names in CBs and electronics. Their CB units range from simple to extravagant. Prices start at $50 for 40-channel, full legal power handhelds. A mobile unit for your car minus the antenna starts at $70.

Mobile CB antennas range in price from $20 to $60, and up.

Many catalogs offer CB radios, such as the following:

DAMARK sells a Midland 40-channel handheld model with instant access to emergency channel 9. It's powered by 8 AA batteries or 10 rechargeable NiCad AA batteries. It comes complete with a 12-volt cigarette lighter adapter, and features 7 watts input with a 4-stage bar graph. It has a price tag of $50.

DAMARK also offers a Uniden handheld model. This 40-channel model comes with instant emergency channels and 7 weather channels. It also offers dual watch to monitor two channels at once, comes complete with cigarette lighter power cord and belt clip, and is powered by either 9 AA batteries or 9 rechargeable NiCad batteries. This unit sells for $70.

Heartland America offers a Midland 40-channel handheld delivering pinpoint channel tuning, instant weather updates, two user selectable memory channels, and last channel recall. The unit is powered by 9 AA batteries, and sells for $50.

The Sportsman's Guide offers a Maxon handheld CB radio with three National Weather Service Frequencies, last channel memory, cigarette lighter plug, low battery indicator and belt clip. Powered by 8 AA batteries or 10 rechargeable NiCad batteries, it retails for $40.

General Mobile Radio Service

The General Mobile Radio Service band in the 462-MHz range is an evolution in Citizens Band radio. It was designed for semi-professional use as with security forces and large groups. GMRS radios have a channel for citizens involved with search and rescue activities. This radio does not require a radio operator's license, but does require a valid FCC equipment license. The paperwork for this license is included in the packaging when you purchase the radios. The five-year equipment license costs $75. Contact the FCC for information, 888-225-5322.

http://www.fcc.gov

Motorola sells TalkAbout Distance and Distance DPS radios which operate in the GMRS band. These radios have a five mile range, 10 channels, and built-in VOX hands-free operation.

The Sportsman's Guide sells the TalkAbout Distance for $389 per pair, which is quite a bit better than the $520 per pair suggested retail price. The TalkAbout Distance operates either on the included NiCad rechargeable battery pack or six AA batteries. The battery life is 10 hours per charge with the NiCads or 20 hours with the AA batteries.

Family Band Radios

There are 14 Family Radio Service channels in the 462-MHz range located between the normal GMRS channels. They are set aside for low-power, unlicensed use on simple short-range radios for families. The maximum legal power output for FRS radios is 0.5 watt, and the effective range is from 1 to 2 miles, depending on terrain and conditions. FRS radios are an excellent, inexpensive means of local two-way communication.

Handheld FRS radios start at under $50 each. You can find Family Band radios in your neighborhood sporting goods store, gun shop, department store, Radio Shack, etc. We found low prices and a good selection in a number of mail-order catalogs.

They all have the same number of channels and interference eliminator codes. Before making your purchase, consider the *power output, effective range,* and *power source* of the model you select.

Power output is measured in watts. The greater the output, the stronger the signal and the farther the range. FRS radios are all 0.35 or 0.5 watts, and all have a range of from 1 to 2 miles. We recommend you only buy FRS radios with 0.5 watts power output for maximum range.

Effective range, or talk range, is dependent upon the surrounding terrain. If your radio has a 2-mile range, you can transmit and receive signals for 2 miles line of sight—straight line, unobstructed. This range is decreased substantially if tall buildings, trees, or other obstructions are between the transmitter and the receiver.

Power source refers to the type of battery that powers the unit. Some use rechargeable nickel cadmium batteries, while others use three or more AA alkaline batteries. Disposable batteries are more convenient than rechargeable ones. If you suffer a sustained power loss, it may be difficult to recharge batteries unless you have a solar battery recharger. AA batteries are inexpensive if purchased in bulk, and good quality alkaline ones have a five-year shelf life.

We purchased a pair of Motorola TalkAbout PlusOne model FRS radios from The Sportsman's Guide for $260. This model has a large LCD channel indicator, comes with an unbreakable fixed antenna, and weighs 7 oz. Three AA batteries give the user approximately 20 hours talk time.

The TalkAbout series permits use of an optional Ear Bud with Microphone or Headset with Microphone, for hands-free operation. Both options are available from the Sportsman's Guide for $27 and $29 respectively.

The TalkAbout 250 model has a scanning mode to monitor all FRS channels. It's suggested retail price is $170 each.

Motorola has a website describing the TalkAbouts which lists prices, specifications and suppliers.

http://www.motorola.com/talkabout

Many less expensive handheld FRS models are available which will do the same job. DAMARK offers the following choices in handheld FRS radios:

Two-Way Family Radios come with an automatic power saving mode, low battery indicator, and an automatic squelch feature. Slightly larger than the Talkabouts, they sell for $200 a pair.

Midland's model #75-501 has a 2-mile range and a call button to notify other FRS radio users in your group. Powered by 3 NiCad batteries or 3 AAs, they are priced at $100 per pair.

Northwestern Bell Phones make two-way FRS radios that come with a key lock feature and channel monitor and require 4 AAA batteries. Model 99141 retails for $130 a pair. We purchased a pair for $100 on sale at a electronics discount store.

Heartland America, 800-229-2901, offers a Whistler FRS radio, featuring automatic squelch and low battery indicator. It operates on 4 AA batteries and costs $100 per pair.

http://www.heartlandamerica.com

LICENSED TWO-WAY COMMUNICATION

Anyone can listen to almost any radio frequency at any time. All you need is the proper equipment, such as a shortwave receiver discussed earlier. But, in order to transmit or talk over distances greater than 20 miles, you need to get an FCC amateur radio license. If you want the ability to converse over long distances during Y2K-induced communications outages, this option is for you.

With a little training, you can take a test and become licensed to broadcast on the long-range or mid-range radio frequencies controlled by the FCC. A ten-year FCC Amateur Radio license is free; the only cost is a $6.50 examination fee.

However, if you will be using your radio in any money-making activity, you must pay $75 for a five-year Business Radio license, and use frequencies assigned to you.

Amateur radio transceivers are more expensive than shortwave receivers, but they add the factor of two-way communication. For an overview of amateur radio with good links see:

http://www.irony.com/ham-howto.html

Amateur radio operators (hams) cooperate with the authorities in the event of emergencies by participating in the relaying of emergency information. Hams use Orbiting Satellites Carrying Amateur Radio (OSCARs) to communicate worldwide on voice and through computer! Some satellite systems may fail due to embedded chip problems, but others may continue to function.

Low-power short-range handheld radios used in conjunction with repeater stations let hams communicate within distances of 150 miles. Hams also communicate globally on high frequency (HF) long-range equipment.

If interested in amateur radio, you can contact The American Radio Relay League (ARRL) at 800-326-3942 or 888-277-5289. They publish ham license study guides to assist you in learning what's necessary to pass the exam. A good overview is found in *Now You're Talking! All You Need To Get Your Ham Radio Technician License*, published by the ARRL.

http://www.arrl.org

Amateur Radio Options

In an emergency there will be networks of amateur radio operators communicating regionally and nationally. They may even be asked by FEMA to provide local and long-range emergency communications. If you want access to this valuable information, you'll need the training and equipment amateur operators use.

You don't need a license to listen to ham radio, and in a genuine emergency, anyone is allowed to talk on any radio at any time to protect life and property. But to enter into regular two-way communication with your ham radio, you'll need to get licensed.

Local-Range Amateur Radios

With a handheld amateur radio, you have access to two-way local communications over a distance of from 20 miles unassisted to 150 miles using repeater stations. This is a much greater range than that of Family Radios or CBs.

For local communications, use 70-centimeter or 2-meter handheld radios. Many models are available from the ham radio suppliers listed here. You can also buy less expensive, used ham equipment from sources such as The Ham Trader-Ham Radio and Electronics Swap and Shop:

http://www.hamtrader.com

Handheld amateur radios: We recommend the new 5-watt Yaesu VX5R handheld transceiver. It provides 70-centimeter, 2 and 6-meter transceiving, as well as shortwave listening. It uses rechargeable lithium ion batteries (recharger included), and is built to military specifications with a metal case. Available for $360 from the Ham Radio Outlet, 800-644-4476.

http://www.hamradio.com

Contact Yaesu at 562-404-2700

http://www.yaesu.com

The 5 watt ICOM W32 handheld costs $290 from Amateur Electronic Supply. It has both 70-centimeter and 2-meter channels and will monitor 70-centimeter while transceiving on 2-meter, and vice versa. It uses rechargeable NiCAD or nickel metal hydride (NiMH) batteries. Contact ICOM at 425-454-8155.

http://www.icomamerica.com

When combined with the 12 VDC MAHA MHA201 Dual Channel amplifier for $150 from Ham Radio Outlet, it puts out 45 watts on 2-meter and 35 watts on 70-centimeter and becomes an effective mobile radio for your car. The $30 MFJ 1729 is a dual 2m/70cm mobile antenna.

Long-Range Amateur Radios

The high frequency (HF) ham bands travel the farthest for global communications. These radio signals bounce between the layer of the atmosphere called the ionosphere and the earth and literally can skip around the world.

Ham Radio Outlet sells the 12 VDC, 100 watt ICOM 706 MK II Mobile/Base radio. It covers the standard ham bands as well as shortwave, 2 and 6-meter, and handles all modes. It does it all in a box the size of your car radio for $970. Use it in your car, then carry it into the house for use as a base station.

With the $310 ICOM AH4 mobile antenna automatic tuner, it makes any piece of wire 8 ft. or longer a perfect antenna.

Amateur Radio Antennas

Investing in an antenna tuner such as the AH4 above is the most cost-effective way to improve the performance of any radio. When attached to an 80 ft. piece of any insulated 10 to 18 gauge copper wire draped in a tree, your base station reception problems are solved. AARL also offers several books on building your own antennas, such as the *Antenna Compendium* series.

POWER SUPPLIES

In the event of regional electrical power failures or brownouts, you'll want a stable, renewable source of power for your radios.

DC vs. AC

Having a radio transceiver which can operate on an alternative 12 volt DC system powered by solar panels and a battery bank may be your most independent power solution.

If your equipment requires 110 volt AC, the use of a DC/AC inverter will permit you to take your 12V DC source and convert it into 110V AC. See Chapter 7, page 256, for details.

Batteries

Handheld radios typically use AA-type batteries. Your best bet to power the handheld portable radios discussed in this chapter is to stock up on the indicated batteries and purchase a solar battery recharger. See Chapter 7, page 262.

Mobile radios are powered by an automobile's lead-acid wet-cell battery. Base station radios utilize the gel cell or wet cell types used for solar systems, or deep cycle lead-acid batteries used in boats. Be sure to purchase the proper batteries for your equipment. Your radio club or supplier will give you advice on what to use.

Information on batteries for ham radio use is available at:
http://www.qsl.net/ke3fl/htm/BATTERY.HTM

In conclusion, even if you're on a budget, you can prepare to keep informed if the normal channels of communication are disrupted. For as little as $40, you can purchase a shortwave receiver and listen to worldwide transmissions. Starting at $40, you can buy a pair of handheld CB radios, for two-way communication up to a range of 20 miles. If you need to communicate over longer distances and can spend more, purchase Amateur Radio equipment.

Over and out!

COMMUNICATIONS CHECKLIST

_____ Buy an AM/FM/shortwave receiver

_____ Buy a *Shortwave Listener's Guidebook*

_____ Upgrade your SW antenna

_____ Buy a scanner to monitor emergency communications

_____ Buy *Police Call*, a scanner frequency guidebook

_____ Buy a power-free radio, such as the BayGen Freeplay SW Radio manually-powered model

_____ Buy one or more matched pairs of two-way local transceivers from this list:

    ___ Communicators

    ___ Citizens Band

    ___ General Mobile Radio Service

    ___ Family Service Radio

_____ To communicate over long distances, consider two-way amateur radio

_____ Take an amateur radio class from ARRL

_____ Get an FCC amateur radio license

_____ Buy a handheld or mobile local-range amateur two-way radio

_____ Buy a long-range HF base station amateur two-way radio

_____ Upgrade your amateur radio antenna

_____ Purchase necessary power supplies

    ___ Alkaline batteries

    ___ Rechargeable batteries

    ___ Solar battery recharger

_____ Practice with your radios!

CHAPTER 9

Medical

If there isn't more action, I'm afraid this Y2K problem could have the nation's health care system on a respirator come January 2000.

Senator Christopher Dodd
Co-chair, Senate Y2K Committee

Of all the sectors of our economy, the national health care system is one of the least prepared for Y2K. One of your major Y2K-related concerns should be, "What do I do if I get sick and can't get to the hospital, or if when I get there the hospitals aren't functional?"

Though you can't resolve the poor status of hospital Y2K readiness, there are proactive steps you can take to promote good health and handle some basic medical problems yourself. We're not doctors, and are not making recommendations for your health care, but the following material will give you some ideas as to where to focus your attention regarding medical issues.

PERSONAL MEDICAL STEPS TO TAKE NOW

First, take care of all medical problems you can resolve in 1999. Utilize your medical insurance coverage fully this year; make sure you're in the best health possible going into the Year 2000.

Medical Exam

Get a thorough physical examination, including blood work, X-rays and cardiac evaluations. Your doctor or insurer may try to brush you off. Don't let them. You want to have a clean bill of health in 1999, or have enough time to resolve any problems before 2000. If your insurer refuses to pay for a complete physical exam and you are over 50 years of age, seriously consider paying for it out of your own pocket.

Surgery

If any elective or necessary surgery is indicated, be sure to have it done as soon as possible. That will give you time to heal and/or deal with any potential complications prior to the millennium. If you can, avoid all surgery in the six months both preceding and following Y2K.

Medical Devices

Some medical devices such as Pacemakers and Implantable Automatic Cardioverter-Defibrillators are totally contained in the body. These must be evaluated to insure they will not malfunction due to date-sensitive embedded computer chips. These devices need their implanted batteries replaced every few years. If you or someone you know has one, get the battery replaced in mid-1999. You can't be certain when you'll be able to get these batteries, and have them surgically implanted, after 2000.

If the power grid is disrupted, personal medical equipment requiring electrical power must have reserve batteries and/or generator backup. This includes home ventilators and other personal use medical equipment such as oxygen concentrators. Stand-by generators will start up automatically if your power fails, then turn off automatically when power is restored.

Institutional medical equipment and services such as kidney dialysis may become inaccessible after 2000 due to infrastructure problems.

It's possible that people with chronic or acute illnesses may not be able to maintain their health through a protracted Y2K crisis. These individuals should consider resolving all personal issues prior to 2000, and prepare themselves and their families, should the stresses of Y2K prove too great to sustain life. They could ask to be referred to social workers or psychologists, who would help the patient and family work through these issues and concerns in a healthy way.

Prescription Medicines

Talk to your doctor about your prescriptions. Explain your concerns about not having a consistent supply in early 2000. Ask for his or her advice. Ask to be weaned off all medications not crucial to your health. Ask your doctor to supervise a "drug holiday" for you. This is a common technique used to see how well you will do without many of your prescriptions, or with smaller doses. Wean medications only when being closely supervised by a doctor. Do not do this yourself.

If you don't feel your doctor is giving you the support you need, or if he/she refuses to help, find another doctor. Remember, the doctor is your employee—contracting with you for medical services rendered.

Once you have decreased the drugs and dosages, ask your doctor for prescriptions for a year's supply of medications. Diabetics especially need ample insulin and related supplies.

Fill your prescriptions by mid-1999. It is likely to be a volatile year, so be prepared and stock up early! Medicines do have a limited lifespan. Ask your pharmacist about your particular medicines;

check the expiration dates. Also find out the length of time after expiration that you can still safely use the medication. Be certain your medication doesn't break down over time into dangerous chemicals, as some do.

Unlike many countries, the pharmaceutical supply in the U.S. is strictly controlled by law. Only those licensed to prescribe medications, such as Doctors, Dentists, and some Physician's Assistants and Nurse Practitioners can provide them to you. It is illegal to have non-prescribed medications. Don't put yourself at risk.

Some physicians are trying to ensure that prescription medications not run out in the event of prolonged medication supply problems. Y2K Meds provides inexpensive bulk quantities of medications. Y2K Doc is trying to get permission to write primarily antibiotic prescriptions for Y2K supplies.

http://www.bonners-ferry.com/y2kmeds
http://www.y2kdoc.com

Narcotic Analgesics

Tylenol with codeine, Darvocet or other narcotic pain relievers would be helpful for cases of severe pain, if you couldn't get to a doctor. Your doctor might give you a prescription.

Antibiotics

During disasters such as 1998's hurricane Mitch in Central America, many of those affected died immediately. Others died from exposure, but most people died from preventable problems such as infected wounds and epidemics of infectious disease.

Obtain a prescription for antibiotics from your physician, if he or she agrees. Try to persuade your doctor to give you a supply of amoxicillin, sulfa, erythromycin and tetracycline antibiotics.

In an emergency, if you don't have access to a doctor for prescribing medications, the book *Where There Is No Doctor* contains antibiotic dosing and usage information.

Vaccinations

Get all your vaccinations brought up to date. Consider including those for diseases normally found in Third World countries. The military vaccination protocol for worldwide deployment includes Yellow Fever, good for 10 years; Tetanus, also effective for 10 years; Typhoid, good for 3 years; Anthrax, with a booster shot every 2 years, as well as annual flu vaccinations. See to it that your children's immunizations are current as well.

Vision Care

If you are concerned that Y2K disruptions could last for an extended period, purchase an extra pair or two of prescription eyeglasses. Get the same style as your current pair if possible, so you can exchange parts, or order sturdy frames.

Get polycarbonate lenses, as they are the strongest, most scratch-resistant type available. Buy an eyeglasses repair kit with extra screws, screwdriver and nosepads. Keep your old glasses for spares.

Dental Care

Complete all dental work and any indicated dental surgery in early 1999. Have your dentist replace all old and suspect fillings. The older white composite fillings have a limited lifespan. They should be replaced with the newer more durable versions of the composites. The older style "silver" amalgam fillings are durable, but they leach mercury into your blood stream and are believed to have a negative effect on your nervous and immune systems. Have your wisdom teeth X-rayed and consider having them removed if there is a possibility of an impaction.

Physical Conditioning

Physical activity and regular exercise are extremely important and beneficial for long-term health and well being. Exercise reduces stress and increases endurance. This is especially true when you consider preparing for Y2K. Imagine facing all the possible problems ahead of us, while huffing and puffing trying to get everything together, because you're out of shape.

It won't be too difficult to get into tip-top condition for Y2K. Begin with something as simple as briskly walking for 20 minutes three times a week. Or, try aerobics or jogging. Some strength training such as with free weights is also appropriate, especially if you're going to lug 40 lb., 5 gal. pails of water any distance!

If there ever was a time to begin an exercise program, the time is now. Join a health club or run around your neighborhood. Just get back in shape!

PREPARING FOR MEDICINE AFTER 2000

In a worst-case Y2K scenario, our medical system could resemble a battlefield. In a national emergency or prolonged civil disruption, hospitals may be forced to adopt the military triage system where the care goes first to those deemed to be survivable with medical treatment.

The ability of medical providers to give citizens current levels of care could be impaired. Many high-tech medical diagnostic systems such as MRIs and CT Scanners are likely to be compromised. Potential reimbursement failures from nonfunctional federal government bureaucracies could cause severe cash flow problems. The capacity to continuously resupply hospitals with generator fuel, equipment, medical supplies and pharmaceuticals after 2000 is in serious question.

Medical Providers

You'll want to establish an alternative medical plan. Your best solution to any potential medical shortages is to make friends with a physician and keep him or her well-fed and happy! Otherwise, consider working with alternate medical practitioners.

The U.S. Public Health Service suggests a list of doctor substitutes. In an emergency you can turn to: Veterinarians, Physician Assistants, Nurse Practitioners, Dentists, Paramedics, EMT Specialists, Registered Nurses, Pharmacists, Combat Medics, Licensed Practical Nurses, Basic EMTs, Podiatrists and students of any of these medical disciplines.

If you're participating in a preparedness community, at least one member is likely to have had some medical training. Your group should also have funds available to invest in an array of medical equipment and supplies.

Realistically, it's not likely that you'll always have someone nearby who has both medical skills and supplies. A better option is to be prepared to provide your own simple medical support.

Emergency Medical Library

Building an emergency medical library is a crucial preparedness step. The book *Where There Is No Doctor* by David Werner is great for low-tech medical solutions. Though designed for Latin American and African communities, it clearly describes what you can appropriately handle in a primitive setting and how to do so. It also explains which medical conditions require expert intervention.

Get a book or two on "field medicine." We recommend *Ditch Medicine: Advanced Field Procedures for Emergencies* by Hugh Coffee and *Wilderness First Aid: Emergency Care for Remote Locations* by the National Safety Council and Wilderness Medical Society. Both may be helpful during Y2K.

Even if you've been fortunate to team up with a doctor, most physicians will not have had exposure to working in primitive conditions, or a working knowledge of the related effective techniques. The DoD's *Emergency War Surgery* would give a doctor a wealth of information, and will show you what not to try to do! An excellent series of Emergency Medical textbooks is published by Brady-Prentis Hall, 800-638-0220. *Emergency Care* and *First Responder* are good examples. *First Responder* is written in simpler language, making it more understandable.

http://www.bradybooks.com

Another good source is a pocket *EMS Field Guide* by Jon Tardiff. This small flip chart reference manual sells for $16.50 from booksellers or Time Emergency Equipment, 248-852-0939.

International Medical Guide for Ships: Including the Ship's Medicine Chest by the World Health Organization was written for the medical staff of ocean-going ships. It covers problems and how to deal with them while away from hospitals. You can purchase this book, and the others listed here, from Amazon.com.

For good information on common medical issues, a list of Medical Frequently Asked Questions (FAQs) is available at:

http://www1.oup.co.uk/scimed/medint/medint1emedfaq.html

Survival Medicine FAQs are available at:

http://www.survival-center.com/med-faq/index.htm

First Aid Training

Obtain basic training in first aid, so you can provide supportive care to keep an injured person alive until you can get him or her to a qualified medical provider. Once you've been trained, you'll also have a barterable skill.

You can take the American Red Cross first aid class in your local area. The "Community First Aid and CPR" 10-hour class covers standard first aid, adult Cardio-Pulmonary Resuscitation and infant/child CPR for a modest fee. Call them at the number in your phone book or at the national headquarters, 800-HELP-NOW. The national website has a link to local service centers.

http://www.redcross.org/where/chapts.html

At a minimum, learn basic CPR. The Red Cross has classes for this as do most local hospitals and clinics. A basic Red Cross Emergency Handbook is available online at:

http://www.lifelink.com/emergenc.htm

If you have time and want further training, the Red Cross and some community colleges offer First Responder Advanced First Aid classes. Advanced First Aid is a 60-hour class which culminates in State licensure as a First Responder, someone who can offer simple emergency support.

The Basic Emergency Medical Technician training at community colleges is about 180 hours, with 20 to 30 additional hours of clinical time or "on the job experience" depending on the school. You will be eligible to take the exam for EMT licensure at the completion of the course.

Beyond that is the EMT Specialist which has training in intravenous therapy and airway intubation. Finally, the Paramedic classification requires a year's instruction, including Advanced Cardiac Life Support from the American Heart Association.

First Aid Supplies

Where There Is No Doctor recommends every family keep on hand a stock of medicine and medical supplies for emergencies. A list in the book was created with the expectation that replacements could be purchased at any time for restocking. This may not be the case for you.

We suggest buying enough of the supplies to have extra available. The items on our list are available from your local pharmacy or from the suppliers listed in this chapter:

- large waterproof first aid kit box (from Major Surplus)
- large fishing tackle box with waterproof seal (Plano brand)
- manual blood pressure cuff
- stethoscope
- Ambu bag and mask
- rigid plastic back board for immobilizing and transporting patients or 3/4" plywood with 3 sets of handholds
- 3 sets of straps for back board (car seatbelts can be used)
- stretcher ($30 from The Sportsman's Guide)
- body bag (Military surplus from Major Surplus)
- bags of normal saline intravenous solution, tubing and needles
- flashlight
- otoscope, to examine ears
- 5.5 in. or larger EMT shears
- hypothermia thermometer (goes below 95° F)
- oral and rectal thermometers
- eyedropper
- metalized emergency blanket
- packages of sterile gloves
- box of clean gloves
- disposable face masks
- cervical collar/neck brace, head blocks or towel rolls (to immobilize the neck)
- full size and Jr. size SAM splints
- inflatable splints or 1 in. x 3 in. wooden boards
- nail clipper
- sterile scalpel with replacement blades
- 2 pair of hemostats
- surgical tweezers
- surgical scissors

- several 3/0 sutures with needles
- sterile wound closure strips ("butterflys")
- small, medium and large airways, or a 6-size set
- small and medium nasal airways
- abundant bandaids, various sizes
- large bulky wound dressings, 18 in. x 36 in.
- triangular bandages
- Tegaderm 3 in. x 3.5 in. adhesive second skin plastic dressing
- 4 in. x 4 in. sterile gauze pads
- 2 in. x 2 in. sterile gauze pads
- sterile eye pads
- non-adherent dressings (Telfa)
- gauze rolls
- clean cotton batting
- adhesive tape rolls, cloth and paper, 1 in. and 2 in.
- various sizes of elastic bandages
- moleskin
- Dermaplast spray
- irrigation squeeze bottle
- irrigation piston syringe
- suction device or turkey baster for suction
- bottled sterile water
- tincture of benzoin
- isopropyl alcohol pads
- 3% hydrogen peroxide
- benzalkonium chloride antiseptic towelettes
- Betadine antiseptic iodine solution
- colloidal silver solution
- liquid antibacterial soap
- water soluble lubricant (K-Y Jelly)
- tube of glucose paste

- instant chemical ice packs
- instant chemical heat packs
- cotton-tipped applicators
- tongue depressors
- emesis (kidney) basin
- bedpan
- urinal
- safety pins
- plastic bags

Other lists of medical supplies can be found at:
http://www.millennium-ark.net/News_Files/LTAH_First_Aid(8).html
http://www.ionet.net/~rbrocato/MedicalSupplies.html
Medical Kits

Purchase a comprehensive Emergency Medical Kit including basic surgical equipment and suture material. Prepackaged first aid kits range in price from $20 to $470. We recommend buying one of the comprehensive kits and getting additional items such as extra gauze bandages, tape, bandaids, clean gloves, isopropyl alcohol and Betadine antiseptic iodine solution. Kits usually contain first aid manuals and emergency action information cards.

Both Major Surplus and B&A Products sell a variety of first aid kits as do most preparedness suppliers. The Expedition for $80 was designed for long-term backcountry use where evacuation would be difficult, making it appropriate for Y2K disruptions. The Atwater Carey EMT Mini costs $230 and The Mountain Rescue backpack kit costs $470.

Adventure Medical Kits from Campmor or SafeTrek Outfitters are rated the most comprehensive and innovative medical kits available. The Comprehensive Kit has 190 items for $145, the Expedition Kit costs $230. The Mountain Medic Kit is designed for wilderness rescue professionals, it costs $350.

The Special Op's Shop sells the Atwater Carey 3.0 Medical Kit for $80. It's rated as serving medium sized groups on multi-week trips. They also sell individual boxes of sutures, syringes with needles, inflatable splints, medical instruments, surgical instruments, airways and other items.

Emergency Essentials sells a Surgical Care Kit which includes nine stainless steel instruments for more serious injuries, it costs $40. They also sell a Burn Care Kit for $30.

Nitro-Pak sells a Deluxe Suture & Syringe Kit for $73, a Medic Surgical & Suture Kit for $50 and a $19 Emergency Childbirth Kit.

Emergency Medical Equipment Suppliers

Look in your Yellow Pages for "First Aid Supplies-Retail." The following suppliers also sell equipment and first aid kits used by EMTs, as well as more common medical supplies.

Dixie USA, 800-347-3494.

http://www.dixieems.com

Laerdal Medical, 888-562-4242, sells a variety of emergency equipment including portable defibrillators, resuscitators, a BaXstrap Spineboard for $190 and three sets of straps for $20.

http://www.laerdal.com

Masune, 800-831-0894

http://www.masune.com

Michigan First Aid and Safety Supplies, 800-221-9222, is another mail-order medical supply company with a huge selection and discount pricing. Their largest five-shelf industrial first aid kit costs $282. A First Responder's kit costs $82.

http://www.mfasco.com

Over-the-Counter Medications

If the drug stores aren't open in early 2000, you may soon run

out of aspirin for the splitting headache you'll likely get from Y2K.
So stock up on the following medications:
- activated charcoal
- aloe vera gel
- antacid (Maalox)
- antibiotic ointment (Neosporin)
- antifungal treatments for vaginal yeast infections (Gyne-Lotrimin or Monistat)
- acetaminophen (Tylenol)
- aspirin
- antidiarreals (Immodium AD)
- antiemetic (Compazine)
- antihistamine (diphenhydramine, Benadryl)
- burn ointment (hydrocortisone, Derm-Aid)
- Calamine lotion
- DEET bug repellant or Avon Skin So Soft oil or lotion
- ephedrine
- epinephrine 1:1000 mg injection for severe allergic reactions (Epi-pen)
- eye drops (Visine, Liquid Tears)
- ibuprofen (Motrin)
- laxative
- lice shampoo (Nix or Rid)
- lip balm (ChapStick, Blistex)
- oil of cloves
- sodium bicarbonate (baking soda)
- SPF 15 sunscreen
- syrup of Ipecac
- topical anesthetic (viscous lidocaine, Lanacane)
- topical antifungal ointments and creams (Lotrimin)
- white petroleum jelly (Vaseline)

Antibiotic Alternatives

If you can't get prescription antibiotics, use alternatives.

Colloidal Silver

Colloidal silver is a safe and nontoxic antibiotic. Silver has historically been used for its bactericidal properties and is used today in Silvadene, a topical burn treatment. As discussed in Chapter 3 regarding water purification, pathogens including viruses, bacteria and fungi die in the presence of colloidal silver, and no organisms have been shown to develop a tolerance to it.

Studies demonstrating the effectiveness of colloidal silver are currently underway at major medical research centers. The book *Colloidal Silver: The Natural Antibiotic Alternative* by Zane Baronowski discusses this subject, and is available from Amazon.com.

See Chapter 3, pages 129 to 131, for information on purchasing or making your own colloidal silver.

Veterinary Antibiotics

In an emergency, veterinary antibiotics could be used by physicians to treat people. The chemical quality is the same as that prescribed for humans. It's legal to buy and own veterinary antibiotics for your animals. Buy only the types listed in the back of the book *Where There Is No Doctor*.

Jeffers Veterinary Supply, 800-JEFFERS, sells veterinary antibiotics.

http://www.1800jeffers.com

Alternative Medical Therapies

Probiotics

Most antibiotics work so well that they also kill normal intestinal bacteria, necessary for optimal health. *Probiotics* promote and restore a balanced intestinal environment.

A supply of freeze-dried probiotics including Acidophilus,

Bifidus and soil-based organisms would make a good health-promoting supplement. These have a good shelf life if kept cool and are available at most health food stores or from Arise & Shine, 800-688-2444.

Homeopathy

Homeopathy is a 200 year old system of medicine which the World Health Organization rates as the second most widely used method of medical treatment in the world. It works with the immune system to stimulate healing. Since it was cheap, effective, and safe, it was quite popular in the U.S. during the late 1800's, before it was legislated out of existence by allopathic medical supporters.

Homeopathic remedies are effective on both acute and chronic conditions. Homeopathic medical supplies can be extended without losing their potency, an important factor when restocking may be difficult or impossible. You can multiply and indefinitely extend the individual remedies with some brandy and plain lactose tablets.

Get a homeopathic first aid kit of common remedies, such as those listed in Maesimund Panos, M.D.'s *Homeopathic Medicine At Home*. Or, get a more comprehensive kit of remedies with a *Materia Medica with Repertory* book written by Kent or Boericke which both documents the use of the remedies and acts as a cross reference and diagnostic tool. A comprehensive book on homeopathy is Dr. Andrew Lockie's *Family Guide to Homeopathy*.

Boiron, 800-258-8823, makes all remedies and sells Travel Kits with 36 remedies for $90. Boiron Comprehensive Kits with 36 remedies of varying potencies as well as tinctures and ointments are available for $100.

http://www.boiron.fr

A source of homeopathic first aid kits or variety packs of commonly used remedies is Homeopathy Overnight, 800-ARNICA3.

http://www.homeopathyovernight.com

You can get information on homeopathy by accessing the Homeopathy Home webpage.

http://www.homeopathyhome.com

Herbology

Certain Chinese herbal formulations have demonstrated antiviral, antifungal and antibacterial activities. Yunnan Paiyao is an herbal combination which helps stop severe bleeding and infection. It was used internally and externally by the North Vietnamese to treat gunshot wounds. In the West, combinations of Echinacea and Goldenseal can be used similarly to fight infection.

A Barefoot Doctor's Manual is the translation of a manual written by Chinese doctors for paramedics in that country. It offers practical solutions which utilize Western as well as Chinese medical techniques such as accupuncture.

Survival Medicine: Nature's Way by Marilyn Moore is an herbal remedy book available for $13 from Major Surplus & Survival. Other good books are Mark Bricklin's *The Practical Encyclopedia of Natural Healing*, Charles Millspaugh's *American Medicinal Plants* for $16 and Andrew Chevallier's *Encyclopedia of Medicinal Plants* for $28. The *Peterson Guide #40: Medicinal Plants* by Foster and Drake contains excellent photos and line drawings of medicinal plants, so you can collect your own.

Nitro-Pak sells an herbal first aid kit for $43; Real Goods for $55.

Online sources of herbs and herbal combinations are:

Phyto Pharmica, 800-553-2370,

http://www.phytopharmica.com

The Apothecary, 800-869-9159,

http://www.the-apothecary.com/catalog/Herbs.html

MayWay Corp., 800-262-9929, sells inexpensive medicinal herbs.

http://www.mayway.com

Bach Flower Remedies

Other herbal medications include Bach Flower Remedies. Rescue Remedy, one combination, has been widely used for relief of trauma-related shock.

Nelson-Bach, 800-314-2224, sells Bach Flower Remedies.

http://www.nelsonbach.com

Essential Oils

Medicinal-quality essential oils are concentrated herbal extracts which have powerful health-promoting effects. Lavender oil has demonstrated pain-relieving qualities. Essential oil books and supplies are available from Nelson-Bach and AromaTherapy International, 800-722-4377; e-mail eurolink@umich.edu.

AromaTherapy sells an Aroma Therapy Starter Kit which contains 10 essential oils as well as supplies for $100.

A good book is Shirley Price's *The Aromatherapy Workbook.*

Additional books on alternative medicine are available at bookstores and health food stores.

Dental Supplies

Be sure to buy plenty of toothbrushes and dental floss. You can manage without toothpaste, a good substitute being equal parts salt and baking soda. But without a toothbrush, you are sure to start losing friends, as well as teeth!

The book *Where There Is No Dentist* by Murray Dickson does for dental care what the book *Where There Is No Doctor* does for medical care. It gives an in-depth overview of basic therapeutic dental techniques used in third world countries, provides materials and equipment sources as well as information on creating your own equipment.

An instrument and temporary filling material list is included, which will enable you to create a dental preparedness kit. It also recommends ECHO as a source of inexpensive dental instruments. Contact them at ECHO, 4 West Street, Ewell Surrey KT171UL, England.

Cheaper Than Dirt! sells a dental inspection mirror for $2.25 and a set of four cleaning picks for $5.

Major Surplus and Nitro-Pak sell a Dental Emergency Kit for $20, which includes Cavit temporary filling material if one of your dental filings falls out, as well as oil of cloves and topical anesthetic for toothache pain. Campmor sells the same kit for $16.

In conclusion, get medical and dental checkups and resolve any problems in mid-1999. Have your doctor wean you off as many medications as possible, then get a year's worth of prescriptions. Buy a comprehensive medical preparedness kit and establish a medical library. Get trained to administer first aid. Consider buying a homeopathic first aid kit and colloidal silver generator.

Then, exercise and get in shape in 1999!

MEDICAL CHECKLIST

Personal medical steps to take now:

____ Address any medical problems prior to 2000
____ Get a thorough physical examination
____ Schedule any necessary surgery as soon as possible
____ Replace implanted batteries for pacemakers
____ Obtain reserve batteries for home medical equipment
____ Consider generator backup for home medical equipment
____ Ask your doctor to supervise a "drug holiday"
____ Ask your doctor for a one year supply of medicine, or more
____ Request a supply of antibiotics
____ Get all your family's vaccinations up to date
____ Get vaccinated for Third World diseases
____ Purchase extra prescription eyeglasses
____ Complete all dental work and dental surgery in 1999
____ Exercise regularly in 1999 and get in shape

Prepare for medicine in 2000:

____ Build an emergency medical library
____ Get basic training in First Aid
____ Keep medicine and medical supplies on hand
____ Purchase a comprehensive Emergency Medical Kit
____ Purchase a colloidal silver generator
____ Stock up on alternative medical supplies:
    ___ Probiotics
    ___ Homeopathic First Aid Kit and book
    ___ Medicinal herbs
    ___ Bach flower remedies
    ___ Essential oils
____ Buy plenty of dental supplies
____ Buy a Dental Emergency Kit

CHAPTER 10

Transportation

Imagine the disruption if one million traffic signals were to fail, if buses or trains couldn't run...if cargo backs up at ports or rail terminals...or if highway-rail grade crossing signals stop. The delays and risks to safety are potentially enormous.

Mortimer Downey
Deputy Secretary, Dept. of Transportation

We all rely on transportation—automobile, bus, train, airplane, etc. We take for granted that these forms of travel will be available whenever needed.

All modes of transportation share one thing in common—they consume fuel. Y2K-related problems may disrupt fuel manufacturing and distribution. Yet, the fuel problem is only one of many that could interfere with our getting around.

POTENTIAL TRANSPORTATION PROBLEMS

Transportation is a crucial issue in America. We are highly dependent on these systems to get us where we need to go, and to bring us food, fuel and all the various supplies which make our lives possible. Few of the things we use are manufactured in our local area; most are shipped in from remote factories which supply large regions of the country. Let's look at the effect Y2K problems could have on various sectors of the transportation industry.

Automobiles

The question on many people's minds is, will my car cease to function due to problems with the on-board computer, or date-sensitive embedded chips located throughout the vehicle? Chip problems could range from annoying dashboard digital display glitches to more serious braking, suspension, or fuel mixture problems.

There is great debate on this issue. Auto manufacturers claim embedded chip failures won't impact vehicle operability. Yet, as of this writing, no written guarantees have been issued, due to litigation concerns.

In the course of our research, we've received off-the-record information from automotive engineers which has eased our concerns somewhat. They assert that no date-sensitive functions are programmed into chips in automotive applications. Yet, many generic chips used by manufacturers have internal clocks, which could be vulnerable, even if not utilized in the chip's programming instructions. Our engineer friends also assure us that even if cars' computers fail, cars are designed with a "limp mode" which allows them to run without the computer's fine tuning. With this issue as with many others associated with Y2K, only time will tell.

Microprocessor problems aren't the only obstacle to automobile transportation after 2000. If gasoline isn't available at the pumps, cars won't run even if the embedded chips work.

Will gas be available? Testimony before congress has illustrated it may not be. Up to 70% of U.S. fuel refineries may be at risk of Y2K failure. Y2K-related problems in the shipping industry raise doubts that imported crude oil can reach our shores. Chevron Oil has 12,000 suppliers for its shipping division alone; no one knows if each will be Y2K-ready in time.

If cars run, and gas is available, does that mean we'll be able to drive in the new millennium? Maybe not.

Traffic Management Systems report and measure traffic levels throughout metropolitan areas. Y2K could corrupt data derived from these systems, used for traffic control and reporting, as well as emergency management purposes. Traffic Signal Control and Intelligent Transportation Systems are also at risk. Timed or co-ordinated traffic signals, automated vehicle message signs, and information kiosks could malfunction.

If the traffic lights don't work, computer-controlled bridges and tunnels are on the blink, or traffic enforcement breaks down, automobile transportation may not be a viable option.

Buses

Buses face the same problems as automobiles—faulty micro-processors and potential fuel unavailability. Worse yet, highly com-puterized bus scheduling systems and the attendant communica-tions involved may well be disrupted by Y2K problems.

Scheduled transportation services—buses, trains, subways, and airplanes—could be halted due to Y2K related problems in date-sensitive computer systems. Schedules could be confused, route maps could disappear. Dispatchers may have to scramble and manually generate schedules.

If you rely on bus transportation, you may have to make al-ternative plans after the new year.

Subways

Subways, like all transportation sectors, are computer depen-dent and face a significant embedded chip problem. Unlike other sectors of the transportation industry, subways rely on electrical power, compounding their Y2K challenges. Studies on the Y2K sta-tus of subway systems of major U.S. cities, such as Washington, D.C. and New York City, reveal little hard evidence of progress toward compliance. It remains to be seen whether the subway systems will function in the Year 2000.

Trucks

The trucking industry is the backbone of modern society. In our home state of Michigan, this industry employs one of every 11 workers in the state and moves 90% of the total manufactured freight each year.

Nearly every major business and industry today is based on the *just-in-time* truck delivery system, made possible by computer technology. Throughout the manufacturing and retail industry, inventories are kept to a bare minimum. Stores of nuts and bolts, parts, food products, etc., are ordered via computerized scheduling, linked through massive computer networks. The items are delivered on a daily basis, hourly in many cases—"just-in-time" as needed. This keeps inventories and carrying costs at a minimum.

Before the advent of computer-based ordering and distribution, companies depended on warehouse space availability, and kept a week or two of inventory in stock. If delivery trucks were a day or so late, it didn't stop production. Now, a single late shipment could mean a shutdown for an average company. The question that must be asked is—can these computerized ordering and distribution systems have alternative work-arounds put in place and be made Y2K-ready? If not, our modern manufacturing system could be brought to its knees.

Trains

The railroad industry is highly computer dependent. Both passenger and freight lines rely on computerized scheduling, routing and switching. Railroads move food to the cities, coal to coal-fired electrical power plants, and parts and supplies to the manufacturing industry. In January 1999, U.S. Y2K Council Chairman John Koskinen summarized the Y2K threat to this industry when he said, "We are deeply concerned about the railroads. We have no indication that they are going to make it."

Train travel could be unreliable after 2000. Slowdowns could occur if automated functions have to be carried out manually. It could also be risky, if fail-safe mechanisms malfunction.

It's a normal occurrence for two trains to occupy the same track. In the past, the trains were rerouted through manual switching. The advent of computer technology has replaced the human element with computers. Computers now automatically control and switch the vast network of tracks, utilizing date dependent microchips. A computer glitch causing erroneous data to be reported could result in head-on collisions.

We recommend avoiding rail travel after 1-1-2000, until safety can be guaranteed.

Airplanes

The airline industry faces difficult and complex challenges in achieving Y2K compliance. Three main areas of concern must be addressed. Chief among them is the issue of Air Traffic Control.

Air Traffic Control

In 1997, IBM informed the Federal Aviation Agency that the IBM 3083 Host Mainframe Computers, currently used in Air Traffic Control Centers, would not work after the Century Date Change. Furthermore, this obsolete equipment could not be made Y2K compliant. The FAA must install a new nationwide Air Traffic Control System by 1-1-2000. The National Air Traffic Control Association has expressed grave doubts this can be accomplished in time.

On top of that, 23 of the newly purchased ATC systems, intended to replace the IBM 3083 Host Mainframe system, have not been guaranteed to be Y2K-compliant! In late 1998, the FAA tested the new system at five U.S. airports, with alarming results. Planes disappeared from radar screens, and air traffic controllers had to alert pilots to take evasive action to avoid mid-air collisions. One controller was quoted as saying, "It was sheer terror." FAA scrapped the new system, and returned to the old. At present, the old non-compliant system continues to be used. How long it will take to ready the new system is unknown.

Airplanes and Airline Companies

Airplanes and the airline companies must also be made compliant. Airplanes are among the most computerized pieces of machinery in the world. Boeing 747 jetliners contain up to 16,000 embedded chips each.

Airline companies face a massive task, guaranteeing the safety of thousands of passengers after the date rollover. Some airlines have announced they may cancel flights to foreign countries that haven't made Y2K repairs to their ATC systems.

Many people will elect not to fly at that time. In late 1998, Reuters News reported, nearly half of all Americans surveyed said they would avoid traveling by plane on or around January 1, 2000.

Airports

The third concern is the Y2K readiness of the airports themselves. As of December 1998, a survey of 34 airports revealed that their level of awareness about Y2K problems varied widely. Many airports still had no Y2K project in place.

Seattle's Sea-Tac International Airport is in the forefront of Y2K-readiness among U.S. airports. After five years of Y2K work, Sea-Tac is not yet compliant. How will our nation's 550 airports prepare in time, when most did not begin as early as Sea-Tac?

These problems worry airline insurers. Some insurance companies state they may not insure airlines which can't guarantee compliance. Whether airlines will operate beyond December 31, 1999 may be entirely in the hands of the insurance industry.

We don't find these facts to be reassuring. If you must fly, don't plan any flights in late December 1999, or January 2000! We won't fly from September 1999 to well into the new millennium.

Ships

Shipping is critical to international trade. Fully 95% of imported goods entering the United States come on board maritime shipping. Y2K problems could paralyze these supply lines.

More than 80,000 ships sail the world's waters. Today's commercial vessel is increasingly dependent on computer technology for all phases of operation. Propulsion, engine controls, communications, navigation, distress and safety systems, and more, rely on computer control.

On land, port authorities also depend on embedded chips to manage cargo, run elevators and maintain security. The Rotterdam Port, the world's largest, demands that all ships using its facilities after 2000 must be Y2K compliant. Other ports plan to follow suit.

Y2K awareness is low in the shipping industry, and progress lags. Only time will tell if this transportation sector will meet the date rollover successfully .

ALTERNATIVE TRANSPORTATION

If Y2K impacts the transportation sector, life will change drastically. Interrupted vacation trips and cross country business travel won't be our biggest problems. Most people couldn't even make it to work if automobile, bus, and subway transportation were disrupted.

In considering the use of non-fuel-dependent alternative transportation after the date rollover, we are basically limited to "personal" transportation mechanisms—walking or bicycling.

Motorized transportation such as small motorcycles could also be a useful strategy if adequate fuel is stored.

Bicycles

Bicycles are the most efficient form of human-powered transportation. We recommend you purchase a good sturdy bike, if you don't already own one. It may come in handy, if Y2K problems make our cars difficult or impossible to use. Bicycles could temporarily fill the transportation void.

Bicycles have been with us for quite some time. In 1817, Baron von Drais invented the walking machine, to get him around the royal gardens faster. The evolution of the bicycle continues to the modern day. Three-speed bikes were popular in the 1960s, 10-speed derailleur bikes became the norm in the 1970s, and today the mountain bike enjoys popularity. Metal alloy frames now make our bicycles extremely light and sturdy.

Most of us have ridden a bicycle at least once in our lives. As children our bikes gave us freedom and were our primary method of transportation. We utilized our bikes for short neighborhood trips and for longer trips to the shopping malls. As adults we sometimes ride bikes with our children, but they're no longer considered a standard mode of transportation as they are in other countries.

It's time to change our thinking. In light of Y2K, it's wise to have a bike for each member of your family. A three to five mile bike trip isn't difficult, even if you're not in great physical shape. Bikes could get many of us to work, if we couldn't use our cars.

Bicycles require no fuel, only the muscle power provided by the rider. Good bikes don't cost much, starting at about $100, and can be purchased in department stores, bicycle shops, through catalogs, and websites on the internet. Internet sites for bicycle products and suppliers are:

http://www.bikecrawler.com/
http://www.bicycle.com/

Mini-Cycles/Folding Bikes: Folding bikes are similar to standard bicycles, but can be folded small enough to fit in the trunk of your car. This makes them handy for use in a Y2K emergency situation. With a folding bike in your trunk, if you run out of gas or get stuck in a traffic jam, you're still mobile.

Folding bikes can be found in some bike shops. Dahon offers a wide selection. They have models ranging from 16 in. wheel size compact bicycles to full size and full performance mountain bikes. Contact Dahon at 818-305-5264 for distributor information.

http://www.dahon.com/

Saddlebags: Saddlebags or panniers are standard equipment for carrying supplies on bike tours. They'd be very helpful when bringing home groceries from the store with your bike.

Schwinn, 800-SCHWINN, and most bike and recreational equipment suppliers such as Campmor sell sets of bags which strap onto the bike and carry as much as a large suitcase. Saddlebags which hang down from a rack on either side of the rear wheel cost $70. Bags are also sold which hang from the handlebars, seat, and from the frame.

http://www.schwinn.com

Child trailers: Two children up to several years in age can be towed a in bike trailer such as the Schwinn Joyrider Trailer for $325. We have also seen trailers from other manufacturers sold new for as little as $250. Trailers attach to the frame of a bike with a long hitch. Bike trailers can carry as much as 125 lbs. of cargo, if you choose to carry groceries instead of children. Used trailers may be available through classified ads.

Safety equipment: Helmets and lights are crucial when riding bikes. Proper maintenance is also important.

Since you are fully exposed to injury while riding a bike, it's prudent to take precautions. A bike helmet costs $20 to $40 from Campmor or other suppliers and should be worn at all times to protect your head in case of an accident.

Use lights and reflectors even during the day to increase your visibility. High quality rechargeable lighting systems are available for night riding. They cost from $70 to $270 from Schwinn and other suppliers and produce excellent illumination from low and high beam lamps.

Bicycle maintenance: To perform properly, your bicycle must have proper maintenance. The most frequent and most important bicycle maintenance involves tightening, lubricating, adjusting, and cleaning the different parts of your bike. Most tasks are labor intensive, but require few parts.

Becoming your own bicycle mechanic is not difficult. Start by purchasing a good book on bicycle maintenance. We recommend Bicycling Magazine's *Complete Guide to Bicycle Maintenance and Repair, Including Road Bikes and Mountain Bikes,* from Rodale Press. It's comprehensive, and priced at $17.

Store two extra tires and inner tubes for each bike, as well as a hand air pump. A hand air pump costs $15 from Campmor or Recreational Equipment Inc., and can be attached to your bike.

Having the proper tools to perform the necessary maintenance is another consideration. Bike components may vary somewhat in structure and size between manufacturers and models.

Park Tool Company, 651-777-6868, makes a mini tool kit you can take with you on your rides. The kit includes:

- 2 tire levers—lightweight, made of glass-injected nylon for strength
- 3 glueless patches
- Multi-spoke wrench—fits the 3 popular spoke nipple sizes

- Mini chain tool
- Multi tool—This tool has 3,4,5,6 & 8 mm hex wrenches; 8,9, & 10 mm socket wrenches; and a flat blade screwdriver.

The Park Pack sells for $35.

http://www.parktool.com

Electric Assist Bicycles

Electric bikes are everyday bicycles with an add-on battery-powered motor. The motor assists your pedaling, taking the strain off your legs. Electric bikes are limited to a range of about 8-20 miles, with top speeds of 20 mph.

Any bike can be motorized for about $200. Electric bikes are the least polluting motorized vehicle on the market, and don't require a license, insurance, or vehicle registration. An excellent source is Zap Electric Bikes and Scooters, 408-262-8975, website:

http://www.electric-bikes.com

Jade Mountain sells the following electric bikes:

The Cruizer claims to be "The most efficient and affordable transportation on earth." The Cruizer operates like a conventional bike, but comes with a 15 mph turbo boost. It provides a boost for hills, headwinds, or whenever you desire assistance. The Cruiser comes with a 6 speed grip shift, cantilever brakes, factory installed electric assist, maintenance-free battery, automatic 110 volt charger, and a 1 year warranty. It's priced at $650.

The EROS Bicycle generates its own electricity on downhill slopes or flats which you can use for going up steep hills and into headwinds. The EROS (electric regenerative operating system) utilizes a 3/4 HP electric motor add-on that can be used on any bicycle. A 12 amp-hour 12 volt battery attaches to the top cross tube of your bicycle and provides enough power to travel 15 mph without pedaling, for a distance of 8 miles. Installation requires only a wrench and screwdriver. For recharging, use a 12 VDC charger or use the included 120 VAC Smart Charger. The EROS sells for $200.

The Charger Electric Bicycle is a true electric assist bicycle—stop pedaling and the assist stops immediately. An out of shape husband can keep up with his athletic wife at the + 1/2 setting. At + 3, the ordinary rider surpasses an Olympic cyclist. The 18 in. frame size accommodates riders from 5 ft. 3 in. to 6 ft. 3 in. tall. You get 20 miles from each 4 hour charge. The price: $1500.

The Power Rider Collapsible Electric Bike has an important feature the others lack—it weighs only 49 lbs., and folds small enough to easily fit into the most compact trunk. The Power Rider has a removable power supply for convenient recharging. You can use the Power Rider for up to 2 hours between charges. The Power Rider Collapsible Bike sells for $600.

Mopeds

Motorized bicycles called *mopeds* became popular in the U.S. in the 1970s. Mopeds come equipped with up to 2 HP motors, which don't exceed 50 cc in size, and have a maximum speed of 30 mph. Their advantage lies in their fuel efficiency, generally 100 miles or more per gallon, depending on the engine size. See your individual state laws governing moped registration and licensing.

Mopeds are excellent alternatives to bikes. They require less physical exertion, are faster than bikes, are reasonably priced and require little fuel. Some models can be pedaled like a bicycle—advantageous if you run out of fuel. We recommend models which can also be pedaled.

The Kinetic TFR has a 49 cc engine, gets 150 mpg, and can achieve a top speed of 30 mph. This model can be pedaled. Northern Tool and Equipment sells it for $825.

The 1998 Tomos Targa is a 2 speed automatic with a 49 cc, 1.5

HP, oil-injected engine. We found it locally for $1400.

Another model we like is the Mosquito. It features a 0.2 gal tank that gets one hour of use at 20 mph. The Mosquito has a 1.2 HP two-stroke motor, pneumatic tires, caliper brakes, and a chain drive that allows you to ride on dirt paths. It folds flat for storage, making it an attractive transportation alternative. Like a folding bike, it can be stowed in the car, and used in an emergency. Available from Northern Tool and Equipment for $450.

For further pricing and information on mopeds contact AAA Moped, 305-223-2041. They offer mopeds starting at $800.

http://www.aaamoped.com

Go-Peds

The Go-Ped design features a "chromoloy" frame combined with a lightweight folding handle system, for maximum strength and portability. Go-Peds are similar to mopeds, but have no seat. The rider stands on a platform similar to a skateboard, and holds onto handlebars. To start the Go-Ped, just step on and push forward. Go Peds are powered by two-stroke engines, achieve speeds of 20 mph and can be stored in the car for emergencies. Jade Mountain sells the Zappy PowerBoard model for $650.

The Blatino is a cross between a folding moped and the Go-Ped. It has more power and can zip along at 28 mph. The platform is made from a fiberglass board and it features a seat, front and rear disc brakes and 4 in. pneumatic tires. It costs $875 from AAA Moped.

Scooters

Scooters are similar to mopeds in appearance, but are more like little motorcycles, equipped with engines 50 cc or larger. The Yamaha Zuma II line features "ultra reliable" engines, electronic ignition, variable speed and automatic transmissions. One model is the Three-Wheel Electric Scooter, which is more stable and therefore safer than two-wheel models. A solar panel provides supplementary charging of the on-board batteries and it comes with a charger for full charging overnight. It has an adjustable seat, and the entire unit folds up. It's priced at $1200 from AAA Moped.

Motorcycles

Motorcycles are by far the fastest and most rugged of all the two-wheeled vehicles. They require more maintenance than other two-wheeled vehicles, and use more fuel. Motorcycles are the fastest alternative means of transportation, but along with the speed advantage comes the major drawback—they're more dangerous.

Motorcycles come in both on and off-road styles. The off-road versions, like the ATVs, could be useful in rough terrain. Motorcycles cost significantly more than the methods of transportation described above, but there is a greater availability of used models. Visit your local motorcycle retailer for more information.

All-Terrain Vehicles

All-Terrain Vehicles have 4 or 6-wheel drive. Polaris states its ATVs are "user friendly and come in a variety of engine sizes and models for the sport rider, to the avid hunter or farmer." They range in price from $3600 to $7000, depending on options. The Polaris Xpress 300 4-wheel drive model costs $3775 from AAA Moped. ATVs are good for those in rural areas.

Other Alternate Forms of Transportation

There are other alternate forms of transportation available. Some are indigenous to specific regions or climates, such as snowmobiles and boats. We feel those listed above are the most practical forms of alternative transportation for use during a Y2K emergency.

Assess your own situation, and determine the best choice for you.

PREPARING YOUR CURRENT AUTOMOBILE

Your most cost-effective short-term Y2K transportation solution will be to keep your car in good condition and store sufficient fuel to enable you to get around for a few weeks.

Fuel Supply

As the millennium nears, be sure to have a full tank of gas at all times. Y2K-related infrastructure problems may make it difficult, if not impossible, to purchase fuel.

Fuel Storage Containers

Fuel shortages after 2000 are likely. Service stations may suffer delays in fuel deliveries. In addition, the stations may have trouble dispensing fuel because of electrical and/or electronic problems. In preparation, store what you safely can at home. Review the fuel container and storage information on page 252.

Fuel Preservatives

If you want to store gasoline for long periods, it should be preserved with chemicals to prevent it from oxidizing and losing octane. Automobile diesel also can be treated for longer life. A variety of fuel stabilizers and preservatives are referenced in Chapter 7, pages 250 to 251.

Plan Ahead With Alternate Routes

Be prepared. Have alternate routes planned for all of your trips, whether within the city or cross-country. Most traffic signals are controlled by microprocessors, and they may suffer disruptions or malfunctions due to Y2K. Traffic jams, or panic-induced accidents may cause severe delays. Pre-planning alternate routes could save a lot of time and ease travel discomfort.

Get county maps for your travel routes, as you may have to use back roads. If you must travel near or after the new year, plan alternate routes, bypassing major cities wherever possible. State and Federal highways may be closed in a national emergency. The more alternate routes you have planned, the more choices you will have available in a crisis situation.

Communication Devices

A Citizens Band radio in your vehicle could prove invaluable, especially near a traffic jam. A CB radio will enable you to communicate with other drivers who have CBs, and provide you with timely information you can use to make logical, informed choices. CB Channel 9 is an emergency channel monitored by the police and REACT members. If you have problems, you can ask for help via CB.

If digital or cellular mobile phones work after 2000, they would also be helpful to contact family members, road service, or other emergency services.

Safety Kit

An auto safety kit is something every car should carry at all times. This kit should contain useful and necessary emergency items. Your regional climate conditions and personal preferences or requirements will determine the contents of your emergency auto kit. A basic kit should contain:

- Flashlights and extra batteries
- First aid kit
- Extra medications
- Maps
- AM/FM/Weather Radio and extra batteries
- Citizen's Band radio, extra batteries, and 12 VDC adapter

- Flares
- Blankets and/or sleeping bags
- Fire extinguisher
- Extra clothing—cold weather gear, rain gear
- Tool kit
- Instant tire repair (Fix-A-Flat)
- Battery jumper cables
- Shovel
- Tire chains
- Bottled water
- Nonperishable foods
- Compass

One device we recommend for any auto safety kit is the Auto Starter. This sealed 5 amp alkaline battery recharges in 30 to 120 minutes, and provides enough recharge power to start your vehicle. Plug it into your car's cigarette lighter and within minutes you're able to start the car. It's compact, and can be stored in your glove compartment, Available for $50 from D-Mail.

In summary, avoid utilizing commercial transportation services during and around Y2K. Buy bicycles for each family member and consider having fuel-efficient alternative transportation available.

Treat and store sufficient fuel to meet your expected automobile needs in early 2000. Have a safety kit in your car. Keep a CB radio in your car for emergencies. Finally, plan alternate routes for your travel and buy county road maps for your routes.

TRANSPORTATION CHECKLIST

Evaluate current transportation alternatives:

_____ Automobiles

_____ Buses

_____ Subways

_____ Trains

_____ Airplanes

_____ Other

Purchase alternate transportation for 2000:

_____ Bicycle

     ___ Accessories

     ___ Safety gear

     ___ Tools and spare parts

_____ Electric assist bicycle

_____ Moped

_____ Go-Ped

_____ Scooter

_____ Motorcycle

_____ All-Terrain Vehicle

_____ Other alternate forms of transportation

Prepare your current automobile:

_____ Ample fuel supply

_____ Treat the fuel for storage

_____ Alternate routing and county maps stored and ready

_____ Store a safety kit in your car

_____ Store communication devices, including CB radio, in your car

CHAPTER 11

Community

There are some very responsible Americans coming forward and saying that our communities have got to come together....As a community...you might store some extra food in a local school building. Or make sure there is a building that has a generator where people could go as a shelter.

Janet Abrams
Executive Director, President's Y2K Council

If you implement every preparedness strategy in this book for your family, but are surrounded by unprepared neighbors, you have not completed your preparations! You'll find yourself in the untenable position of being called upon to provide assistance to all those around you.

It's far better to help your neighbors now, so they can be prepared for Y2K disruptions. Once all of you are Y2K-ready, you'll be in position to support each other and weather the storm together.

Beyond your neighborhood, you can work alone or with a team to educate the public about Y2K, and to galvanize your town's officials to respond proactively.

Or, you can start your own cooperative preparedness community. There are many benefits to working with a group. Within the context of a larger preparedness team, such as a church group or circle of friends, you'll be able to more efficiently prepare your family for Y2K.

We'll examine community from three perspectives, with regard to Y2K preparedness: why community is important, what others are doing to promote and strengthen community Y2K readiness, and what you can do to help prepare your community.

WHY COMMUNITY IS IMPORTANT

We can't afford to ignore our neighbors. We'll all need to work together and help one another to minimize Y2K disruptions. Since everyone will be simultaneously affected by the century date change problem, there may not be resources available from unaffected regions to provide disaster relief and assistance, as is usually the case in emergencies such as earthquakes and hurricanes. We'll have to make do with the personnel and supplies we have on hand.

More and more local communities and their leaders are educating themselves, planning and preparing for Y2K disruptions. They see the potential for problems, and are actively working to put responses in place which will minimize dangers to community members.

It's enlightened self interest to help your local community prepare for Y2K! While you can count on people to rally in a crisis to help one another, good will and helpfulness after the fact won't substitute for effective advance preparations. It's important that all municipalities make comprehensive plans and take specific steps to become ready for Y2K. You can be an effective voice for prompting your community leadership to address the issues and take action.

WHAT OTHERS ARE DOING

People all over the world are joining with others and taking steps to prepare for Y2K.

Government Response
Federal Efforts

On the national level, efforts to assist communities include those being planned by the Federal Emergency Management Agency. Observers believe the Federal government will focus available resources on the 120 largest U.S. cities, which house 80% of the nation's population.

If conditions warrant, the President could declare a state of national emergency. Martial law empowers the government to conscript civilian manpower, supplies and material to support the general populace.

As mentioned earlier, the National Guard is preparing for mass mobilization during Y2K. It could be federalized and used in those 120 cities to maintain order. State efforts could be folded into the national command structures. Yet, immediate assistance to individual civilians may still be minimal as these efforts will have to be coordinated over the entire nation.

Municipalities

In some municipalities, community leaders are directing their constituencies in Y2K preparedness.

Local government planners such as those in Miami-Dade County, Florida are preparing to respond to and recover from Y2K threats to the local infrastructure. Planner Chuck Lanza offers the Miami-Dade County preparations as a template any municipality can duplicate. He has written a series of articles describing work being done to "coordinate and facilitate local Y2K planning and response activities of the utilities and the food distributors."

http://www.y2ktimebomb.com/GL/CL/g19903.htm

Lubbock, TX has already held city-wide Y2K drills. After being hit by a class F-5 tornado in 1970, that city doesn't want to be unprepared for any potential disaster.

The mayor of St. Paul, Minnesota asked the city's churches to help citizens in January 2000, by providing shelter and assistance.

Community Emergency Response Team

The Federal Emergency Management Agency is coordinating the regional preparation of Community Emergency Response Team trainers, who will train citizens in disaster preparedness. CERT evolved from a Los Angeles Fire Department project which trained citizens to handle disasters, such as earthquakes, until professional Fire and EMT personnel arrive on the scene.

CERT trains citizens to help themselves and their neighbors in Y2K-induced emergencies. FEMA says, "If a community wants to supplement its response capability after a disaster, civilians can be recruited and trained as neighborhood, business, and government teams that, in essence, will be auxiliary responders. These groups can provide immediate assistance to victims in their area, organize spontaneous volunteers who have not had the training, and collect intelligence that will assist professional responders with prioritization and allocation of resources following a disaster."

http://www.fema.gov/emi/cert/prog.htm

For further disaster preparedness study, FEMA's Emergency Management independent study course is also available online at:

http://www.fema.gov/emi/ishome.htm

Community Preparedness Activities

Momentum is developing in communities all over the country regarding preparedness activities. Organizations have been established to encourage and direct this work.

Cassandra Project

Paloma O'Riley and Cathy Moyer of the Cassandra Project have made it their goal to prepare neighborhoods, one by one, to maintain the integrity of society. O'Riley says, "individual preparedness is for those who can; community preparedness is for those who can't." And, "the best security you have is a prepared neighbor."

The Cassandra Project has an extensive listing of over 200 Y2K Community Preparedness Groups around the world.

They also have a Neighborhood Organizing site detailing steps to take in working with your community. The information includes suggestions on how to talk to your neighbors and conduct meetings; with materials and information you can print out for use.

http://cassandraproject.org
Y2K Citizen's Action Guide

The Utne Reader magazine has edited a *Y2K Citizen's Action Guide* on Y2K preparedness with input from many well-known preparedness leaders. It has sections on the "Y2K Neighborhood," "Public Citizenship," "Community Organizing," and "Household & Neighborhood Preparedness." Available for $5 at bookstores nationwide, or read it online at:

http://www.utne.com/y2k
Churches and Religious Communities

Church communities in large numbers are preparing for the century date change. A small community based on love and/or shared values may be the best environment in which to weather any Y2K storms. These churches believe the social challenges which will come from Y2K will magnify the importance of the church as a bulwark of social stability, a provider of services for the needy, as well as a vehicle of salvation. They are preparing to feed and assist their surrounding communities both physically and spiritually.

The Y2K issue is increasingly being addressed by religious organizations. The Christian Broadcasting Network's "700 Club" began reporting on Y2K in June 1998, and has aired several programs on the subject. CBN spokesperson and former Presidential candidate Rev. Pat Robertson has encouraged his one million strong membership to start preparing immediately.

You can request a Y2K fact sheet from CBN at 800-716-FACT. Their website has links to other preparedness sites.

http://www.cbn.org

A story released by CBN called *"Community Preparation: Coming Together for the Common Good,"* describes the efforts of the Harbor Light Community Chapel in Harbor Springs, Michigan. They have had a storehouse for their community since 1992. In 1998, they began an extensive Y2K ministry.

This church has been buying wheat, grinders, beans and honey, and has built another storage building. Twice weekly, they provide classes on preparedness. They are applying for an FCC license to establish a radio base station which will permit the congregation to stay in touch with each other via handheld radios. They turned off their power for a week this winter to test their preparations, while there was still time to make adjustments.

The book entitled *Y2K: The Millennium Bug—A Balanced Christian Response* addresses strategies for churches, church leaders and parishioners in preparing for Y2K. Author Shaunti Feldhahn outlines her Y2K ministry action plan:
- Offer to organize meetings for church leaders in your area
- Offer to organize a general awareness meeting for members
- Offer to develop and lead part of your church's Y2K project
- Plan how to spiritually and physically reach out to your neighborhood
- Provide important articles and factual material to your church newsletter
- Develop a strategy for partnering 'sister churches'
- Develop a strategy to partner higher-risk households

Feldhahn created the Joseph Project 2000, dedicated to helping churches organize community-based Y2K preparations. Feldhahn's Y2K education events have been attended by thousands.

http://www.josephproject2000.org

There are also several Internet sites where pastors discuss their efforts to network with other churches and church leaders to coordinate community-wide preparations, including:

http://www.hebronministries.org/samaritan2000.htm
http://www.liberty-revival.org/y2k/

Preparedness Safe-havens and Communities

A June 1998 article in *U.S. News and World Report* featured urban planner Russ Voorhees, architect of a Year 2000 survival colony in the White Mountains of Concho, Arizona. Voorhees hopes to create a "cohesive Y2K community" to weather the anticipated Year 2000 storms.

http://www.heritagewest2000.com

With the expectation that Y2K will disrupt the social fabric, many people are moving to locations they feel will be safer or better able to provide a supportive environment. Joining with others of like mind on this issue has strong appeal. Y2K preparedness communities are spreading across North America and the world.

The following Internet sites discuss groups who are working to establish preparedness communities or "safe-havens:"

http://www.safehaveny2k.com
http://www.webpal.org/Registry.htm
http://y2kfind.listbot.com
http://www.ethell.com/kgriffith/
http://www.garynorth.com/y2k/detail_.cfm/2510
http://206.67.59.5/wwwboard13/index.html
http://www.millennium-ark.net/News_Files/Community/Community.html

WHAT YOU CAN DO

There are many ways you can help others prepare for Y2K. Everyone who understands this issue has an important part to play in facilitating the preparation of their larger communities.

Educate Your Family and Friends

Your family is the one community in which you will always share common ground. In the event of future social dislocations, you may find your relatives sharing your house!

Educate your family members. Begin drawing their attention to Y2K issues. They may not agree with you nor choose to follow your advice, but they will take note as they see Y2K issues dealt with more frequently in the media.

Organize Your Local Community

Citizen's Action Group

In our Metro Detroit area, a concerned citizen organized the Oakland County Y2K Citizen Action Group. The group has held several meetings, giving people the opportunity to learn about Y2K, network, and discuss issues of individual preparedness planning.

Start your own Citizen's Action Group by establishing a team of interested people. Resources to help you are the Cassandra Project and the *Y2K Citizen's Action Guide,* discussed on pages 326 to 327.

You can work with city officials, schedule meetings, post fliers and notify the press. Focus on education by giving a Y2K overview to begin your meetings. Then, have a series of presentations on various preparedness topics. Leave time for questions and answers. Always provide handouts for attendees.

Your Action Group can also branch out into cooperative bulk buying and processing of preparedness supplies. Do whatever you can to facilitate individual and community preparations.

Neighborhood Organizations

Neighborhoods are ideal for implementing a shared, cooperative preparedness program. Having familiarity as neighbors and sharing concerns associated with security issues, you will work together naturally.

Offer to give presentations at your neighborhood's churches or organizations such as the Neighborhood Watch Group, Block Club or Homeowner's Association.

Food Banks

Food is a renewable resource which can be generated by community activity and be shared. We can prepare for food shortages by working with local farmers, organizing community gardens, canneries, and food banks. Some churches are doing this.

Regional Coalition

Develop a Year 2000 coalition for your region. Organize a core group from your community or association to work together promoting Y2K readiness. Establish task groups to follow up on specific areas. Talk to regional officials and try to get them to take steps to address the problem. Partner with other community groups.

Establish Your Own Preparedness Group

If you don't feel that organizing a larger community such as a city or county is what you want to do, you can easily work with a more close-knit community composed of family, friends, church members or your immediate neighbors.

Even if you don't think of yourself as the leader type, consider just getting things started. Others will come forward to take on leadership roles. A group is a dynamic process. Different individuals will assume varied, yet equally valuable roles at different situations and times.

Some projects will require everyone's participation, such as dry-pack canning of grains and beans. These can be scheduled on weekends when you can all devote the day to the process. Other projects, such as purchasing preparedness items, can be delegated. Decide what equipment and supplies you want to buy, establish a budget, and assign individual members to make the purchases.

The most important thing is to get started. Once a group is formed, the union of minds and hearts will create momentum.

Advantages of Group Preparedness

If you are limited by time or money in accomplishing your preparedness plans, there may be areas you'll have to skip in favor of others. You'll achieve more comprehensive preparedness by joining with others, gaining additional man-hours and funding.

Financial advantages: The financial advantages of group preparation include pooling of resources, buying in bulk, and economies of scale. If you pool your funds, you can make bulk purchases of storable food and preparedness supplies, obtaining more quantity and possibly better quality for the same cost. Likewise, you can help each other to prepare and store supplies. It is much more efficient to mass produce than to work alone.

Group shelter, power and water: Costly projects such as a solar or wind-powered electrical generating system are beyond the reach of most individuals. Yet with pooled funds, one shared system can provide dozens of people with light and pumped water. If you work together on shared housing, you can cooperate in utilizing alternative power systems.

Shared labor and specialization: "Many hands make light work." An Amish barn-raising is completed in one day with the help of the whole community. Compare that to the efforts of one individual or one family. Cooperate with others on tasks such as food production and storage.

Divide tasks and responsibilities among your group members, to take advantage of each person's skills. For example, gardeners, electricians or doctors should be encouraged to pursue their specialities. There is a long learning curve to become proficient in certain skills. Don't waste the energies of group members by having them learn jobs which others can already do.

Backup equipment: Buy two of each of your crucial items such as diesel generators. Securing extra equipment and parts will provide a ready supply to keep at least one unit working. Apply this principle to any equipment with multiple components or moving parts, such as communications, lighting or heating systems.

Group communication: Acquiring an Amateur Radio license might not appeal to you, but may to another member of your group. It will also be more economical to share the cost of a Ham radio with others. Likewise, a few pairs of handheld local-use Family Band or Citizen's Band radios will go a long way when shared in a community.

Mutual defense: By banding together you'll be much safer and less likely to be targeted by individuals or groups who may want to take what you have. Devise a mutual defense system if social safeguards, such as police forces, are stretched thin by Y2K-related problems.

Mutual encouragement: If the tasks before you seem daunting, your group members will urge you on. The "esprit de corps" of a goal-oriented group is a big plus!

Child care and education: Cooperative child care will maximize the productive capacity of your group. Providers should rotate or appoint one person who is best suited. One professional teacher can do a better job than a dozen inexperienced parents.

Y2K disruptions will probably close schools. Make plans now to provide for children's education if this occurs.

Obtain standard texts for the various ages of children who may be a part of your community. One option is the Robinson Curriculum, 248-740-2697. Material for grades K-12 can be purchased on 22 CD-ROMs for $195. This set contains the text of 210 books.

http://www.robinsoncurriculum.com

Saxon Math, 800-284-7019, provides a complete set of math books for home schooling, kindergarten through calculus. They also have a phonics program.

http://www.saxonpub.com

Get a Y2K-compliant DC-powered laptop computer with a CD-ROM drive. Or, buy a 12 VDC to 110 VAC power inverter to provide electricity for the computer and printer from batteries. Buy some toner cartridges and a few cases of paper and you can print the books out as needed.

We recommend you print out hard copies of educational materials which are stored on CD-ROM disks in 1999, in case you can't access your computer files after January 1, 2000.

Obtain a current encyclopedia set, such as the Encyclopedia Britannica. Put a want ad in a newspaper for a used set. You can also order an encyclopedia stored on a CD-ROM disc.

http://www.eb.com

Used book stores often carry school books. Teachers' supply stores sell teaching aids. If the school system has a period of disruption, you'll be glad for whatever educational supplies you have on hand with which to occupy your children.

For further information on home schooling, see:

http://www.home-school.org

Home Education Magazine, 800-236-3278

http://www.home-ed-press.com

Preparedness library: As a group, consider purchasing a unique library of preparedness information on microfilm. This comprehensive, practical reference collection consists of 138,650 pages from 1000 books and documents transferred to microfiche, selling for 5% of the original book cost. It includes information on agricultural tools, crop storage, water supply, forestry, aquaculture, improved cook stoves, solar/wind/water power, biogas, transportation, health care, communications, small industries, and other small scale technology topics.

Jade Mountain sells the Microfiche Library for $895, an Economy Microfiche Reader for $225, and a Deluxe Reader for $350.

In addition, many of the books referenced in this volume could be purchased by a group to minimize costs.

Group economics: If the national economic infrastructure comes upon hard times, individual communities can develop sustainable local economies.

Communities can establish a cashless barter system. Computer software is even available to facilitate the record keeping. The *Local Exchange Trading System* is a barter system in use since 1983. It operates in hundreds of communities in Australia, New Zealand, Canada, England and the U.S. It is "a self-regulating economic network which allows its account holders to issue and manage their own money supply within a bounded system."

At the LETSystems website, you'll find a list of Frequently Asked Questions, a design manual, plus materials and software for administrators and users which can be downloaded.

http://www.gmlets.u-net.com

Jim Crowfoot's article, *Developing Local Economies and Currencies: Resources for Sustainable Local Communities* in "Synapse" magazine, is one of an excellent series on local economies.

http://www.nrec.org/synapse45/syn45index.html

More information can be found in the book *Going Local:*

Creating Self Reliant Communities in a Global Age by economist Michael H. Shuman, as well as at the Community Economic Development Centre:

http://www.sfu.ca/cedc

Order the $40 "Hometown Money Starter Kit" from Ithaca Hours by phone, 607-272-4330, or website:

http://www.lightlink.com/hours/ithacahours

In summary, it's important that everyone become Y2K-ready. Working to educate and organize your community creates a win/win situation. You benefit by having prepared neighbors who are an asset to your neighborhood, not a liability. Your neighbors benefit by being empowered through their preparations.

Working together is the most efficient way to achieve Y2K-readiness, preparing the greater community to meet the challenges ahead.

COMMUNITY CHECKLIST

_____ Educate your family and friends
_____ Organize your neighbors to prepare for Y2K
_____ Educate the public about Y2K
_____ Galvanize your town's officials to respond proactively
_____ Develop a Year 2000 coalition for your region
_____ Start a Food Bank or join with an existing one
_____ Investigate joining a preparedness community
_____ Start your own cooperative preparedness community
_____ Pool your preparedness funds
_____ Share big expenses such as alternative power systems
_____ Make bulk purchases of preparedness supplies
_____ Share responsibilities among your group members
_____ Share child care and children's education
_____ Together buy a shared preparedness library
_____ Establish a cashless barter system
_____ Get Community Emergency Response Team training

CHAPTER 12

Records

To ensure against Y2K-related loss of data, financial planner Rich Carlquist recommends securing copies of all vital records and organizing them in a manner worthy of Felix Unger.
theWhiz.com
June 29, 1998

Y2K is like a virus waiting to be activated. Don't trust any part of your life to vulnerable computer systems. Computer data processing problems can corrupt your personal information at any point from now through 2001! A faulty computer calculation attributing wrong data to you could cause serious personal consequences.

Only your eternal vigilance and excellent documentation will help you solve Y2K information problems. These records may become your only proof that your legal and financial world existed as you now know it.

As the American founding father Thomas Paine said in *Common Sense,* "These are the times that try men's souls." With all this record keeping, Y2K will be the time that tries men's patience!

The easiest way to avoid having to deal with many of the documentation issues outlined in this chapter is to simplify your life. Eliminate as many liabilities as possible, and pay off all loans. This will make your life much easier and focused during the century date change period.

IDENTIFICATION

Establish personal identification with passports, multiple picture IDs and personal records such as birth certificates and voter registration cards for each family member, including children.

Your ability to prove your identity will become vital if society becomes crippled by the predicted information services' computer failures. Normal confirmation services for check and credit card purchases will likely become nonfunctional. The subsequent threat of increased criminal activity related to false financial information will probably necessitate a need for at least two pieces of picture ID for business transactions.

Make certain there are no discrepancies or wrong information on the ID. Identification is considered proof of your citizenship. Therefore, your driver's license, birth certificate, voter's registration card, passport, etc. are very important.

Picture ID

Work gate cards, association membership cards and other picture ID should be kept available for photographic proof of identity.

Driver's License

Driver's licenses or state identification cards are obtained at your Secretary of State office. Make sure they are kept up to date with new addresses as needed.

Passports

Passports are good for 10 years and are recognized internationally. If your's is within three years of expiration, get it renewed. Your Post Office has passport forms, and you can also get passports at Federal office buildings. To obtain a passport you will need to provide a certified birth certificate and your photograph. Passports cost $60.

Non-Picture ID

Non-picture ID such as fingerprints, DNA records, occupational license, association membership cards, insurance cards and certificates, etc. will also help prove your identity if that should ever prove necessary.

Fingerprints

Your local Police Department will fingerprint your children for you as a public service, if you ask. This provides proof of their identity, if they ever become separated from you. Keep these fingerprints, plus each child's infant footprint, in your identification files.

DNA Record

A blood specimen specially preserved on blotter paper for each child can be obtained from your doctor. Some hospitals are providing these records to new parents.

Birth Certificate

Get at least two certified copies of each family member's birth certificate. These should be notarized with the raised or embossed official seal. They are available from the clerk at the city or county of birth for a nominal fee.

Voter Registration

Retain your Voter Registration Card. Be sure the address and name are identical to that on your Driver's License. This is obtained free of charge at a Secretary of State office.

Social Security Card

Obtain a free replacement Social Security card from the Social Security Administration.

http://www.ssa.gov/replace_sscard.html

DOCUMENTATION

Most businesses aren't revealing the state of their readiness for the century date change, and how this may affect your accounts. If companies even respond when asked for this information, expect them to say they'll meet all Y2K deadlines on time. Take this information with a grain of salt. The available industry-wide evaluations show that complete readiness will not be obtained by the deadline. Moreover, those businesses which have been diligently working and expect to be completely Y2K ready, will be severely challenged or incapacitated by the problems of interconnectivity. When businesses fail, they will pull down those connected to and dependent on them. This is especially critical for the public utilities' infrastructure including electrical power, telecommunications, water, sewage and fuel supplies.

We recommend you concentrate on fully documenting your personal situation, and physically preparing your family for all of the potential Y2K scenarios.

It's vital that you document and protect your personal information in all areas which affect you. If Y2K problems corrupt information about you stored in computer files, the documentation efforts you put forth now will be crucial in repairing the damage.

To facilitate your documentation, get a copy of Matthew Lesko's *Info-Power III*, which has 15,000 sources of information available from all areas of government and business.

Documentation Safeguards

You should document, with hard copies, all personal identification and records as well as financial information.

Save all bills and account information from now on, and compare the previous bill's ending statement to any subsequent statement's beginning point. Resolve all discrepancies immediately.

Store all your documentation in a fire-resistant safe in the basement of your home. The basement will be the coolest part of your house in a fire. Sentry is a good fire safe manufacturer. Portable fire-resistant security boxes start at $30 and can be purchased from K-Mart or Walmart.

We recommend getting a large size fire safe, or more than one. If you follow the advice in this chapter, you'll likely be keeping a lot of papers. Buy those with fire protection ratings of at least one hour. If you are able, cement a floor safe into a hidden location in the floor of your basement. This would take care of your valuables' security needs as well. See Chapter 5, pages 201 to 204, for more information on safes.

For all Y2K-related correspondence, use Certified Mail with Return Receipts requested from the U.S. Postal Service. These services cost an additional $2.45 for each letter; but they document that you sent, and that the recipient received your written comunication. Keep copies of your correspondence in your files.

LEGAL DOCUMENTS

Keep in your fire-resistant file certified copies of any legal documents such as adoption papers, court judgements, power of attorney, guardianship papers and advance directives for medical care or living wills.

Personal Legal Documents

Professional License

If you are a licensed worker such as medical professional, cosmetologist, or lawyer, obtain a copy of your entire licensure file, which shows that you have met all criterion for licensure. Holding a license may not provide enough proof of your status, due to continuing education and other requirements. This information can be obtained from the State's Licensure Board, see the license document for contact information. Renew your license early.

Marriage License

Obtain and store official, certified paper copies of your marriage license or certificate. Proof that you are the legal spouse will be important in any next-of-kin issues, such as making medical decisions, as well as in rights of survivorship for estate and insurance claims. These are obtained from the county of your marriage for a nominal fee.

Divorce/Custody Decree

Get a certified copy of any divorce and child custody decree. This proves that you are your child's custodial parent, or have parental rights. The decree comes from the county court in which you were divorced; a certified copy may be obtained for a nominal fee.

Will/Trust

Establish your will or living trust. Have it legally certified and keep copies in several separate locations; one certified copy with each of the parties listed in the document. This process can cost from one hundred to several hundred dollars in legal and filing fees. An excellent sourcebook on this topic is Norman Dacey's *How To Avoid Probate*, which has 598 pages af actual trusts and wills which can be photocopied and filled out.

Guardianship

Legally appoint a primary and secondary guardian, for the proper custody of your children in the event of your death. Better yet, create a list of guardians, in case the primary choices can't fulfill the obligation.

Financial/Property Legal Documents

Keep certified copies of titles, liens and deeds. Document the book and page reference numbers used by the recording clerk.

Mortgage

Make sure your mortgage company is paying your property taxes and insurance on time from your escrow account. If your insurance policy lapses, the provider may chose not to renew it. Analyze your mortgage statements for accuracy and file them. Look for and save IRS Form 1098 at the end of each year. The mortgage company is required to send you this form, which details the interest received by your escrow account and the amount of taxes paid by it. Review the escrow account agreement, to be sure that you aren't contributing more than you absolutely must.

Leases

File your lease agreement and obtain a statement that you are not delinquent in any way regarding your payments. File all payment information and correspondence and keep copies of checks and receipts.

Automobile

Auto, truck, motorcycle or boat titles should be kept in your safe. They are obtained from your Secretary of State office. Keep them with your original financing or leasing agreement and signed receipts. Registration information should be kept in your vehicle or in your wallet. Documentation of your service plan or warranty should have accurate mileage and date information. Keep all maintainance records for your car.

Stock and Bond Certificates

You should physically hold all stock and bond certificates issued in your name. In addition, keep a copy of each in a separate location. Some of your stocks may be issued to your broker in "street name," meaning they are in the broker's name, not in yours. You won't be able to get certificates for these. You may want to sell any street name stocks, and either buy stocks for which you can receive certificates, or convert your funds into more secure assets.

Carefully document your activities, keeping a log of them and checking your account statements against it. Save all paperwork. For tax purposes, keep this information for three years after stocks or bonds are sold.

RECORDS
Personal Records
Academic Records

For students in grades K-12, keep copies of all grades, report cards, grade level completion, immunization and attendance records. Obtain transcripts for all college-level classes, as well as graduation and degree documentation. The institution's registrar will provide copies of these for a small fee. Likewise, current tuition receipts and grade reports should be saved.

Be sure all student loans are paid up to date and payment records are well documented. Obtain and retain all paperwork that shows you have paid in full.

For Student Loan information, call the Federal Student Aid Information Center, 800-433-3243.

http://www.finaid.org/finaid/gov.html#FSAIC

Military Service Record

Obtain your military service record. First, obtain a copy of your discharge papers (Form DD 214) from the Veteran's Administration by filing Standard Form 180.

Then, submit Veteran's Administration Form 26-1880 (Request for Determination of Eligibility and Available Loan Guarantee Entitlement) with form DD214. The information you receive will document your military service and your eligibility for Veteran's Administration benefits.

The VA Internet site states, "To request your own VA record, submit a written request, under the Privacy Act, to the nearest VA regional office (dial the toll-free number, 1-800-827-1000). Please provide as much identifying information as possible to enable the local VA office to identify the requested records. Some examples of useful information include the full name, VA file number, branch of service, service serial number, Social Security Number, exact date [and place] of birth, and enlistment and discharge date. In some cases, it may be useful to provide the home of record at the time of entry into the service. Include as much of the same information listed above, as possible. The most important piece of information, if known, is your VA file number, commonly referred to as the VA claim number."

National Personnel Records Center, 800-827-1000

http://www.va.gov/forms

Selective Service Record

The Selective Service card is another piece of ID you can document. Keep it and all information which comes with it.

Each American male citizen is required to register for the draft within one year of his 18th birthday. You can still register through the age of 25. In the event of a national emergency, you could be drafted. You don't want this to happen erroneously, nor do you want to be considered a draft dodger. Now you can register online.

Selective Service System, 703-605-4000

http://www.sss.gov

Medical Records

Obtain hard copies of treatment records from your Hospital, Clinic, Doctor, Chiropractor, Dentist, Ophthalmologist, Psychiatrist, Psychologist, Pharmacist, and other health care providers and equipment suppliers. Keep copies of your diagnoses, allergies and all prescriptions.

Keep immunization records for all your children. Obtain records of your account number and insurance billing information on letterhead or official printouts from each of your providers. This will encourage them to treat you in the event of a computer failure as they will anticipate getting future payment from an established billing account.

Obtain copies of your recent x-rays and reports from your Radiologist as well as all other reports from recent examinations and blood tests.

Medical Insurance

Request and keep signed proof on your company letterhead that you are a member of your employer's medical, vision, dental, life and disability group insurance policies. Get the actual legally binding policy for each of your individual insured coverages, or of the group policy, from your Insurance Plan Administrator.

Obtain an official agreement from your medical prescription card provider. Keep copies of your policies' statements of benefits, your medical bills, claim forms, the insurance payment notices, and all your related correspondence.

Other Insurance

Home, liability, life, disability, and automobile insurances are very susceptible to computer problems. Safely file away your current ID cards, legally binding original policies, claims information, correspondence, and renewal policies.

Carefully examine and have corrected any inaccuracies in the policies or other data. Obtain a report for any life insurance policy as to its current status, describing beneficiary, cash value and accumulated dividends. Be sure to pay the policies on time, even if you fail to get billed.

Memberships

Obtain an updated membership card and request copies of your membership documents for all your association memberships, such as professional or social associations.

Financial Records

Document your tax, Social Security and pension payment history as well as all insurance policy information.

Business Records

If you are an employer or self-employed, take the time to draft a list of potential problem areas connected to your suppliers and customers. Don't forget to address global infrastructure issues which may directly or indirectly impact your cash flow.

Examine each item on your list and communicate with the individuals involved to plan for Y2K snafus and create contingency plans. Create "work-arounds" or alternative work techniques for each potential problem. Document all relevant commitments and agreements. Save copies of all business data such as customer files, accounts receivable and payable, and personnel records.

Obtain a copy of your occupational license or business license, as well as your licensure file from the regulating agency. Be sure to renew your license well in advance. Document all required continuing education data.

Bank Records

Secure official copies from your bank or credit union of all original loan documents, credit card agreements and safe deposit box contracts. Document all account numbers, ID numbers and statements for each account you have. These should include checking and savings accounts, certificates of deposit (CD's), loans, tax-deferred retirement accounts, trusts, investment accounts as well as credit and debit cards.

Save your monthly account statements and reconcile your savings and checking accounts promptly each month, to catch any glitches swiftly. Examine interest and fee calculations. Keep your canceled checks for the previous three years. Closely monitor automatic deposits such as those from payroll deductions.

Investment Account Records

Keep statements from your Mutual Fund, 401(k), TSA, IRA and other investment accounts. Watch that the number of shares remains constant and the interest accrued is correctly calculated.

Tax Records

We recommend keeping copies of your income tax records for the current and previous three years. If the Internal Revenue Service actually survives as a government agency past late 1999, any mathematical errors could insert incorrect date-related information into your file. This could result in fines, penalties and even liens on your property, if the IRS computer calculates that you haven't paid on taxes due since 1900.

Obtain certified copies of your IRS files, to be sure they are correct. Thoroughly review the material. Then, if you should ever get an audit generated from subsequent computer errors, you will have proof of your correct information.

These certified copies cost $23 each and take at least 60 days to arrive. Use IRS Form 4506, "Request for Copy or Transcript of Tax Form" to order the current and previous three year's returns.

You can order the free computer printout transcripts of your returns by using the same form. These are somewhat less helpful in determining if everything on file from your return is exactly as it should be, but the transcripts may be adequate if you kept copies of everything you sent the IRS.

http://www.irs.gov
ftp://ftp.fedworld.gov/pub/irs-pdf/f4506.pdf

Documentation should be maintained of all interactions with city, county and state government taxing authorities. Like your federal income tax returns, save your state and city income tax returns for four years. If a computer concludes that you haven't paid your property taxes, you can be considered as delinquent.

Obtain certified Paid Tax receipts from the authority that taxes your property, even if your mortgage company pays your taxes from an escrow account. Ask for an official statement stating there aren't any prior delinquencies. Keep and file your property valuations.

Social Security

For every $100 you make, $15 gets paid to your Social Security account, half directly from your withholding taxes and half from your employer. That is a huge pool of money. To maximize the possibility that you will get your share, keep good records of your Social Security contributions.

Order a free copy of the Social Security Administration's "Request for Earnings and Benefit Estimate Statement" (SSA-7004). Compare this to any future statements to insure that the data you and the SSA have is correct. If there is ever a problem, this data will help you prove your claim for future benefits. The information in SSA reports is typically one year behind the current date.

Contact the Social Security Administration at 800-772-1213 or 410-965-7700; see your phone book for a local number.

http://www.ssa.gov/online/ssa-7004.pdf

Bills and Statements

Starting now, keep reference files for all bills and statements. If errors crop up, you will have a paper trail of previous statements to help refute the error and prove your case.

The Y2K-related problems which you should look for will be those affected by corrupted date-based computations. Interest and fee calculations, as well as payment and billing schedules will be the primary areas where these issues will surface. Watch for these, do your own calculations to cross-check what you receive, and compare previous bills or statements to subsequent ones. The last figures reported in your statements should match those at the beginning of your next ones. Check these figures for accuracy. Resolve all discrepancies immediately.

Review your phone calls to be sure they are all yours. Look for usage and billing amounts out of their normal ranges. If you keep getting billed the same exact amount, this could indicate that you are being billed at an estimated service level and there is a problem with your account.

Credit Cards

Save and file your credit card statements. Monitor the interest calculations and compare the statement's beginning balance to the previous statement's ending balance. Keep a list of all your credit cards, with the full name of the provider, complete account information and an 800 number for the service department.

Credit Reports

Request a credit report now, and again in December 1999, from the three major credit reporting agencies. If your credit data is corrupted by Y2K computer glitches, it may destroy your credit rating. Compare the old to the updated files, to see if any errors have slipped in. Estimates are that up to half of all current credit reports have errors in them. Think what that percentage could be like after Y2K!

One copy of your credit report per year is free. If you've been denied credit, another copy is free within 60 days of that event. Additional copies cost about $8.00 each.

The three major credit reporting agencies are:

Equifax, 800-685-1111

http://www.equifax.com

Experian (TRW), 888-397-3742

http://www.experian.com

Trans Union Corporation, 800-888-4213

http://www.transunion.com

There may also be smaller local credit-reporting companies in your area. The service department of your bank should be able to assist you in contacting them.

Employment Records

As part of your planning strategy, find out what your company is doing to prepare for Y2K. Insist on having complete hard copies of your pay and personnel records. Update them in December 1999.

Document your employment date, sick time and vacation hour accumulations, performance reviews, bonus calculations, profit sharing, stock purchase plan, pension plan records, health insurance agreements, payroll deductions, payroll savings plans, 401(k) plan, union dues, and pretax medical or child care reimbursement accounts.

It is currently estimated that 20% of U.S. businesses will go bankrupt due to century date change problems. Be prepared!

In summary, get all the identification you can, and establish a practice of documenting your life well. Obtain and save official copies of all legal documents and store them in a fire-proof safe. Review your bills, and watch for Y2K-induced problems.

Good identification and documentation may save you much grief as we pass through Y2K. Be proactive in your record keeping. You'll be glad you did!

RECORDS CHECKLIST

Obtain picture ID:

____ Update your driver's license

____ Get passports for all family members

Obtain non-picture ID:

____ Birth certificates

____ Voter registration card

____ Social Security card

____ Fingerprints

____ DNA records

Document all records and financial information:

____ If licensed, obtain a copy of your entire licensure file

____ Obtain marriage license

____ Obtain divorce/custody decree documents

____ Establish wills and trusts, obtain documentation

____ Establish child guardianship, obtain documentation

____ Document all mortgage information

____ Document all lease agreements

____ Obtain all vehicle titles

____ Physically hold all stock and bond certificates

____ Obtain all academic records

____ Obtain military records / Selective Service card

____ Obtain all personal medical records

____ Obtain all medical insurance records

____ Obtain all other insurance records

____ Get updated membership cards

____ Obtain all business records

____ Obtain all bank records

____ Obtain all investment account records

____ Obtain all tax records

_____ Obtain your Social Security account statement
_____ Keep reference files for all bills and statements
_____ Save and file your credit card statements
_____ Request credit reports from all credit reporting agencies
_____ Get hard copies of your employment records

Obtaining and storing your documentation:

_____ Use Certified Mail with Return Receipt to obtain documents
_____ Review all documentation for accuracy
_____ Purchase a fire resistant safe
_____ Store all your documentation in your fire resistant safe

Epilogue

The greatest antidote to worry, whether you're getting ready for a spaceflight or facing a problem of daily life, is preparation.
Senator John Glenn

We want to leave you with the message which is the theme of our book: It's not too late for you to prepare for Y2K!

The Year 2000 problem can seem overwhelming. It's a challenge bigger than any of us have had to deal with before. Yet, many people are taking positive steps to prepare themselves for the problems we might have to face after the century date change. They are finding that it can be done. You can, too.

There are concrete steps that all of us can take, starting today, to get ready for Y2K. In this book, we outlined those steps, categorized them, and explained what to do and how to do it.

Now that you've read the book, you have an overall view of what Y2K preparedness involves. It's time for you to examine your situation, and decide how you can put these preparedness steps into practice in your life.

Use the checklists at the end of the chapters as a guide. This will help you see at a glance what you need to consider as you make your plans and start carrying them out. It will also show you which areas are unclear, so you can go back to those chapters and review, or do further research with the recommended books and websites.

Preparation prevents panic, and as John Glenn stated, it's the greatest antidote to worry. We'll attest to that! The steps we've personally taken to prepare have made all the difference in how we view the Y2K situation.

The Year 2000 computer problem will be recorded in history as either a catastrophe, or as a challenge met by all of us, and won. We trust it will be the latter.

We in the United States are fortunate to live in the country which leads the world by example, with a range of freedoms that exist nowhere else. Our nation is a technological forerunner, marshalling global preparation for Y2K. America's history of triumph in the face of adversity will help assure that the Year 2000 problem is overcome in like manner.

To succeed, we must heighten the awareness of our neighbors and surrounding communities. We need to use the tried and true methods that have worked in the past—cooperation, teamwork, and unity. By working together, we can overcome all repercussions of the millenium bug.

We wish you all the best in your preparedness efforts!

Supplier Contact Information

Supplier information is arranged in alphabetical order. Access the Internet web sites for free at your local library. You can get info on products and prices, and with a credit card, even place your order on-line. When you contact the suppliers listed here, mention that you read about them in **Y2K-It's Not Too Late.** *Some are offering a bonus.*

AAA Moped - *motorized bicycles*
305-223-2041   http://www.aaamoped.com

Adsorbents & Desiccants Corp. of America - *food desiccants*
800-228-4124   http://www.thomasregister.com/olc/adcoa

AGM Container Controls - *food desiccants*
800-995-5590   http://www.agmcontainer.com

Amateur Electronic Supply - *radio equipment*
800-558-0411   http://www.aesham.com

Amazon.com - *on-line bookstore*
800-201-7575   http:/www.amazon.com

American Freedom Network - *preparedness supplier*
800-205-6245   http://www.amerifree.com

American Security Products Co. - *safes*
800-421-6142   http://www.wbmkt.com/amsec

AmeriGas – *propane*
610-337-7000   http://www.amerigas.com

Antique Electronic Supply Co. - *crystal radios*
602-820-5411   http://www.tubesandmore.com

The Apothecary - *discount medicinal herbs and vitamins supplier*
800-869-9159
http://www.the-apothecary.com

Arise and Shine - *medicinal herbs supplier*
800-688-2244

AromaTherapy International - *alternative medicine*
800-722-4377   eurolink@umich.edu

B&A Products - *preparedness supplier*
918-696-5998   http://www.baproducts.com

Bags On The Net - *plastic bags*
888-638-2247   http://www.bagsonthenet.com

Bags USA - *plastic bags*
888-646-2247   http://www.bagsusa.com

Baker Manufacturing - *hand water pumps*
800-356-5130

BioLet Composting Toilets - *composting toilets*
800-5BIOLET   http://www.biolet.com

Boiron - *homeopathic medicine supplier*
800-258-8823   http://www.boiron.fr

Brady- Prentis Hall - *emergency medical books*
800-638-0220   http://www.bradybooks.com

Bronson Pharmaceutical - *discount vitamin supplier*
800-235-3200

CDF - *container supplier*
800-443-1920   http://www.cdf-liners.com

Campmor – *camping supplies*
800-230-2153   http://www.campmor.com

Cell Tech - *food supplements*
800-800-1300   http://www.celltech.com

Centipede Industries - *hydrogen peroxide*
800-433-0348

Cheaper Than Dirt! - *preparedness supplier*
888-625-3848   http://www.cheaperthandirt.com

China Diesel Imports - *generators*
800-341-7027   http://www.chinadiesel.com

Clivus Multrum - *composting toilets*
800-962-8447   http://www.clivusmultrum.com

Code Three Fire and Safety - *fire safety products*
707-429-5323   http://www.quickpage.com/c/code

Commercial Stored Food Suppliers
See list on pages 147 to 148

Costco - *discount wholesaler*
800-774-2678   http://www.costco.com

Cover-Your-Basics - *plastic liners*
509-935-0375   http://www.theofficenet.com/~covyrbas

Creative Solutions - *diatomaceous earth*
713-433-3182

CS Pro Systems - *colloidal silver generators*
888-710-2773   http://www.csprosystems.com

Cumberland General Store - *preparedness supplier*
800-334-4640   http://www.cumberlandgeneral.com

D-Mail - *electronic supply catalog*
800-686-1722   http://www.d-mail.com

DAMARK - *electronic supply catalog*
800-827-6767   http://www.damark.com

DeepRock – *well drilling kits*
800-333-7762   http://www.deeprock.com

Delta Light - *LED lamps*
612-980-6503   http://www.stpaulmercantile.com/deltalit.htm

Desiccare - *food desiccants*
800-446-6650 http://www.desiccare.com

Diamond Brands - *wooden kitchen matches*
800-777-7942 http://www.diamond brands.com

Diamond Farm Book Publishers - *farming books*
800-481-1353 http://www.diamondfarm.com

Dixie USA - *medical supplier*
800-347-3494 http://www.dixieems.com

Eaton Metal Sales - *fuel storage tanks*
800-208-2657 http://www.eatonmetalsales.com

ECHO - *inexpensive dental instruments*
4 West Street, Ewell Surrey KT171UL, England

Elixa - *colloidal silver generators*
800-766-4544 http://www.elixa.com

Emergency Essentials - *preparedness supplier*
800-999-1963 http://www.beprepared.com

Excalibur - *food dehydrators*
http://www.excaliburdehydrator.com

Fisher Scientific - *hydrogen peroxide supplier*
800-766-7000 http://www.fishersci.com

Fossil Shell Supply Company - *diatomaceous earth*
800-355-9427 http://www.amaonline.com/fssc

Freeman Marketing - *self-defense supplier*
888-GO-STUNGUN   http://www.freeman-mkt.com

Freund Can Co. - *container supplier*
773-224-4230 http://www.freundcan.com

General Fire Equipment Co. - *fire safety products*
800-293-6641 http://www.generalfire.thomasregister.com

GlitchProof - *plastic liners*
877-302-0706 http://www.glitchproof.com

Golden Genesis - *alternative energy systems*
800-544-6466   http://www.goldengenesis.com

Gourmet Mushroom Products - *mushroom spawn supplier*
800-789-9121   http://www.gmushrooms.com

Grain-Power Products - *preparedness supplier*
612-545-7240

Ham Radio Outlet - *radio equipment*
800-644-4476   http://www.hamradio.com

The Ham Trader - *radio equipment*
http://www.hamtrader.com

Harbor Freight Tools - *tools and generators*
800-423-2567   http://www.harborfreight.com

Heartland America - *electronic supply catalog*
800-229-2901   http://www.heartlandamerica.com

Homeopathy Overnight - *homeopathic medicine supplier*
800-ARNICA3 http://www.homeopathyovernight.com

Ithaca Hours - *local economic system*
607-272-4330   http://www.lightlink.com/hours/ithacahours

Hot Products, Inc. - *wood-fired water heaters*
707-444-1311   http://www.hotpro.com

Ives-Way Products - *manual canning equipment*
847-740-0658

Jade Mountain - *alternative technology products*
800-442-1972   http://www.jademountain.com

Jeffers Veterinary Supply - *veterinary medicine supplier*
800-JEFFERS   http://www.1800jeffers.com

Kansas Wind Power - *alternate technology products*
785-364-4407

Kidde Safety - *fire safety products*
800-880-6788   http://www.kidde.com

Laerdal Medical - *medical supplier*
888-562-4242   http://www.laerdal.com

Lehman's - *preparedness supplier*
330-857-5757   http://www.lehmans.com

L&H Vitamins - *discount vitamin supplier*
800-221-1152   http://www.bvital.com

Long Life Food Depot - *preparedness supplier*
800-601-2833   http://www.longlifefood.com

Loompanics Unlimited Publishing Co. – *self-defense books*
800-380-2230   http://www.olympus.net/egi-form

Maxi Container - *container supplier*
800-727-6294   maxirsr@aol.com

Major Surplus & Survival - *preparedness supplier*
800-441-8855   http://www.majorsurplusnsurvival.com

Masune - *medical supplier*
800-831-0894   http://www.masune.com

MayWay Corp. - *medicinal herbs supplier*
800-262-9929   http://www.mayway.com

Meilink - *safes*
800-MEILINK   http://www.fireking.com

Michigan First Aid and Safety Supplies - *medical supplier*
800-221-9222   http://www.mfasco.com

Miller Nurseries - *tree supplier*
800-836-9630   http://www.millernurseries.com

Military Logmars Plus - *preparedness supplier*
800-922-1717   http://www.oxygenabsorber.com

Millennium Power Systems - *alternative energy systems*
410-686-6658   http://www.offgrid.com

Mr. Solar - *solar power supplier*
435-877-1061   http://www.mrsolar.com

Multisorb Technologies - *food dessicants*
800-445-9890   http://www.multisorb.com

Nelson-Bach - *alternative medicine*
800-314-2224   http://www.nelsonbach.com

Nitro-Pak Preparedness Center - *preparedness supplier*
800-866-4876   http://www.nitro-pak.com

Non-Hybrid Seeds
See list of suppliers on pages 178 to 180

Northern Tool and Equipment - *tools and generators*
800-533-5545   http://www.northern-online.com

North Farm Cooperative - *bulk food distributor*
888-632-3276   http://www.northfarm-coop.com

Nutraceuticals 2000 - *container supplier*
800-929-9972   http://www.nutraceuticals2000.com

O'Brock Windmills - *windmill supplier*
330-584-4681   windmill@cannet.com

Off Line Independant Energy Systems - *alternative energy*
209-877-7080   http://www.psnw.com/~ofln

Omega Systems - *storage tanks*
301-735-8373   http://www.omega-inc.com

Out-n'-Back - *preparedness supplier*
888-533-7415   http://www.citysearch.com/slc/outnback

Park Tool Company - *bicycle tools*
651-777-6868   http://www.parktool.com

Perma-Guard, Inc. - *diatomaceous earth*
800-813-9641   http://www.permaguard.com

Phyto Pharmica - *medicinal herbs supplier*
800-553-2370   http://www.phytopharmica.com

Poly Lam Products - *food desiccants*
800-836-9648   http://www.foodsave.net

Precious Metals Distributors - *precious metals bullion and coins*
See list on pages 224 to 225

Radio Shack - *electronics equipment*
800-THE-SHACK http://www.radioshack.com

Ram Co. - *water pump supplier*
800-227-8511 http://www.theramcompany.com

Real Goods - *alternative energy supplier*
800-762-7325 http://www.realgoods.com

Recreational Equipment, Inc. - *camping supplies*
800-426-4840 http://www.rei.com

Rife - *water pump supplier*
800-RIFERAM http://www.riferam.com

RKS Plastics - *plastic bags*
800-635-9959 http://www.allsizepolybags.com

Robinson Curriculum - *home school curriculum*
248-740-2697 http://www.robinsoncurriculum.com

Rodale Press - *farming and health books*
800-914-9363 http://www.rodalestore.com

SafeTrek - *preparedness supplier*
800-424-7870 http://www.safetrek.com

Sam's Club - *discount wholesaler*
888-733-SAMS   http://www.samsclub.com

Sancor Industries - *composting toilets*
800-387-5126   http://www.envirolet.com

Saxon Math - *math and phonics home school curriculum*
800-284-7019 http://www.saxonpub.com

Schwinn - *bicycle supplier*
800-SCHWINN   http://www.schwinn.com

Sentry - *safes*
800-828-1438 http://www.sentry-grp.com

Sharefin's Internet Links - *preparedness website links*
http://www.cairns.net.au/~sharefin/Markets/Alternative.htm

Shomer-Tec - *self-defense supplier*
360-733-6214

Silver Solutions - *colloidal silver generators*
888-505-6005   http://www.silversolutions.com

Solar Chef - *solar cookers*
806-794-2150   http://www.solarchef.com

Solar Extreme - *alternate energy*
888-477-4717, ext. 298   http://www.solarextreme.com

Solar Solutions - *alternate energy*
888-44SOLAR   http://www.solarsolns.com

Special Op's Shop - *preparedness supplier*
877-852-2486   http://www.compfxnet.com/opshop

Suunto USA - *preparedness supplier*
800-543-9124   http://www.suuntousa.com

The Sportsman's Guide - *preparedness supplier*
800-888-3006   http://www.sportsmansguide.com

The Sausage Maker - *food processing supplier*
888-490-8525

Storey Books - *gardening books*
800-441-5700   http://www.storeybooks.com

Stark Brothers - *tree supplier*
800-775-6415   http://www.starkbros.com

Statpower - *electrical inverters*
800-994-STAT   http://www.statpower.com

SunlightWorks - *alternative energy supplier*
520-282-1202   http://www.sunlightworks.com

Sun-Mar Corp. - *composting toilets*
800-461-2461   http://www.sun-mar.com

Swanson Vitamin Discounts - *discount vitamin supplier*
800-437-4148   http://www.healthy.net

Topper Co. - *water-pumping windmills*
800-775-3277

Turner Tanks - *fuel storage tanks*
800-672-4770   http://www.turnertanks.com

US Carburetion, Inc. - *propane conversion kits*
800-553-5608   http://www.uscarb.qpg.com

U.S. Cavalry - *safety supplies*
888-88USCAV http://www.uscav.com

The Vitamin Shoppe - *discount vitamin supplier*
800-223-1216   http://www.vitaminshoppe.com

Walton Feed - *preparedness supplier*
800-269-8563   http://www.waltonfeed.com

watertanks.com - *container supplier*
877-H2O-TNKS   http://www.watertanks.com

Y2K Grub - *preparedness supplier*
877-Y2K-GRUB   http://www.y2kgrub.com

Zap Electric Bikes and Scooters - *electric bicycles*
408-262-8975   http://www.electric-bikes.com

Y2K Internet Research

If you're interested in researching the Y2K problem further, we recommend the following websites. Several offer free e-mail subscription services; sign up, to recieve Y2K news updates and information. Keep up to date on the Year 2000 issue as it evolves!

The Cassandra Project

This site is dedicated to fostering neighborhood and community-based Y2K preparedness. It teaches steps of group organization for Y2K education and action.

http://cassandraproject.org

Dr. Ed Yardeni's Y2K Reporter

Dr. Yardeni is the Chief Economist of Deutsche Morgan-Grenfells Securities in New York. His popular web site contains vital information, much pertaining to Y2K's impact on the financial sector. At his site, you can download his free "Y2K Netbook."

http://www.yardeni.com

Electric Utilities and Y2K

Created by Rick Cowles, author of Electric Utilities and Y2K, this site disseminates information on the status of the nation's electric power grid as it is impacted by Y2K.

http://www.euy2k.com

Gary North's Y2K Links and Forums

This is Dr. Gary North's site. While he is an outspoken doomsayer and not politically correct, his site is among the best Y2K resources on the web. It has links to thousands of articles written on all aspects of the Y2K problem, conveniently organized by category. It also has forums for online exchange of Y2K information.
http://www.garynorth.com

Heath's Exhausive Y2K Congressional Testimony Links

This site links to transcripts of Congressional testimony that has been given in the numerous Y2K hearings held since 1996.
http://home.swbell.net/adheath/testimony.htm

U.S. Federal Government Gateway for Year 2000 Information Directories

Links to official U.S. government sources of Y2K information, plus more.
http://www.itpolicy.gsa.gov/mks/yr2000/y2khome.htm

U.S. Senate Special Y2K Committee Site

This site links to news and testimony transcripts from the Senate Special Y2K Committee.
http://www.senate.gov/~y2k

Westergaard Year 2000

This site provides a daily commentary on Y2K-related news, with strategic analysis of the Y2K problem. Several prominent Y2K authorities provide ongoing columns to this online news service. Be sure to sign up for their daily e-mail service.
http://www.y2ktimebomb.com

Year 2000 Computing Crisis—GAO Reports

This site contains links to General Accounting Office reports and Congressional testimony transcripts on the Y2K problem. Over 50 documents are listed. To get a feel for the seriousness of this situation, read some of these reports.

http://www.gao.gov/y2kr.htm

Year 2000 Information Center

Peter de Jager's website, containing links to current Y2K news articles plus commentary.

http://www.year2000.com

Y2K Newswire

Articles and commentary on Y2K; e-mail subscription service.

http://www.y2knewswire.com

Y2K Today

Updates, articles, and commentary on the Y2K problem.

http://www.y2ktoday.com

Y2K Watch

This site, home of the "Y2K Weatherman," helps you gauge the winds of the upcoming Y2K storm, and prepare. Sign up for free e-mail updates.

http://y2kwatch.com

Y2K Women

Geared for women, this site explores topics of concern in preparing for Y2K. Sign up for the free e-mail newsletter.

http://www.y2kwomen.com

ORDER FORM

To order additional copies of:

Y2K–It's Not Too Late
Complete Preparedness Guide

_____ copies at $19.95 each = $_____

Add 6% sales tax for orders
shipped to Michigan addresses   +_____

Add $4 shipping for the first
book and $2 for each additional   +_____

Total   =_____

Name _____

Address _____

City_____State_____ Zip_____

Phone _____

E-mail _____

Send to:
Mercury Publications
P.O. Box 1714
Royal Oak, MI 48068-1714

Internet: http://www.y2kredy.com
E-mail: mercurypub@aol.com

or call toll-free:
1-877-Y2K-REDY